4. Herriard Park

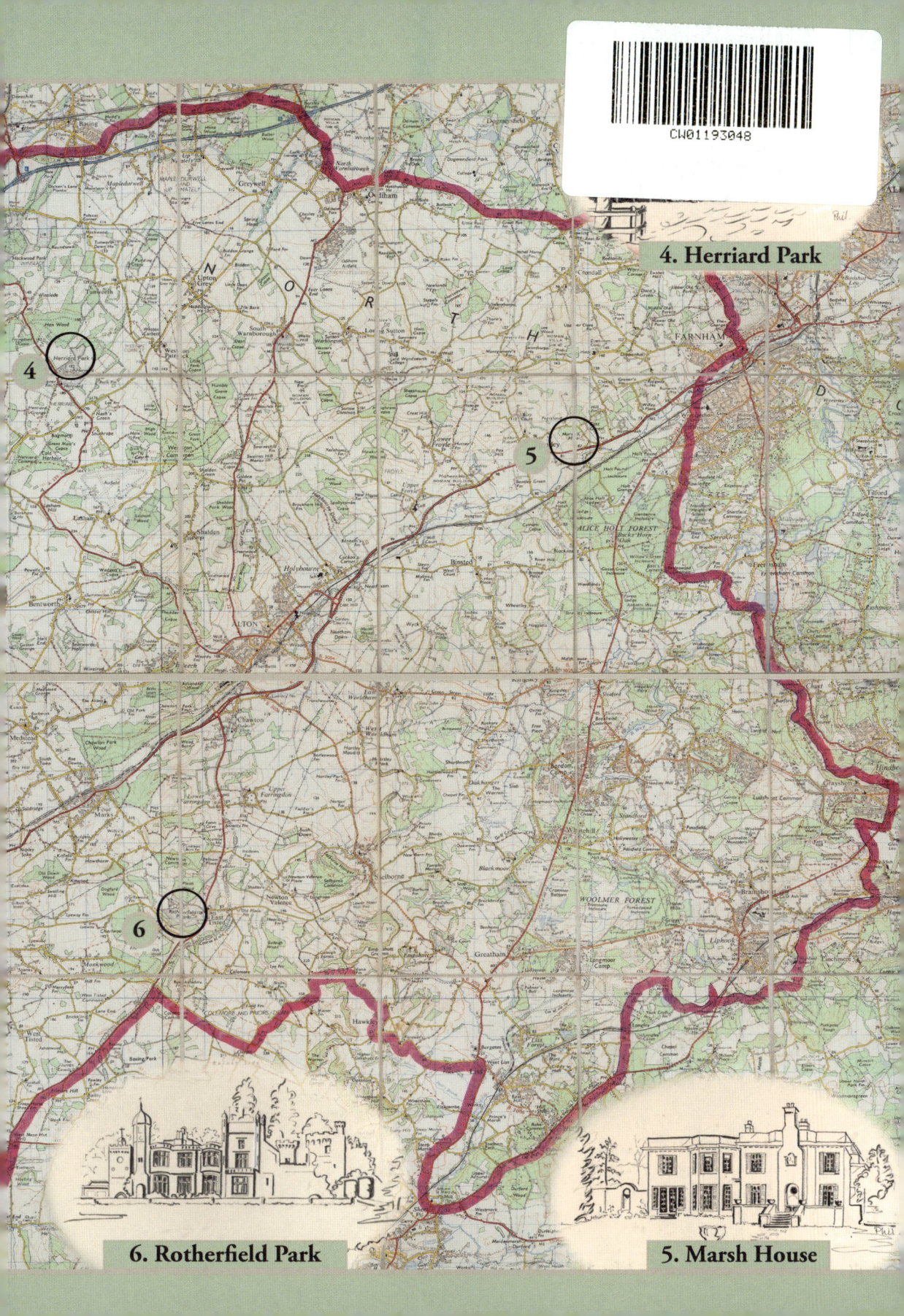

6. Rotherfield Park

5. Marsh House

PARSONS.

The HAMPSHIRE HUNT
1749–2022

His Royal Highness George, Prince of Wales, in 1792.

The HAMPSHIRE HUNT
1749–2022

Adrian Dangar

Muscoates Publishing

The Trustees of the Hampshire Hunt Club are extremely grateful to the following, who have made the publication of this book possible:

Mrs Mark Andreae
Peter Andreae Esq.
Mrs Penny Aikenhead
Mrs John Andrews
The Lord Ashburton
Luke Axel-Berg Esq.
Mrs Luke Axel-Berg
Mrs Anthony Bird
Miss Poppy Burnyeat
Mrs Peter Butler
Mrs Peter Caplan
The Hon John Cavendish
The Hon Mrs John Cavendish
Mrs Cherida Cannon
Mrs David Church
Anthony Cooke Esq.
Johnny Cowper-Coles Esq.
Mrs Johnny Cowper-Coles
Charlie Corbett Esq.
Mrs Charlie Corbett
David Cowley Esq. CBE
Kevin Coker Esq.
Mrs Sarah Daniels
Adrian de Ferranti Esq.
Mrs Peter Dennis Goodman
Derek Edwards Esq.
Miss Sally Evans MFH
Derick Faulkner Esq.
Mrs Noel Fisher
Tom Floyd Esq.
Mrs Tom Floyd
George Gray Esq.
Mrs Clive Gregory
Mrs Adrian Hardman
The Harrap Family

Rupert Harvie Esq. MFH
Mr & Mrs Peter Humphrey
Guy Hurst Esq.
Anthony Jervoise Esq.
John Jervoise Esq.
Ralph Kanter Esq.
Mark Kemp-Gee Esq.
Dougie Lowe Esq.
John MacMahon Esq.
Mr & Mrs Charles Marriott
Mrs Anthony Maxse
David Mayhew Esq. CBE
Charlie McCowen Esq.
Simon McCowen Esq.
Nigel McNair Scott Esq.
Mrs Frank Momber
Martin Moore Esq. KC
Jonathan Moseley Esq.
The Lord Northbrook
Mrs Charles Petre
Mrs Rocky Petre
The Earl of Portsmouth DL
Mr and Mrs Peter Price
Mr and Mrs Ben Robinson
Peregrine Rowse Esq.
Mr & Mrs Giles Rowsell
Mrs Nick Rowsell
Sir James Scott Bt.
Mrs David Sinclair
William Swan Esq.
Tim Walters Esq.
Nigel Webb Esq.
Mrs Nigel Webb
Bill Welling Esq.

The Hampshire Hunt 1749–2022

is a Limited Edition of 500 copies

of which this is number...175......

Contents

Subscribers to the book		iv
Foreword		ix
Introduction		xi
1.	The Earliest Days 1745–1795	15
2.	The First Golden Age 1795–1837	21
3.	Seasons of Discontent 1837–1862	33
4.	An Angel in Top Boots 1862–1884	41
5.	The Coryton and Jervoise Era 1884–1909	53
6.	Cometh the Hour, Cometh the Man 1909–1914	69
7.	The Great War 1914–1918	81
8.	An Uphill Road 1919–1926	93
9.	The Magician's Wand 1926–1939	107
10.	A Time of Gifts 1939–1953	131
11.	The Goschen Era 1953–1965	145
12.	The Quartermasters and Beyond 1965–1975	159
13.	A New Broom Sweeps Clean 1975–1981	173
14.	The Best of Times 1981–1991	185
15.	The End of an Era 1991–1996	195
16.	Listen to Us! 1996–2005	207
17.	Stormy Waters 2005–2016	221
18.	The Music of the Hounds Will Never Die 2016–2022	231
	Bibliography	247
	Index	249
	About the Author	254
	Acknowledgements	255

Foreword

Possibly the only time I have ever responded to a public consultation was when Lord Burns was inquiring into hunting with dogs at the turn of the century. As something of an insider/outsider I tried to convey to him the place of hunting in country life (even in SW60) and a feeling for its history, which in my family's case dated from soon after the future George IV granted the Hampshire Hunt Club the right to wear the Prince of Wales's feathers.

It is that history which Adrian Dangar has revisited and brought up to date in this special volume commissioned by the HH, supported by generous subscribers and, most importantly, driven forward by the joint enthusiasm of Hopper Cavendish, Charlie Corbett and Nigel Webb to whom we all owe an enormous vote of thanks and appreciation.

Almost 100 years on it is hard to imagine what it must have been like to be one of the 5,000 well-wishers at the legendary George Evans's wedding in Ropley. As the happy couple left the church my grandfather's head keeper, Harry Healey (whose son was killed in North Africa in 1943), presented the groom with a silver hunting horn as a present from all the keepers in the HH country. But history is often only one step away. In 1966 that very same Healey did his best to teach my brother and me to shoot.

Although there have always been some tensions between the two main field sports, enough landowners have understood that it is possible to accommodate both. I have a clear but inadequately exact recollection of an article from *The Field* which Mark Andreae had framed in the downstairs loo at Moundsmere describing certainly sequential if not quite simultaneous sport on his family's estate.

We had a beagle meet at Rotherfield the day before the ban on hunting with dogs came in, and I gave them champagne because I thought that was the end of hunting. In fact, of course, hunting within the law has gone from strength to strength, with enormous support from all those who relish the camaraderie it engenders. That support will be needed more than ever as we seem to be revisiting some of the economic and financial challenges which caused such havoc 50 years ago.

Reading Adrian's account of close to 300 years of the Hampshire Hunt will help keep morale up during the difficult times ahead. I thank him for it and commend it to you.

Sir James Scott Bt.

Introduction

Writing the history of the Hampshire Hunt has been a fascinating journey, but as to be expected with an institution of such antiquity, there are differing views on when the Hunt actually started. Squire Evelyn is known to have hunted the country with a private pack from 1745, although their quarry has never been established and there is nothing to link his hounds with the current Hunt. The same cannot be said for Thomas Ridge, who maintained a pack of foxhounds at Kilmeston Manor for 46 years from 1749 and accepted subscriptions during the latter years of his Mastership. The earliest surviving records of the HH date from a list of Members in 1782, and by 1784 the *Hampshire Chronicle* was also referring to Mr Ridge's pack as the Hampshire Hunt. Since Thomas Ridge did not retire until 1795 it is reasonable to assume that the current Hunt began life under his stewardship.

This appeared to be the consensus of Members who celebrated the 200th anniversary of the Hunt in 1949 with a dinner at Moundsmere Manor, although a previous chronicler of hunting in Hampshire has suggested that the anniversary was delayed by four years due to the Second World War. To further confuse the issue, the Hampshire Hunt Club celebrated its bicentenary with a dinner at Winchester College in 1995, which was actually the 200th anniversary of the first recorded minutes. For the purpose of this book, which is the intertwined history of both the Hampshire Hunt and the eponymous Club, the Hampshire Hunt dates from 1749. In that year Thomas Ridge established an organisation that, by the end of his tenure, was universally referred to as the Hampshire Hunt.

In many ways the Hunt's unfolding narrative is a metaphor for the history of hunting itself, a sport that has successfully overcome seemingly insurmountable difficulties by constantly adapting and evolving. I was somewhat surprised to discover that many of the challenges facing contemporary hunting were also very much in evidence during the nineteenth century. Members of the HH Club have always been preoccupied with raising sufficient money to run the Hunt, and the current Masters will doubtless recognise some of the frustrations experienced by Henry Deacon when organising hunting to fit in around shooting during his Mastership from 1862–1884. The arrival of barbed wire in the late 1800s was greeted with horror by many, including the incumbent Masters who threatened to resign on its account. Disputes over hunt boundaries, compensation for damage, and constant repairs to the stables and kennels at Ropley, where hounds have been kennelled since 1846, are issues that may never disappear.

The Hampshire Hunt's high standing in the local community and the willingness of its Members and subscribers to embrace charitable causes have also shone brightly throughout my research. Hunt records from 1795 onwards reveal that many of Hampshire's most prominent members of society, several of them decorated for great military achievements, have also been Members of the Hampshire Hunt Club. The tradition endures, for since the Millennium year no less than five of the county's High Sheriffs can also claim membership of what is one of the oldest and most distinguished hunt clubs in the land. The importance attached to fox coverts throughout the Hunt's long history is especially poignant given that some are no longer open to hounds. Today it is hard to imagine the Forestry Commission unlocking gates for hunt access, the National Trust maintaining woodland rides for the benefit of mounted followers or the County Surveyor requesting the loan of a hunt horse for the purpose of mapping out bridleways. But despite so many changes to land ownership, attitudes and the Hampshire countryside, hounds continue to be welcomed warmly by enough farmers, landowners and shoots to be able to regularly cross much of the same enduringly beautiful landscape Thomas Ridge hunted between 1749 and 1795.

The countryside is much changed since those days, the towns and villages too. The first recorded meetings of the HH Club were held at an unnamed venue in Winchester, but by the beginning of the nineteenth century they had moved to the Swan Inn at Alresford, which remained a favourite rendez-vous for the next hundred-odd years. On a bitterly cold afternoon last November, I called into the same hostelry where Members had once met to discuss the affairs of the Hunt by candlelight. As I searched for the merest hint of the inn's hunting past, shirt-sleeved guests relaxed in a warm fug that would have been unimaginable two centuries earlier, and piped music pervaded every space. There was no trace to be found until I entered a dimly lit side room and discovered an old black and white photograph of the Hampshire Hunt's top-hatted followers riding up Broad Street.

If you care to look beneath the surface, similar clues to the county's longstanding involvement with hunting are not hard to find. A wooden plaque beside a narrow country lane pays lonely tribute to a 'beloved little pack of bloodhounds' that existed between 1888 and 1902. A tombstone in the graveyard beside the deserted village of Hartley Mauditt, where hounds ran a fox to ground in 1888, celebrates the life of 'a true hunting gentleman', and the legend HH Inn 1801 to 1884 is displayed in bold white lettering on the façade of a red brick house in Cheriton that was once the Hampshire Hunt public house. There will be scores, possibly hundreds, of other subtle reminders to reaffirm the interwoven histories of the Hampshire Hunt and the county from which it takes its name.

There would be no history to write were it not for the hounds, which over the years have been transformed just as dramatically as the landscape over which they hunt. John Villebois's tough and wiry 70 couple kennelled at Harmsworth in the early 1800s were much admired by the leading hunting correspondent of the day, and improved by stallion hounds from Sir Thomas Mostyn, Squire Osbalderton, and the Brocklesby and Milton Hunts. Things had deteriorated so badly by 1909, when George Evans became Master for the first time, that he was obliged to send 22½ couple to Rugby sales and replace them with draft hounds from the Belvoir, Grafton and Puckeridge. The reinvigorated pack were soon catching foxes in style, but the First World War put them back to square one, and when George Evans returned for a second innings in 1926 he once more transformed the conformation and working qualities of a much diminished pack. The revolutionary introduction of Welsh blood from the Curre and Carmarthen Hunts was such a success that in 1933 the Master claimed his pack would have caught twenty brace more each season than the hounds he handled before the War. Nearly a century later the Hampshire Hunt hounds, still kennelled at Ropley, have adapted most successfully to the challenges of hunting under the 2004 Hunting Act and continue to impress on the flags and in the field. Long may they continue to do so.

Adrian Dangar

Chapter One 1745–1795

The Earliest Days

Squire Evelyn, 1745–1749, Thomas Ridge Esq., 1749–1795.

The meet at The Grange in 2021, Squire Evelyn brings his hounds to Harmsworth in 1745, Thomas Ridge establishes a pack of foxhounds at Kilmeston in 1749, early references to hunt dinners, transition from a private to subscription hunt, the Prince of Wales and the Kempshott Hunt, some notable hunting runs and anecdotes, The Prince of Wales's heraldic badge and the Hampshire Hunt button.

Winter arrived early in Hampshire on the morning of Saturday November 27th 2021, with leaden skies, and a biting north-easterly to ruffle the long, sinuous lake that is overlooked by The Grange near Northington, an imposing nineteenth century mansion widely acknowledged as being the finest example of Greek Revival architecture in England. As the morning light slowly banished dawn, men and women dressed to turn the bitter cold started to assemble on foot beneath the building's eight gigantic columns, soon joined by mounted Members and subscribers to the Hampshire Hunt. All were beautifully turned out, and several wore dark blue coats offset with brass buttons displaying the three ostrich plumes from the Prince of Wales's heraldic badge. Shortly before 11am the hunt staff and hounds arrived on the lawn, the former sporting buttons of gleaming brass from the backs of quality hogged-maned hunters, the latter lean, fit and raring to go. After the assembly had been photographed for posterity, the sizeable throng moved off across Lord Ashburton's parkland in a snowstorm and ten minutes later the landscape reverberated to the joyous sound of hounds in full cry, just as it had done every winter since the mid eighteenth century.

The same dramatic setting featured in an historic painting of the Hampshire Hunt executed by Mr G. B. Spalding in 1845, less than thirty years after a 17th century brick building had been transformed by the architect William Wilkins into the glorious temple it is today, although the parkland trees depicted in Spalding's painting are young and recently planted. In keeping with the 19th century painting, the 21st century photograph includes a key to identify the individuals present, some of whose ancestors featured in Spalding's original painting. However it is necessary to go back a further century to find the first recorded pack of hounds in Hampshire, which were brought into the county when Squire Evelyn moved from his St. Clere estates in Kent to Harmsworth[1] near Alresford in 1745. In those days hunting establishments were privately financed by their owners for hunting the country surrounding their place of residence, which in Squire Evelyn's case was less than three miles to the east of The Grange at Northington.

Little is known of the sport provided by the Squire's pack, or even their preferred quarry, but his kennels appear to have been dissolved after only four seasons, the vacuum being filled in 1749 by Thomas Ridge who lived at the beautiful Kilmeston Manor and is credited with starting the Hampshire Hunt as it is known today. Up until 1784 his pack of foxhounds were loosely referred to as the Kilmeston Hunt, but in March of that year 'Members of the Hampshire Hunt Society' and 'Gentlemen of the Hampshire Hunt' are mentioned in the *Hampshire Chronicle*, which dates from 1772 and is one of the oldest publications in England. Reference to the Hampshire Hunt Society clearly indicates the existence of an association of individuals who enjoyed hunting together and meeting up for dinner every month in the style of an eighteenth century club. These dinners were served at 3.30pm in the afternoon, often at Mr Vernon's Wheatsheaf Inn on Popham Lane just south of Basingstoke and enlivened by hunting songs composed by the Rev. C. Powlett of Itchen Abbas, an illegitimate son of the third Duke of Bolton, known as the Poet of the Hampshire Hunt. One of his most enduring compositions runs to six hearty verses and refers to the Wheatsheaf Inn by name, which along with the White Hart at Winchester and the Swan Inn at Alresford was a venue for both Hunt meetings and dinners during the second half of the eighteenth century.

Towards the end of his hunting career Thomas Ridge was offered a small subscription by his friends and supporters to defray the cost of maintaining a private pack of hounds. With a remarkable 21 children to his name – eighteen of whom lived to adulthood – Thomas needed some financial support if he were to continue providing his neighbours with sport. His expenses included paying, and dressing in blue livery, his professional huntsman, Joe Hall, first whipper-in, Phil Gosling, and a fiery character known only as Hellfire Jack, who was the second whipper-in. Thomas Ridge's decision to accept financial assistance effectively marks

---

[1] Eighteenth century Harmsworth is now known as Armsworth.

THE EARLIEST DAYS 1745–1795

The Hampshire Hunt at The Grange 1845 by Mr G.B. Spalding and key.

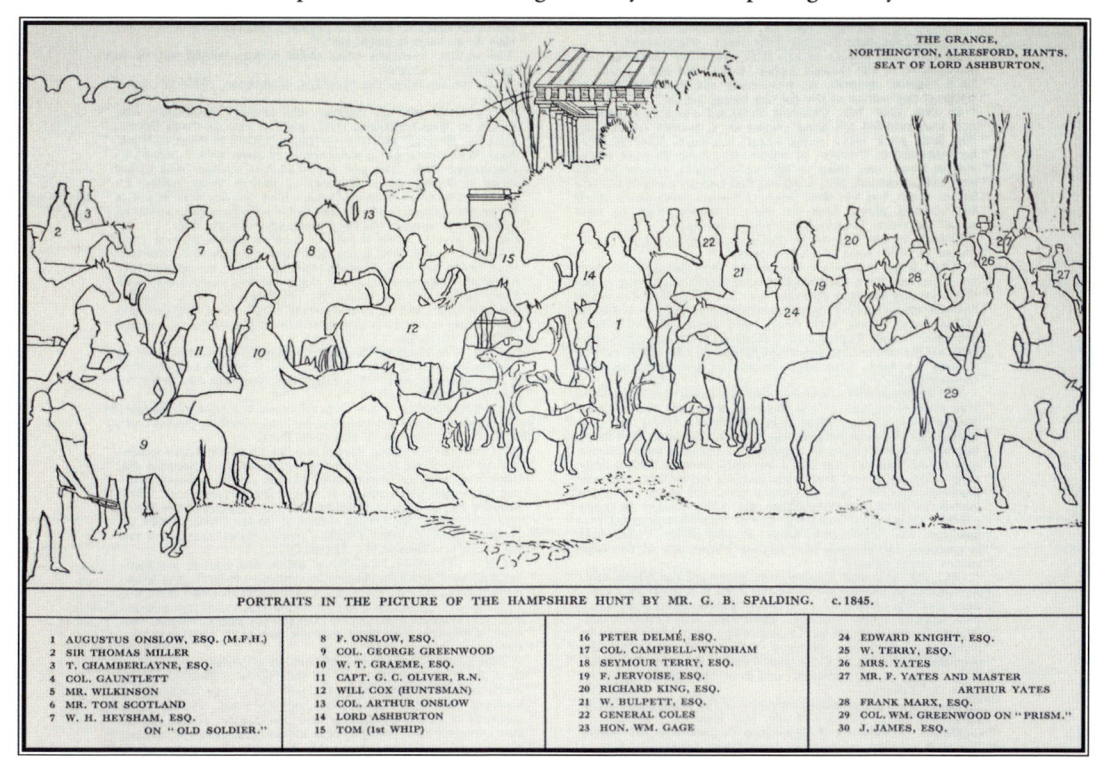

THE GRANGE, NORTHINGTON, ALRESFORD, HANTS, SEAT OF LORD ASHBURTON.

PORTRAITS IN THE PICTURE OF THE HAMPSHIRE HUNT BY MR. G. B. SPALDING. c.1845.

1 AUGUSTUS ONSLOW, ESQ. (M.F.H.)	8 F. ONSLOW, ESQ.	16 PETER DELMÉ, ESQ.	24 EDWARD KNIGHT, ESQ.
2 SIR THOMAS MILLER	9 COL. GEORGE GREENWOOD	17 COL. CAMPBELL-WYNDHAM	25 W. TERRY, ESQ.
3 T. CHAMBERLAYNE, ESQ.	10 W. T. GRAEME, ESQ.	18 SEYMOUR TERRY, ESQ.	26 MRS. YATES
4 COL. GAUNTLETT	11 CAPT. G. C. OLIVER, R.N.	19 F. JERVOISE, ESQ.	27 MR. F. YATES AND MASTER ARTHUR YATES
5 MR. WILKINSON	12 WILL COX (HUNTSMAN)	20 RICHARD KING, ESQ.	28 FRANK MARX, ESQ.
6 MR. TOM SCOTLAND	13 COL. ARTHUR ONSLOW	21 W. BULPETT, ESQ.	29 COL. WM. GREENWOOD ON "PRISM."
7 W. H. HEYSHAM, ESQ. ON "OLD SOLDIER."	14 LORD ASHBURTON	22 GENERAL COLES	30 J. JAMES, ESQ.
	15 TOM (1st WHIP)	23 HON. WM. GAGE	

– 17 –

the transition of the private Kilmeston Hunt into the marginally less exclusive Hampshire Hunt, which had to rub shoulders with other private packs in the county, that came and went according to the fortunes of their proprietors. These included the Prince of Wales's staghounds, or Kempshott Hunt, which evolved during the latter years of Thomas Ridge's long tenure. The future King George IV, who had been introduced to staghunting by his parents in his early twenties, appreciated the certainty of finding a quarry to hunt. The stag was invariably semi-domesticated and often re-captured alive and unharmed at the end of the day, a practice that eventually came to be known as 'hunting the carted stag.'

The Prince's lawyers concluded negotiation for the lease of Kempshott House in 1789, and the earliest records relating to the Prince of Wales hunting with his own staghounds date from the following year, when a stag was turned down in front of hounds at Hackwood Park on January 26th 1790. Hounds were hunted by a professional named George Sharp, and a terrific run ensued after the quarry crossed the River Loddon near Basingstoke and ran to Farleigh, Preston Oakhills, Herriard Common and Lasham before taking sanctuary in the kitchen of a humble cottage. The Prince wore the blue livery of Thomas Ridge's Hampshire Hunt, although he missed the latter stages of the run having been thrown off at Preston Oakhills. Only four followers saw the finish of this fine hunt, during which there were several nasty falls and both of Sharp's horses were exhausted. The Prince finally returned to Kempshott at 7pm that evening and later expressed his high satisfaction with the quality of the sport and the Hampshire landscape.

The Prince joined a field of eleven other riders, including Lord John Russell and Sir Henry St John Mildmay for a meet of his staghounds, now known as the Kempshott Hunt, on January 7th 1791. Hounds flew from the turnpike gate at Kempshott to Hackwood Park, via Hatch Warren, Farleigh Paddocks, and Upper Kempshott Wood, continuing to Ashe Park in the dark. That evening the Prince and his companions dined at the Wheatsheaf Inn, Popham Lane, where the proprietor maintained a cellar of port for the benefit of the Hampshire Hunt, whose members were joined by the Prince at a meet of their foxhounds the next day. Three days later Thomas Ridge returned the courtesy when joining the Prince and 22 others, including the Royal Hunt manager and archivist, William Poyntz, and the Royal jockey, Samuel Chifney, in pursuit of a stag named Unicorn. The hapless beast was released at Weston Down and taken in a field 'near the road leading from Alresford to Winchester' having been coursed by a cur dog and suffered a crashing fall leaping over a tall hedge.

THE EARLIEST DAYS 1745–1795

With two fine packs on their doorstep, sportsmen and women in Hampshire were spoilt for choice when it came to following hounds, especially when both hunts met on the same day, as they did on January 26th 1791. The Hampshire Hunt hunted a fox near Tichborne to the east of Winchester, whilst the Royal Staghounds ran to the outskirts of the same city from Kempshott. No doubt guests attending the Ball at Hackwood Park given in the Prince's honour by the Duchess of Bolton that evening debated the merits of their respective hunts. On May 6th 1791 His Royal Highness hosted a large dinner at the Wheatsheaf Inn to thank the Hampshire farmers over whose land he had ridden the previous season, thus starting a tradition of appreciation that has endured in various guises ever since.

Although the relationship between two hunts covering much of the same country was largely harmonious, occasional complaints were directed against the Prince's Hunt manager and archivist, William Poyntz, who was reputed to be no respecter of hunt boundaries; 'as water will find its way into every vacant place, so his hounds were sure to appear wherever they were not carefully stopped out' wrote one critic. Echoes of similar sentiments have reverberated across Hampshire ever since, for disputes over the precise location of boundaries is a theme woven into the history of every Hunt in the county. The situation must have become rather more delicate during the latter stage of the 1792–1793 season, when, for reasons that are not entirely clear, the Royal Staghounds converted to hunting the fox. Perhaps the Prince had been won over to the merits of the smaller quarry after Thomas Ridge accepted his invitation to bring the Hampshire Hunt foxhounds to a meet at Kempshott the previous season on February 11th 1792, which was recorded for posterity by Poyntz, and attended by several of the Prince's female admirers, amongst them Ladies Jersey and Cunynghame.

The Prince's first hunt of the 1793 season ended when the fox ran into a farm brew-house, which must have given guests something to talk about at the next Hunt dinner. The Royal Hunt's conversion from stag to fox did not appear to cause acrimony, however it was destined to last for less than three years as the expenses of maintaining a private hunting establishment, which in 1793 included 37 hunters and 33 couple of hounds, escalated. The demise of the Kempshott Hunt has also been attributed to its patron's rapidly expanding girth and the consequent inability to ride effectively to hounds. With the notable exception of a loyal local press in Hampshire, the Prince's corpulence was mercilessly exploited by the media. On March 30th 1794 a mounted field of seventeen followed the Prince's hounds for what transpired to be not just the last day of the season but also the end of the

Kempshott Hunt, which was disbanded shortly afterwards. Many of the hounds on secondment from the Dukes of York, Beaufort, and Bedford, and Lords Stawell, Egremont, Craven and Fitzwilliam, were most likely returned to their original owners. Their huntsman took up a new position with the King's staghounds, married the daughter of the Queen's huntsman, and received a life pension from his former employer. After a long and distinguished career in hunt service, George Sharp, one-time professional huntsman to the short lived Royal Kempshott Hunt, was buried back in Hampshire at Dummer.

Before giving up the Kempshott estate the future King George IV bestowed on the Hampshire Hunt an honour that has been renewed by successive heirs to the throne. In recognition of the close fellowship of his Hampshire friends and gratitude for the sport he had enjoyed across their land the Prince of Wales granted Members of the Hampshire Hunt the right to wear the three ostrich plumes from his heraldic crest on their Hunt buttons.[2] The awarding of this honour also ensured that the role played by the Prince's own hounds in the county's history would be acknowledged for evermore. Thomas Ridge retired in 1795 after nearly five decades in office during which he had hunted a large swathe of country between Farnham, Alton, and Romsey. Under his leadership the Hampshire Hunt had evolved from a private pack into a subscription hunt, which would soon be formalised under the auspices of the Hampshire Hunt Club. The fox's position as the premier beast of the chase had also been proven, accepted, and embraced by the ladies and gentlemen of Hampshire. Thomas Ridge, founder of the Hampshire Hunt, died at home at Kilmeston in 1798.

---

[2] The original button in 1783 was made of silver and inscribed with the initials HH. In 1785 the button changed to brass with the same letters until adopting the Prince of Wales's ostrich plumes.

Chapter Two 1795–1837

The First Golden Age

W. Powlett Powlett Esq., 1795–1802, J.T. Villebois Esq.,
Admiral Calmady, and T. Kingscote Esq., 1802–1805,
J.T. Villebois Esq., 1805–1837.

First minute book and rules of the HH Club in 1795, William Powlett Powlett appointed Perpetual President in 1795, The HH Cup and hunt races, change from blue livery in the hunting field to red, John Villebois, Admiral Calmady, and Thomas Kingscote become Masters in 1802, Hampshire Hunt country, hounds, and horses, Nimrod's observations on the Hampshire Hunt, Dick Foster as huntsman, great and unusual hunts, death of John Villebois in office in 1837.

After the retirement of Thomas Ridge, those who had enjoyed hunting and dining together during his long tenure resolved to formalise hunt protocols under the banner of the Hampshire Hunt Club. The inaugural meeting was held in Winchester on April 25th 1795, at which sixteen resolutions were agreed and recorded in black copperplate ink inside a leather-bound minute book with the legend *Hampshire Hunt 1795* inscribed in gold lettering on the cover. The first resolution states, 'A club be now formed to consist of 25 Members besides the President paying annually 25 guineas.' No mention is made of how this sum is to be collected, but within two years it was necessary to insist that subscriptions be paid direct to Messrs Knapp's at Alresford or Walker's at Winchester in order to avoid 'many inconveniences both to the President and to the gentlemen who make up the accounts.'

Ensuing resolutions declare the Club to be called the Hampshire Hunt and that Members should meet on the first Friday of every month between October and April inclusive. Most significantly, it was agreed that the hounds must be kennelled during the hunting season at Bishops Sutton and that their ownership be vested in the Members of the Club. The Prince of Wales's recent granting of the right to depict his ostrich plumes on the hunt button is recognised by its inclusion in the evening dress uniform of a blue coat and white waistcoat. Other rules set out

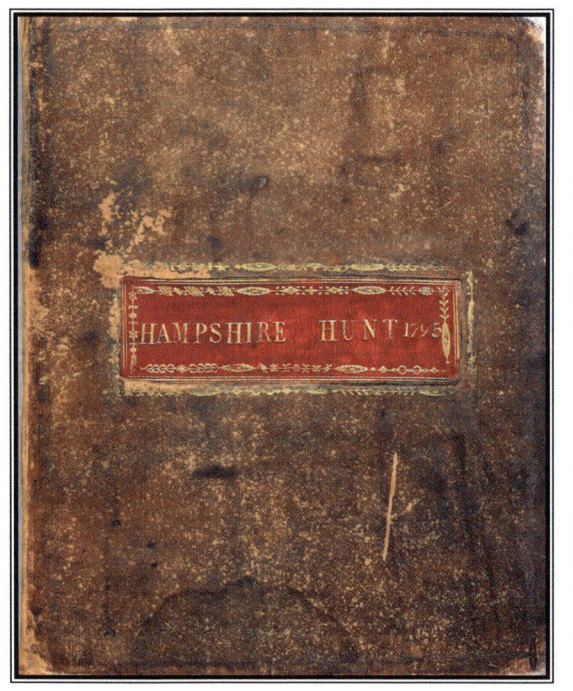

THE HAMPSHIRE HUNT 1749–2022

Front cover of 1795 minute book.

Members of the HH Club in 1782.

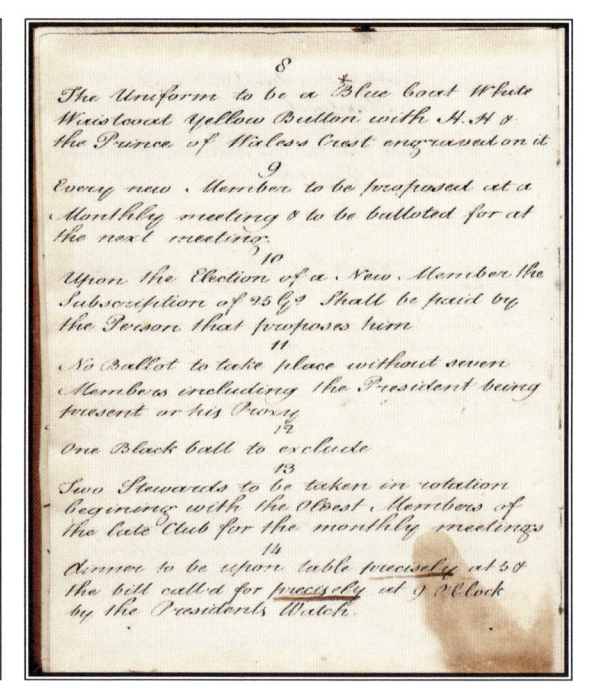

First recorded rules of the HH Club in 1795.

procedures for electing new Members, including the proviso that one black ball[1] excludes membership, and the stipulation that dinner must be served at precisely 5pm, and the bill called for by the President exactly four hours later at precisely 9pm, each reference to *precisely* being underlined in heavy black ink. The thirteenth regulation refers to stewards being taken in rotation for the monthly meetings, beginning with the oldest Members of the *late* Club. This illuminating reference to a former club implies that the Hampshire Hunt Club formed at Winchester in 1795 evolved from an existing association[2] dating from Thomas Ridge's time. The thirteenth regulation also confirms that Friday meetings during the winter months were for dining, and not hunting purposes.

Mr William Powlett Powlett from Little Somborne was elected as Perpetual President, with sole responsibility for directing hunt staff and hounds, strengthened by the proviso that no member may interfere with him in this matter. Whilst Mr Powlett Powlett is described as President in the minutes, it is clear his responsibilities were similar to those of a Master, and that he fulfilled the modern interpretation of the role. William suffered from lameness sustained when his leg struck a gate out hunting, after which he was compelled to use crutches and was quite unable to mount his horse without assistance. He wore a laced-up boot to protect his injured limb and a long grey coat with a blue spencer[3] and leather breeches out hunting, the ensemble offset by a jaunty hat designed to turn the rain.

Races for the Hampshire Hunt Cup had been run during Mr Ridge's Mastership, but not recorded in print until the *Hampshire Chronicle* reported on the 1794 meeting at Worthy Down on April 7th, when the HH Cup was won by a horse belonging to Mr Graeme called Bruiser. That evening racegoers celebrated at a ball given by Mr Hayne at St John's House, which was the precursor of many hunt dances to come, including one given by the bachelors of the HH to 150 fashionables of the neighbourhood at the Swan Inn, Alresford, in March 1817 that lasted until 6am. The *Hampshire Chronicle* faithfully recorded many of these glittering social occasions and their attendees for posterity.

In 2003, more than two centuries after the local paper had first recorded the Worthy Down races, a descendant of Mr Powlett Powlett contacted Hampshire

---

1 A prospective Member was blackballed or denied entry into the Club if an existing Member placed a black ball or bean into the No compartment of the ballot box. Please see final chapter for a more detailed explanation.

2 This reference to a former club almost certainly refers to the organisation described by the *Hampshire Chronicle* in 1784 as the Hampshire Hunt Society.

3 A spencer is a waist length double breasted jacket invented by the second Earl Spencer in the 1790s.

County Council with a request to examine archives held at the Hampshire Record Office. Mr Barton William-Powlett's research had led him to Winchester after he inherited three ornate silver cups, each egg-shaped trophy decoratively embellished and engraved with the initials HHC. The oldest stands 19 inches high and was awarded to the owner of Bagshot, who beat Thomas Ridge's Pretender over two mile-long heats to win the 1789 Hampshire Hunt Cup. The engraved initials HHC further confirm that Thomas Ridge's hounds were referred to as the Hampshire Hunt prior to the commencement of formal records in 1795, and the 1789 inscription predates the earliest previous record of the HH races by five years.

In subsequent years the races for the HH Cup were contested at Worthy Down, Soberton, Tichborne or Abbotstone Down, and by 1815 a tureen worth 100 guineas was Mr Nunez's prize for winning the forerunner of a modern day Members' race. In 1820 the race for the HH Cup was run at Abbotstone and won by Mr Trodd who resided at Romsey and hunted regularly on three of the finest horses that were ever seen. Described as a heavy man and a good sportsman, he ran out of money and ended his career as a porter on the railway at Romsey. After the races were over 250 farmers and gentlemen sat down to a celebratory dinner inside the Swan Inn at Alresford.

In the late eighteenth and early nineteenth centuries the Hampshire Hunt Cup was a prestigious and important event at the very heart of the Club's ethos, usually held on the first Friday in April. There is no record of how the magnificent silver cups in Mr Barton William-Powlett's possession were paid for, but from 1795 onwards every Member of the Club subscribed a guinea towards the purchase of a Challenge Cup, which was initially contested over the Winchester course at Worthy Down in three heats of two miles. Even in the earliest days of hunt racing there was a strong bias against professional competitiveness; horses carried a gentleman's weight of 12 stone and in order to qualify had to be owned and hunted regularly with any pack in Hampshire by a Member of the Hampshire Hunt Club. Members were allowed one entry only at a cost of five guineas, which was submitted for approval in March when the right to participate was granted by a subcommittee of three Members provided they agreed that the horse had been fairly hunted the previous season. Horses in training between October and March were debarred entry, as was any horse to have won £50 or more in a plate, match, sweepstake or a previous HH Cup.

During William Powlett Powlett's reign hounds were hunted by a clever young professional named Green, who must have been delighted by the performance of his charges in 1798 when they found a fox in Beauworth Woods that sought refuge in a bed of artichokes amongst the gardens of Twyford village before being refound and killed near Compton after swimming the River Itchen. Green hunted hounds that day wearing Thomas Ridge's blue livery, but the following year Members were in unanimous support of Charles Graeme's proposal to adopt red coats in the field whilst retaining blue for evening dress, a code that was to remain unchanged for more than two centuries. William Powlett Powlett resigned the Management of the Hounds[4] after seven seasons in February 1802. According to rules agreed in 1795 the hounds and country remained under the jurisdiction of the Club. William went on to hunt what is now the western part of the Hambledon country from 1807 to 1816.

Within a month of the Perpetual President announcing his intention to resign Members gathered at the Swan Inn, Alresford on Tuesday 9th March 1802, and appointed John Truman Villebois of Candover, Admiral Calmady of Woodcote, and Thomas Kingscote of Hinton House, to manage the hounds for the following three seasons. John Villebois, who was born in 1772, was by some way the most prominent of the three individuals entrusted with managing the Hunt. He was descended from a French family who had settled in Ireland and was educated at Harrow and Oxford. More importantly for a Master of Hounds in the early nineteenth century, he was also the joint heir to a brewing fortune which had provided the funds to finance a private pack of harriers from his home at Preston Candover. Their quarry was the humble hare, but John was converted to foxhunting after his pack changed onto a fox near Preston Wood and ran straight as a die for nearly ten miles to kill between Alton and Shalden above Amery Wood. A canvas of Villebois dismounting from his horse to retrieve the brush at the end of the run was painted by Marshall and occupied pride of place in the owner's dining room. From that day on, John Truman Villebois aspired only to hunting the fox and was made a Member of the Hampshire Hunt Club when 24 years old.

Confidence at the start of what was destined to be one of the longest and most successful Masterships in HH history cannot have been particularly high, for a month later it was somewhat ominously agreed that the Masters were authorised to sell hounds and horses at the end of the season if it were necessary to balance

---

4   Up until the middle of the nineteenth century the term Management of the Hounds was used in Hunt records to describe the role of Master.

the books. They need not have worried, for with John Major carrying the horn and Will Biggs, Pop Hennessy and John Knight turning hounds, good sport was quickly forthcoming, with a remarkable 40 brace accounted for during Major's best season. Unfortunately this otherwise sound professional huntsman was overly fond of the bottle, which led to his premature departure and replacement by the whipper-in, Will Biggs.

On January 15th 1805 the Masters gave notice of their intended retirement from office at the end of the season, by which time their undertaking to manage the country for three years would have run its course. Uncertain of what the future held, the twelve Members present at the Swan in Alresford agreed to pledge a sum that amounted to £425, led by generous donations of £50 each from Lord Gage, Thomas Kingscote, Charles Graeme and Squire Villeboy[5] himself. The Hon. Secretary, Charles Graeme, was instructed to write as a matter of urgency to the ten absent Members asking how much they would be prepared to commit to going forward; 'as the adaptation of any measures for the continuance of the hounds will depend chiefly on the funds capable of being raised, an early answer is particularly requested.' Members may have been guilty of putting the cart before the horse, for as it turned out John Villebois not only stepped up to the mark as sole Master, but he also declined to accept subscriptions and for the next 32 years ran the Hampshire Hunt at his own expense for the benefit of friends and neighbours. He purchased the entire pack of hounds from the Hampshire Hunt Club, which is recognised by successive entries in the *Foxhound Kennel Studbook* describing the hounds as *Mr Villebois's (HH)*. The Club Trustees invested the proceeds of sale to such good effect that 33 years later their value was recorded as being £3,550.

After Will Biggs left in 1815, he was replaced as huntsman by Richard Foster, who with the assistance of his first whipper-in, Sawyer and second whipper-in, John Jennings, quickly established a reputation for showing excellent sport, with meets advertised for the first time in the *Hampshire Chronicle*. Then as now, the Hampshire Hunt country was heavily wooded and beset with flints on much of the open ground, over half of which was transformed into cold scenting plough by Christmas. Farmland was often criss-crossed with formidable unkempt hedges that were only cut occasionally for fuel. These near impenetrable barriers were quite unjumpable and so thick that the celebrated nineteenth century hunting correspondent, Charles Apperley, who wrote under the pseudonym Nimrod, admits

---

5   By this stage of his career as a Master of Hounds John Truman Villebois had acquired the affectionate moniker, Squire Villeboy.

to getting stuck fast whilst pushing through them on more than one occasion. And that was from the same man who without hesitation charged at, and sailed over, the six-foot-high locked gates into Lord Bolton's Hackwood Park during the course of a fine hunt on November 18th 1822, a feat faithfully recorded by the *Hampshire Chronicle*. Apperley lived at Beaurepaire near Basingstoke but preferred visiting the grass countries of the hunting shires to the woodlands and plough of Hampshire. In the January 1825 issue of *The Sporting Magazine* he rather uncharitably observed, 'I have languished upon a bed of thorns; but to ride a good hunter over a bed of flints was a misery which was reserved for me till I came to Hampshire.'

In order to hunt such a challenging country effectively up to five days a week from September until March, Squire Villeboy kept 70 couple of hounds in purpose-built kennels at Harmsworth, where Squire Evelyn had kennelled his own pack during the previous century. These spacious and airy kennels were complemented by a smaller establishment near Hursley as a base for cubhunting. Hounds were divided into two separate packs, according to size, not sex; members of the smaller pack stood between 20 and 22 inches at the shoulder, and those in the larger one from 22½ to 24½ inches, with the smaller pack chiefly, but not exclusively, comprised of bitches. One of the best hounds ever bred at Harmsworth was Mr Villebois's homebred Pontiff '17 who was used so extensively as a stallion hound that on December 22nd 1822 a special bye day for 16½ couple of Pontiff's progeny took place in the teeming rain.

According to Nimrod the challenges of breeding a pack of foxhounds to hunt a heavily wooded and cold scenting country were considerable, and he was convinced that hounds which seldom missed a fox in easier countries would struggle to kill one in Hampshire. Nimrod points out the difficulty of hounds getting away together from big coverts, and how they are prevented from carrying a good head through being obliged to hunt in single file up deep plough furrows. Thanks to Nimrod we know that John Villebois bred a distinctive stamp of hound, 'very deep in their forequarters, short and straight in their legs, a little arched in their backs, heads well set, rich in colours, and being lightly fed, very wiry in appearance.' Even with these attributes at least half the pack were sometimes cut by flints after a hard run, which necessitated a well-bred horse if its rider was to see the end of a good hunt; 'short in his legs, quick and handy to turn, a good upright leaper and not long in the pasterns on account of the flints. The hair on his heels should be encouraged to grow; he should be drawn fine in his body and set on the muzzle the night before hunting.'

THE HAMPSHIRE HUNT 1749–2022

The Hampshire Hunt at Hinton House 1822 by Mr T. Smith with key.

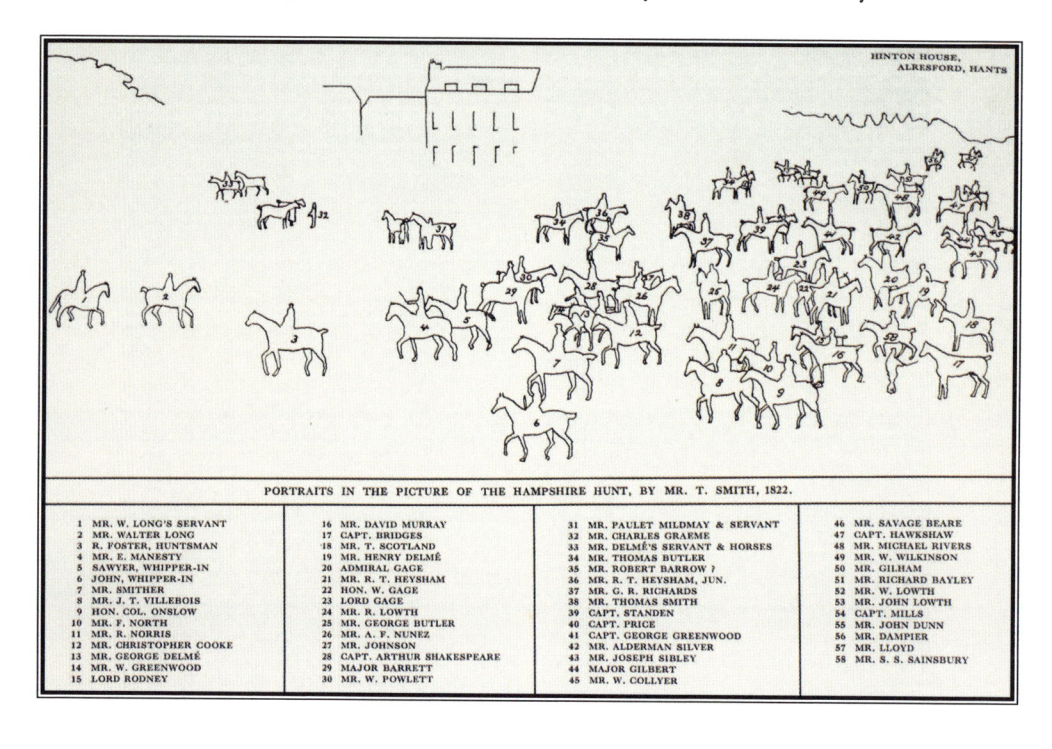

PORTRAITS IN THE PICTURE OF THE HAMPSHIRE HUNT, BY MR. T. SMITH, 1822.

1 MR. W. LONG'S SERVANT	16 MR. DAVID MURRAY	31 MR. PAULET MILDMAY & SERVANT	46 MR. SAVAGE BEARE
2 MR. WALTER LONG	17 CAPT. BRIDGES	32 MR. CHARLES GRAEME	47 CAPT. HAWKSHAW
3 R. FOSTER, HUNTSMAN	18 MR. T. SCOTLAND	33 MR. DELMÉ'S SERVANT & HORSES	48 MR. MICHAEL RIVERS
4 MR. E. MANESTY	19 MR. HENRY DELMÉ	34 MR. THOMAS BUTLER	49 MR. W. WILKINSON
5 SAWYER, WHIPPER-IN	20 ADMIRAL GAGE	35 MR. ROBERT BARROW ?	50 MR. GILHAM
6 JOHN, WHIPPER-IN	21 MR. R. T. HEYSHAM	36 MR. R. T. HEYSHAM, JUN.	51 MR. RICHARD BAYLEY
7 MR. SMITHER	22 HON. W. GAGE	37 MR. G. R. RICHARDS	52 MR. W. LOWTH
8 MR. J. T. VILLEBOIS	23 LORD GAGE	38 MR. THOMAS SMITH	53 MR. JOHN LOWTH
9 HON. COL. ONSLOW	24 MR. R. LOWTH	39 CAPT. STANDEN	54 CAPT. MILLS
10 MR. F. NORTH	25 MR. GEORGE BUTLER	40 CAPT. PRICE	55 MR. JOHN DUNN
11 MR. R. NORRIS	26 MR. A. F. NUNEZ	41 CAPT. GEORGE GREENWOOD	56 MR. DAMPIER
12 MR. CHRISTOPHER COOKE	27 MR. JOHNSON	42 MR. ALDERMAN SILVER	57 MR. LLOYD
13 MR. GEORGE DELMÉ	28 CAPT. ARTHUR SHAKESPEARE	43 MR. JOSEPH SIBLEY	58 MR. S. S. SAINSBURY
14 MR. W. GREENWOOD	29 MAJOR BARRETT	44 MAJOR GILBERT	
15 LORD RODNEY	30 MR. W. POWLETT	45 MR. W. COLLYER	

— 28 —

Despite his patronising views on Hampshire, Nimrod hunted several times with the HH and was fulsome in his praise for the Master, the huntsman, hounds, and inhabitants of the county. John Villebois was a popular Master who commanded widespread respect, and though not a thrusting horseman, had the ability to keep in close contact with hounds throughout a long run thanks to his knowledge of venery and the country. Dick Foster was a gifted woodland huntsman blessed with quick reactions, a remarkable rapport with his hounds and the ability to press his fox like no other. He liked a good holloa to get hounds on through the woodlands and his whippers-in were said to be of similar high quality, Sawyer's piercing holloa signalling the start of many a fine hunt. The first whipper-in and huntsman once quarrelled so badly that they did not speak away from the hunting field for three long years, but neither man allowed their disagreement to compromise the high standard of sport, and Sawyer described his superior as 'the very best woodland huntsman I ever saw.'

Nimrod was so impressed by every aspect of Squire Villeboy's outstanding hunting establishment that he tactlessly opined that 'such fine hounds, able huntsman, clever whipper-in, and a liberal master should not all be transported to a better country. Fortunate it is for the Hampshire sportsmen that they have them.' The establishment was so good that Nimrod even railed against men who left England during winter to tour Europe, as was fashionable amongst high society at the time, suggesting the deserters should be compelled to remain and experience the unique sport provided by Mr Villebois's Hampshire Hunt. It is thanks to Nimrod, *The Sporting Magazine* and the infallible *Hampshire Chronicle*, that we have so many accurate accounts of great hunting runs during this golden era in the Hunt's history. These include a 30-mile run recorded by *The Sporting Magazine* during Dick Foster's second season carrying the horn on December 6th 1817, when hounds raced through thirteen parishes from Woodmancote Holt to Weston Park. A fortnight later they went one better, running forty miles on a fox found at Abbotstone and killing close to Farnham, after the pack had been joined by a goat for the last two miles of the hunt.

In February 1821 the *Hampshire Chronicle* reported that a hard-hunted fox took refuge in a chimney at Ovington, from which he was removed in a sack by the villagers, turned down in front of hounds and killed in fine style. On March 17th 1823 hounds ran so hard and fast that even the brilliant Dick Foster could not live with them, and Edward Knight from Chawton Park was the only man up at the finish. A month later an Abbotstone Down fox was hunted for two hours

The end of a 14-mile point on January 11th 1825 by Mr W. Collyer.

and 50 minutes to College Woods, Bighton where he fell into a well. Mr Scotland of Bishop's Sutton was lowered down 35 feet on a rope and managed to grab the hapless fox by the scruff of the neck, which was then released and quickly caught. Nimrod narrowly missed a tremendous run with the smaller pack on January 11th 1825, having only returned home from a hunting visit to the HH the previous day. Having made a fourteen-mile point[6] from Beauworth to Town Hill three miles from Southampton, the fox took refuge on the bacon rack of a private dwelling house, a scene commemorated in a fine painting by Mr Collyer of Chiffland.

    John Villebois's 30-year tenure is remembered for these and other extraordinary hunts, which would be unimaginable two centuries later; but a

---

6   A point is the distance between the two points that are furthest apart during the course of a specific hunt, and not necessarily the distance between the start and finish of a hunting run.

THE FIRST GOLDEN AGE 1795–1837

John Villebois MFH from 1802–1837.

JOHN TRUMAN VILLEBOIS
MASTER AND OWNER OF THE HAMPSHIRE HOUNDS,
1802-1837.

Just before going to press, the author was enabled by the kindness of Mrs. Bayford of Bursledon, a grand-daughter of Mr. Stephen Terry, owner and squire of Dummer, to obtain an old and faded photograph of a portrait of Mr. Villebois. As the original picture could not be traced, this fine pencil drawing was specially made for this book.

The author is indebted to the same lady for the loan of the very entertaining diaries kept by her grandfather, Mr. Stephen Terry, during the years 1841-1860, containing a number of references to the H.H. Hunt, which are mostly embodied in Æsop's reminiscences.

problem that was to become a recurring theme throughout the Hunt's history was noted for the first time in April 1818. Foxes had been so hard to find during the previous season that a small subcommittee of Members was appointed to liaise with landowners in order to avoid a collapse of the Hunt through having no quarry to pursue. Their efforts must have been successful, for during the 1822 season there were no blank days during cubhunting, and hounds had accounted for eighteen brace by Christmas.

The 1833–1834 season was a poor one, and there were grumblings that the once brilliant Dick Foster was beginning to slow up. Three years later John Truman Villebois died at his home at Harmsworth on April 12th whilst still in office as Master, having steered the good fortunes of the Hampshire Hunt for a remarkable 35 years.

He left annuities to all the hunt staff and his cherished, carefully bred pack of hounds to his brother in the Craven country. His funeral was conducted at Old Alresford by the Bishop of Guildford on a day when the whole town fell silent in mourning, and tradesmen closed their shops as a mark of respect for a man who had endeared himself to every level of society. Sporting correspondents of the time described Squire Villeboy's Mastership of superb sport and political stability as the golden age of the Hampshire Hunt, however in the years to come there would be other, equally eligible, contenders for the accolade.

Chapter Three 1837–1862

Seasons of Discontent

Major Barrett 1837–1842, A. Onslow Esq., 1842–1845, Captain Haworth 1845–1847, Lord Gifford 1847–1850, E. Knight Esq., and a Committee 1850–1852, R. Pearse Esq., 1852–1855, E. Knight Esq., 1855–1856, E. Tredcroft Esq., 1856–1862.

Major Barrett becomes Master in 1837, loan of country to the Hambledon Hunt, Dick Foster replaced as huntsman by Jack Shirley, some good hunting runs, Augustus Onslow becomes Master in 1842, kennels established at Ropley in 1846 on donated land, Captain Haworth becomes Master in 1845, Lord Gifford becomes Master in 1847, Acting Mastership of Edward Knight, James Scott and Francis Jervoise of Herriard in 1850, purchase of new pack of hounds, William Summers as huntsman and hunting anecdotes, Robert Pearse becomes Master in 1852, Edward Knight becomes Master for a second term in 1855, shortage of hounds and Rugby and Tattersalls hound sales, Edward Tredcroft becomes Master in 1856, frequent changes of professional huntsmen, crisis following Edward Tredcroft's resignation in 1862 with no candidate to replace him as Master.

After John Villebois's death his brother-in-law, 64-year-old Major Barrett, took on the Management of the Hounds for the 1837–1838 season and the kennels were moved from Harmsworth to Cheriton. Major Barrett, who was always impeccably turned out both on and off the hunting field, had seen service in the Peninsular campaign as an Eleventh Light Dragoon before retiring with the rank of Major in 1814. The late Master had left his fabulous pack to his brother, Frederick Villebois, who generously lent them to Major Barrett. The loan may have been made permanent in the fullness of time, since there is no record of more hounds being purchased until Mr Napper's pack were sold to the HH Club in 1850. A further consequence of John Villebois's demise was the loan of country to the west of the River Itchen to the Rev Sir John Barker Mill, a keen sportsman and long-standing member of the HH Club. The loan was agreed for three years only but was subsequently extended and led to the formation of the Hursley Hunt as a subscription pack.

The period following the demise of such a long and successful era was followed by a succession of short Masterships and different huntsmen, although Dick Foster remained for two more seasons until his retirement in 1840. Foster continued to show good sport until the end of his career, including a day on November 13th 1838, when hounds ran like smoke from Fulley near Tichborne to kill at Hazely Row between Morestead and Twyford after 55 minutes without a check. Earlier that year the gentlemen and yeomen of Hampshire marked their appreciation of the huntsman's loyal service with John Villebois during race day at Tichborne Down. Michael Rivers of Bishops Sutton presented him with a silver tankard and a silver hunting horn inscribed 'Presented to Mr Richard Foster for uniform good conduct and skill as huntsman during 24 years' service with the late J. T. Villebois Esq., Master of the HH. April 1838.' The money to pay for the expensive silverware was raised by half-crown subscriptions.

Foster retired in 1840 and was replaced by his most capable first whipper-in, Jack Shirley, whose father had been painted by Ferneley when huntsman to Sir Richard Sutton at the Burton. When Major Barrett handed over the Management of the Hounds to Augustus Onslow in 1842, he was presented with a fine piece of silver plate by the grateful Members. Shirley continued as huntsman for the new Master and provided consistently good sport during his four seasons in Hampshire. Notable runs during his time carrying the horn include the 1841 Opening Meet, when a fox found in Cheriton Wood was killed in the lake beneath The Grange within yards of where the HH Club Members and hounds were to be painted by Mr Spalding four years later, the very same lake that nearly defeated hounds during a hunt in November 2021. *Bell's Life* reported a superb Christmas Eve hunt in 1842 when hounds found an outlier near Cheriton Wood which led them over Tichborne Down, through Ropley to Newton Common, Chawton Park and on to Langrish Farm at Greatham, where they ran into their pilot after two hours and ten minutes with only seven riders up at the finish. The fox was not the only casualty of this epic hunt; Mr Gearing's horse later died of exhaustion, not an infrequent occurrence before the invention of mechanical horse clipping machines in the early twentieth century.

Shirley's last great run as huntsman to the HH was a thirteen-mile point from Chilton Wood near Thorny Down to Crabwood near Lainston in two hours and ten minutes on February 8th 1843. During this hunt the pack crossed the railway line above Waller's Ash Tunnel, near King's Worthy, which ten months earlier had been the scene of a terrible accident when stonework collapsed during a routine

Augustus Onslow MFH 1842–1845 at Upton House near Alresford with huntsman Will Cox and whipper-in George Cox. Painted by Charles Spalding.

repair, killing four men employed by the London and South West Railway company. News of Shirley's skills must have travelled far, for he left in May 1843 to take up appointment as huntsman to the Duke of Cleveland. Six years later the professional huntsman met a violent end when murdered by poachers whilst assisting gamekeepers at Raby Castle in County Durham.

Jack Shirley was replaced by Will Cox, who served two seasons with Mr Onslow. In his first season hounds ran from Easters near Horsedown Common to kill in Humbly Grove, during which their new huntsman was said to have 'handled them in a most workmanlike manner.' However the partnership was not to last, for Augustus Onslow resigned after three seasons in office and was replaced by Captain Martin Haworth who brought his own pack from Devon. He hunted them as an amateur, although the West Country hounds were said to be too fast for Hampshire. Their dash and drive was apparent during an historic joint meet with the HH, Hursley and Hambledon at Cranbury Park on February 13th 1846, which took place the morning after a grand ball in Winchester, where Members of the HH

Club wore the evening livery of blue coats with white waistcoats and guests dined on food provided by Gunter's of Berkeley Square in London. The combined pack was hunted by the Hambledon's professional huntsman, John Squires, and a fox was accounted for in thick woodland after a fast 55 minutes; the huntsmen of all three packs rushed in to secure the brush, but it was Squires who emerged with the prize.

Although Aesop describes the Captain's abilities as a horseman, huntsman and diplomat in glowing terms, he gave up the hounds in 1847 after only two seasons due to escalating costs. Captain Haworth may not have remained long at the helm, however the relocation of the kennels from Cheriton to their present-day site at Ropley during his Mastership in 1846 was of momentous significance. Over the years the original acre and a quarter site generously donated by Mr Wilkinson of Alresford has been added to and disposed of in almost equal measure, but Ropley has been home to the Hampshire Hunt hounds ever since. Haworth was replaced by another amateur huntsman in Lord Gifford, a former Master of the Vale of White Horse and Ludlow, who brought his own 60 couple of hounds to the new kennels at Ropley.

During Lord Gifford's three-year tenure of the HH country the well foxed coverts and estates of Farleigh, Nutley, Herriard, Dummer, Tichborne, Brockwood and Beauworth are all singled out for praise by Actaeon writing in *The Sporting Magazine* in 1848. A year later an advertisement appeared condemning unsportsmanlike fox destruction in the Rotherfield coverts, a sinister precursor of a problem that would afflict the Hampshire Hunt in many areas of their country in the years ahead. Thanks to Cecil's observations in the same publication we also know that the practice of holloaing as loudly as possible, much encouraged by Dick Foster during his time as huntsman, was still endemic within the hunt. Cecil opined that there was no county in England to rival Hampshire for what he considered to be a habit of dubious merit, especially when the person holloaing is nowhere near where they saw the fox. 'Every man, woman and child, the instant they get sight of the fox, begins to halloo as if they expected to get paid for it,' he laments. Despite this, or perhaps because of it, hounds continued to show terrific sport including an exceptional hunt following the meet at the Golden Pot in March 1848 when they found in Rowe Wood and killed an hour and 45 minutes later at Mareland's Bridge, having traversed a huge area of Hampshire. The Golden Pot hostelry was a popular meet and is reputed to have been named after a gold receptacle kept especially for the Prince of Wales to relieve himself in when hunting locally in the late eighteenth century.

The hunt's run of short Masterships continued when Lord Gifford gave up after three seasons in 1850 and returned with his hounds to Herefordshire. After George Wall's offer to manage the country was declined the hunt was run by a committee with Edward Knight of Chawton House as acting Master supported by James Scott of Rotherfield and Francis Jervoise of Herriard. The Club purchased Mr Napper's Findhorn pack to replace Lord Gifford's hounds and engaged the Findhorn's former huntsman, Will Summers, to continue in the same role. Summers had previously served with several other hunts including the Surrey Staghounds, the Duke of Cumberland's and West Kent, and was soon being compared favourably with Foster. A tribute to his judgement as a huntsman was recorded by *Baily's Magazine*, which reported that he had trusted a favourite old hound in favour of men cracking whips and claiming the line of a hare. As soon as the old hound opened, he was cheered by Summers to the echo, and a tremendous hunt ensued on a fox that had slipped away from covert long before the hunt had arrived.

The trend of short Masterships showed no sign of abating as men continued to come and go with destabilising frequency. Robert Pearse, who had been hunting the country between Odiham and Alton with his private pack of harriers, gave them up to become Master in 1852 with Charles Roberts as his huntsman. Pearse improved the kennels by introducing draft hounds from Lord Fitzhardinge,[1] but when he moved on left insufficient hounds for his successor to hunt four days a week. On his departure Edward Knight stepped back into the breech with Joseph Orbell hunting hounds, but he was soon to regret the expense of his undertaking. At the annual meeting of the HH Club on April 2nd 1856 Mr Knight explained how he had been compelled to purchase draft hounds out of his own pocket to make up the deficit of only 10½ couple left by his predecessor. He later wrote to the Hunt Club to clarify that only 5½ couple had been bred in the spring of 1853 and that he had spent over £76 purchasing 9 couple of puppies and 16½ couple of entered hounds at the start of the previous season.

The shortage of hounds may not have been entirely the fault of his predecessors, for distemper was rife throughout the nineteenth century and whole litters were sometimes lost to the disease right up until the 1950s when an effective vaccine became widely available. Masters were able to replace losses at Rugby and Tattersalls hound sales, and since many were still privately owned, entire packs of

---

1   Lord Fitzhardinge's hounds were also known as the Berkeley. The 1852 entry in the Foxhound Kennel Studbook describes the pack as 'The Berkeley (Earl Fitzhardinge's).'

Rules of the HH Club in 1853.

List of Members of the HH Club in 1854.

hounds were sometimes offered for sale. Prices varied according to the reputation of the hounds for sale. Squire Osbalderton's Burton hounds made 5,219 guineas when sold at Tattersall's in 1840, which was more than six times the sum he had paid for them 34 years earlier; by contrast the Wheatland pack made just 750 guineas in 1867. Edward Knight was offered £1,300 to manage the hounds despite a deficit in the accounts of just over £18 and was given until May 1st to accept or refuse. In the event of him declining, a committee including Lord Ashburton and Francis Jervoise agreed to 'hunt the country four days a week as usual' for £1,160.

Members met again on May 21st and agreed to reimburse Edward Knight for his outlay in purchasing hounds should funds permit at the close of the year, there currently being no available surplus. More importantly, it was announced that terms had been agreed with Mr Tredcroft of Warnham Court, Horsham, to hunt the country for the following season, 'on the usual days and according to the usual fixtures, keeping a huntsman and whipper-in, paying for the earth stopping and other expenses,' up until April 6th 1857 on a guarantee of £1,130. Mr Tredcroft reserved the right to remove any stallion hounds he had purchased but undertook to leave 50 couple plus puppies at the end of the season. The minutes record that 'The Master of the HH, Mr E. Tredcroft,' was unanimously elected as an Honorary member of the HH Club at a special meeting on November 18th 1856, which is possibly the first time an incumbent Manager of the Hounds is described as 'Master' in the HH records.

Edward Tredcroft remained in office for six seasons until 1862, but his term was beset by squabbles over the size of his guarantee, huntsmen who came and went with suspicious alacrity, and complaints about the manner in which he organised the country. However Mr Tredcroft's resolute determination to remain at the helm ushered in an era of stable Masterships that would endure for many years and ended nearly two decades of turbulence during which two important HH Club minute books were seemingly lost without trace. The subject of the missing books was raised by the Hon. Secretary of the HH Club, A. F. Coryton, nearly a century later during a meeting in November 1949, at which Colonel Mitchell suggested an appeal for the lost books be placed in the *Hampshire Chronicle*. Whatever measures were taken met with some success, for the first minute book dating from 1795 was recovered, however two unique records of the Club's history from 1809–1837 and 1837–1856 have never been found.

Money was in short supply during Mr Tredcroft's Mastership, and Members were unable to offer him more than £1,200 to continue after the end of his first season, although all agreed that additional funds must be raised to cover the cost of replenishing a diminished pack of hounds. Despite protracted negotiations the guarantee did not increase for the 1859–1860 season, although the Master warned Members that the Hunt was costing him £2,500 a year to run, and that unless £1,500 could be found going forward he would have no option but to leave at the end of the season. The Club agreed to this sum for 1861–1862 and decided to raise the extra money by increasing Members' subscriptions.

Given the rapid turnover of hunt staff, it is perhaps surprising that Edward Tredcroft clung on so determinedly to the Mastership. His first huntsman, George Kennet, stayed for two seasons before being succeeded by Henry Nason, who was replaced at the end of his first season after letters from Members expressing dissatisfaction with his performance were read out during a meeting at the Swan Inn on February 8th 1860. Next up was Will Stansby from Badminton, but he also lasted for only one season and was replaced by William Fisher. For the last two years of his Mastership, Mr Tredcroft and Fisher hunted hounds on alternate days, fulfilling an ambition Tredcroft had nurtured from the start of his reign. But it was not to last. In February 1861 three Members reduced their subscriptions and Mr Knight wrote to withdraw from the club. At the same meeting Mr Tredcroft gave notice that 'after the next season he should be prevented from continuing to hunt the country.' There was no bluffing from either side this time, and in January 1862 the Hon. Secretary was instructed to advertise for a new Master and a small selection committee was appointed to interview the applicants. The Club was prepared to offer a suitable candidate £1,150 to hunt the country four days a week provided he employed a professional huntsman and returned 55 couple plus puppies when leaving.

Major Fletcher was offered the Mastership on these terms at the annual meeting in early April but asked for a day to consider the offer. The Major must have got cold feet, for when Members next gathered for a hastily arranged meeting on the racecourse at Abbotstone Down during the hunt races on April 23rd they learnt that Fletcher had declined the Mastership and the selection committee had no further offer before them. With May just around the corner and no prospect of a Master for the coming season, this was a catastrophic turn of events. The powers of the subcommittee were strengthened, and 'in the event of no gentleman coming forward to take the hounds before autumn,' were given full authority to make whatever arrangements they thought best for hunting the country for the 1862–1863 season.

Chapter Four 1862–1884

An Angel in Top Boots

H. Deacon Esq., 1862–1884.

Henry Deacon's history and arrival in Hampshire, his offer to hunt hounds accepted, his skills as a huntsman and diplomat, revision of Club rules and regulations, the decline of the Hampshire Hunt Cup and races, damage complaints, the ascent of driven game shooting, restricted access to hounds and vulpicide, loans of country to the Chiddingfold, Garth and Hursley Hunts, Masters of Hounds committee and Boodles Club, letter to landowners protesting vulpicide agreed but not sent, Henry Deacon's resignation following a fire which destroyed horses and property, Henry Deacon's retirement presentation in Alresford.

May came and went without an applicant for the Mastership, but in early June of 1862 a certain Mr Henry Deacon visited the kennels at Ropley and stated his willingness to take on the hounds provided a residence for his family could be procured in the neighbourhood. Mr Deacon was born in 1823 and educated at Westminster but had been brought up in the shadow of Dartmoor at Holwell, near Tavistock. When eighteen years old Henry carried the horn with a pack of harriers founded jointly with his brother to hunt the Devon countryside and moorland surrounding their home. In 1853 he sold the harriers and purchased Mr Morgan's foxhounds to hunt the modern day Lamerton country for a further five seasons. In addition to his excellent reputation as a huntsman, Mr Deacon was

Henry Deacon MFH 1862–1884

also a consummate horseman and amateur jockey who had won a steeplechase at Totnes riding with his arm in a sling the day after it had been broken in a nasty fall.

Perhaps Mr Deacon had tired of hunting in Devon where greater skill is required to navigate bogs than fences, and the countryside could not be more different than Hampshire. Others have suggested he was disillusioned by a shortage of foxes, but for whatever reason the Deacons decided to chance their arm up country. Having decided to investigate Dorset or Yorkshire they saw an advertisement for the Mastership of the Hampshire Hunt which Caroline Deacon insisted her husband apply for. Henry was to recall her firm intervention with gratitude at his retirement dinner 22 years later, where the Chairman told guests that Mr Deacon came to Hampshire 'with a great reputation as a man who was hard to beat across a difficult country, and a man who knew more about a horse, a hound or a fox than most; better still he had the character of being a thorough sportsman.'

Although the Deacons arrived in Winchester on their first visit to Hampshire – a county where they knew no one – in June, arrangements to hunt the country on a guarantee of £1,400 per annum were not finalised until after the purchase of Ropley Cottage had been agreed in August. Mr Deacon proposed a three year term, but Members were reluctant to pledge a large sum so far ahead, so it was agreed that the arrangement could be terminated by either party at the close of each financial year, subject to 'an honourable understanding on both sides that every effort would be made to continue for the full period originally contemplated.' At this time a disagreement with the retiring Master regarding the disputed ownership of four couple of hounds came to light. Not for the first or last time, Members' diplomacy prevailed, and although they did not believe the validity of Mr Tredcroft's claim it was decided to pay him £25 to 'avoid controversy with a gentleman who had hunted the country with great liability.'

Will Fisher stayed on to hunt hounds but left after one season and was replaced by Charles Pike, who had been a second horseman to Captain Haworth and already knew the country. The new Master was a stickler for punctuality and made it clear during an early cubhunting morning address at Bramdean Common that, with the exception of royalty, during his Mastership hounds would wait for no one. Neither professional huntsman impressed the Master, who observed that both were highly successful in losing the fox. In February 1865 he offered to hunt hounds himself, sweetening the proposition by suggesting a guarantee of £1,400 compared to £1,600 if he employed a professional huntsman. The committee did not like the idea of appointing 'a gentleman huntsman,' Mr Deacon recalled later, 'and if a shell had burst amongst them, they could not have been more frightened.' However reservations were overcome, and a month later the Master's proposal was accepted at a special meeting at the Swan Inn in Alresford.

The new huntsman quickly established a glowing reputation for his skill on the hunting field, even temper, courtesy and diplomacy that contributed to his huge popularity with all sectors of society, especially the farmers of Hampshire. *Baily's Magazine* reported that he could 'ride through any of the farmers' houses without them crying ware crockery,' and there are numerous testaments to his kindness and tact throughout his long Mastership. Henry Deacon is also remembered as a consummate MFH both in kennels and the hunting field, and as good a huntsman as any of his predecessors. Ever modest and self-deprecating, he recalled how everyone would praise him during a run of good sport, but when things were not going so well some would say, 'that old codger is getting slow.' Nevertheless, during the 1868 season the old codger killed a remarkable 41½ brace. Great hunting runs during his time included a three-hour hunt on December 23rd 1880, a straight run from Sheetlands over the River Loddon to kill at Sherfield in November 1881 and on February 5th 1876 a fifteen-mile point from Hen Wood in Herriard Park all the way east to Bentley Station. The fox from Hen Wood was lost that day, however when hounds returned to the same covert shortly before the end of the season they found again and ran due south to ground in Sutton Wood near Alresford having made an eight-mile point.

During Henry Deacon's reign the rules and regulations of the Club were revised and brought up to date, firstly on March 6th 1865 when subscriptions were increased to a minimum of £20 and rule nine amended to reiterate that red coats must be worn in the hunting field, and blue coats and white waistcoats adorned with HH buttons when the occasion called for evening dress. Members were obliged to honour the dress code and forfeit half a dozen bottles of claret if they appeared incorrectly attired, although clergymen were given special dispensation. Since arrangements to hunt the country were normally settled a year in advance and paid for by Members' subscriptions, rule two required Members to give advance notice by the previous February if they wished to leave the Club. Further changes and amendments were considered at subsequent meetings and following a special meeting of the Club at Chawton House on November 5th 1877, printed copies of the latest rules were made and circulated. By and large Members abided by them, although it was sometimes necessary to pursue individuals, such as Lord Ashburton

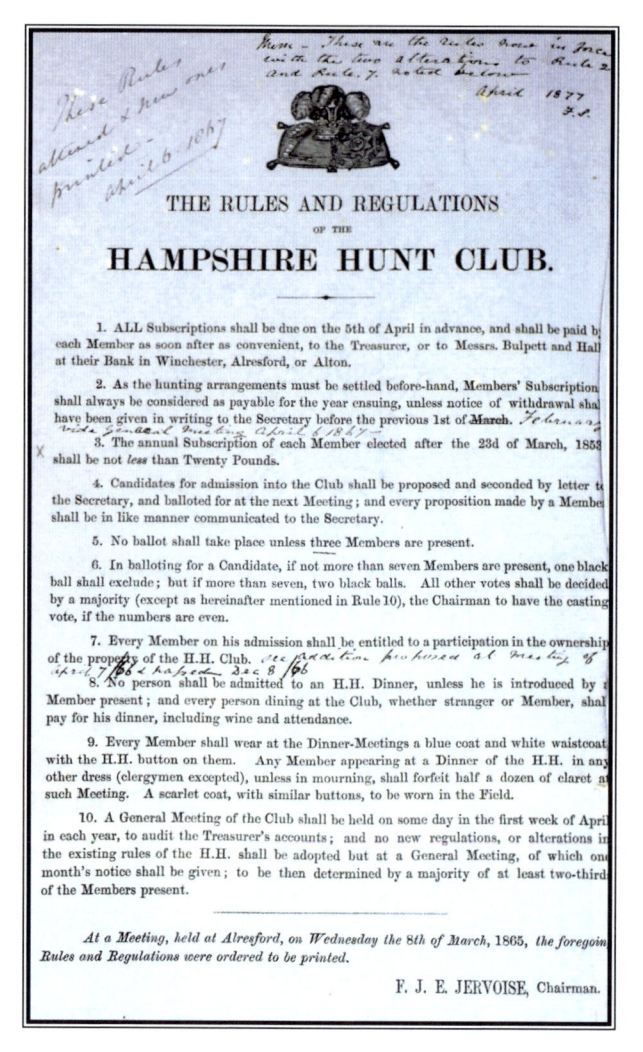

The rules and regulations of the HH Club in 1865.

in 1894, for late or insufficient payment.

The sixteen rules of the Hampshire Hunt Club agreed in 1795 were accompanied by a further eleven Rules for the Cup, however the revised 1877 rules make no reference to the Cup or hunt races, whose popularity appeared to have waned during the second half of the nineteenth century. This is surprising given Mr Deacon's record as a successful amateur jockey, but references to the Hunt Cup during his Mastership are few and far between. There were no HH races at all in 1878, so Members agreed to ask the Hambledon Hunt for permission to hold the

Members of the HH Club in March 1865.

Hampshire Hunt Farmers' Cup at their meeting instead. At the fateful Members' meeting on February 29th 1884 it was also proposed by Captain Pigott that the Hampshire Hunt races be discontinued on two counts. Not only was there no suitable place to hold them, but there were also very few horses in the Hampshire Hunt country 'qualified to run under the new Grand National Rules.' The proposal was carried unanimously and, for the time being, HH races fell into abeyance.

During this time ever more hunts were converting to subscription packs rather than the private enterprises of old, which often sprang up on the whim of wealthy landowners to hunt the country surrounding their place of residence. As hunting arrangements became increasingly formalised an inevitable jostling over hunt boundaries and country followed, with entrenched disputes being referred to the Masters of Hounds Committee, which was the forerunner of the Masters of Foxhounds Association, for consideration at Boodles Club in London. When the Chiddingfold were granted permission on an annually renewable basis in 1869 to draw HH country south of the Farnham and Gosport roads, their Secretary, James Sadler, acknowledged the loan with gratitude and added, 'I hope it will be the means of keeping a few more foxes in that neighbourhood for at present I fear it is a dangerous locality for them.'

Although Members were generous in making country available to hunts less fortunate than themselves, they were quick to claim it back when needed. In 1863 the chairman of the HH Club, Mr Graeme, met with Sir William Heathcote representing the gentlemen of the Hursley country to consider country loaned out after the death of John Villebois 26 years earlier. Mr Graeme wished to reassert the Hampshire Hunt's hitherto undisputed right to hunt the Hursley country on behalf of the Members, however his suggestion that the matter be referred to Boodles was declined by the Hursley. Both sides retired to consider their options, but that was far from the end of the dispute. In 1873 Mr Deacon was asked to arrange for the resumption of the Hampshire Hunt's right to draw all the coverts previously loaned to Mr Garth with the exception of Greywell.

In 1876 Mr Comb of Pierrepont was granted permission to draw parts of HH country east of the Bentley Green to Petersfield road, but the decision did not sit particularly well with the new occupant of Alice Holt, Clement Milward, who politely questioned the wisdom of overhunting the land he owned. The HH's Hon. Secretary, Fred Stephens, wrote to apologise for the oversight – 'the Hunt overlooked the fact that those arrangements might not be acceptable to you' – but explained that whilst Members were unwilling to relinquish their traditional country, they did not wish to withdraw permission to Mr Comb either. He asked if the current arrangements could continue on an annual basis and assured Mr Milward that for the duration of the loan the HH would not meet with the intention of drawing the Holt, and only draw his coverts if they happened to run in. Mr Milward wrote back to confirm the proposal was entirely acceptable and that he was glad Members appreciated he only wished to assist their sport. The arrangement with Mr Comb continued up until 1884 when he gave up his hounds and the HH resumed hunting the Alice Holt country on a regular basis.

Despite Henry Deacon's great popularity and consistently good sport, the early stirrings of problems that were to beset foxhunting in general with increasing regularity began to manifest themselves in the Hunt records. After many years of comparative prosperity, British agriculture was entering an extended period of depression caused by a dramatic decline in the price of grain after the American prairies were exploited for cereal production. The far reaching ramifications would extend to the English hunting field where farmers were faced with a crippling loss of income that led to greater concern over damage caused by the Hunt to crops.

In 1863 the owner of the Beauworth coverts, Mr Mulcock, declined access for a cubhunting meet in September until he had been able to establish new rides through his coverts. Their purpose was to provide an alternative route for the mounted field, which had ridden over the farmer's beans on three occasions the previous season. The Secretary met the farmer to inspect the new rides and gates that he had installed at his own expense. 'Far from wishing to debar the gentlemen of the neighbourhood from their sport,' Mr Mulcock hoped the new rides demonstrated his willingness to assist the hunt and requested written assurance that the field would in future stick to the tracks made especially for them, 'in order to prevent mischief being done on strong land.' All appeared to have been resolved after the Secretary wrote to thank the landowner for his kind assistance and promised him hounds would not draw the Beauworth coverts except when meeting at Four Lanes. However injury to crops elsewhere was inevitable, and in order to address this problem a small subcommittee of Members was appointed in 1882 to assist the Master in preventing unnecessary damage.

The other problem was less easily resolved. When Mr Deacon arrived in 1860 only Rotherfield estate preserved game, but that was all set to change with the mid nineteenth century invention of double-barrelled breech loaders, which were more accurate and powerful than the guns they replaced. As a result, driven shooting involving gamekeepers, reared game and the wholescale destruction of vermin became increasingly prominent and brought the ancient sport of hunting with hounds and the modern one of driven shooting into conflict. Hunts in Hampshire were already used to the fox trapping activities of men who jealously guarded their employers' semi-domesticated rabbits as a valuable source of income. Warreners were paid to desist in vulpicide, but inevitably there were unscrupulous operators who pocketed the bribe but continued to destroy foxes. In April 1866 the Secretary of the Hambledon Hunt wrote to the HH Club requesting they do not pay Stanbrook as usual since they had found a trap near his warren instead of foxes. In

1871 a farmer wrote to the Club to ask them to examine a dead fox discovered on his farm and a landowner came across a brace of foxes with traps still attached. The initialled traps belonged to a Mr Rupells, whose warrener was being paid 50 shillings a year by the Hunt as compensation for fox damage. Shortly after that incident the Hunt Club stopped paying warreners altogether and started to reward gamekeepers with 'find' money instead.

It wasn't just trapping; at a general meeting at Herriard Park in April 1873 the Master stated that if any of his hounds died from poison, he should feel discharged from his liability to make up the agreed number at the end of his tenure. In February 1878 the scarcity of foxes on the Tuesday side of the country was so severe that it was decided to discontinue hunting there for the remainder of the season. A motion proposed by Mr Fitzpatrick and seconded by Viscount Baring to form a committee to encourage the preservation of foxes and to prevail on tenants and gamekeepers to forsake the use of steel traps was carried unanimously. Sport was not only compromised by fox destruction. Certain landowners, including some members of the Club, started restricting hunt access to their coverts until December, and in 1873 a letter to this effect from Lord Ashburton was read out to Members at a meeting. By 1882 the situation had become so worrying that Members agreed a letter should be sent to all covert owners in the country addressing this delicate subject.

For all his immense popularity, skills as a huntsman and fearless horsemanship, Henry Deacon could not resist holding out for an increase in his guarantee with monotonous regularity. The Master invariably settled for less than he wished, but only after resigning his position in a ritual described in the Hunt minutes as his annual resignation. When Mr Deacon asked for £1,500 towards the end of his second season, he had to be reminded that the spirit of the original agreement was for him to serve three years on a guarantee of £1,450 per annum. 'You will observe that our present proposal varies from yours only to the extent of £50' the Secretary wrote, 'but we assure you that in making it, we have stretched our estimate of means to the very utmost.' Mr Deacon accepted.

He resigned in February 1867 on account of escalating costs but settled soon afterwards for £1,600. In 1874 the exasperated Secretary recorded that 'Mr Deacon's letter of February 2nd was read, signifying his (annual) resignation…' As always, an agreement was reached in time. Some years it required the intervention of a wealthy Member, such as Lord Calthorpe in 1879 and Lord Northbrook, who agreed £100 by telegram in 1881, to volunteer the extra funds required to keep Mr Deacon in office. In 1880 Mr Deacon questioned whether he should be paying for dog licences in January, which had been introduced by the Dog Licences Act of 1867, when he was not even sure of continuing as Master for the following year. The Members agreed the licences should be taken out in the name of the Hunt but believed there was nothing unfair about Mr Deacon paying for them. Somewhat surprisingly, the Master agreed to cover the extra cost.

Mr Deacon resigned as usual in January 1884, but the Secretary's written request for him to reconsider fell on stony ground, for the Master wrote back on February 6th complaining bitterly about the shortage of foxes that season and issuing an ultimatum. 'I am much obliged to the gentlemen of the hunt for asking me to withdraw my resignation as Master,' he wrote, 'and I shall be more than happy to do so provided the landowners of different coverts where foxes are scarce will guarantee it shall be better this season. If not, I shall defer explaining as I cannot give satisfaction or sport.' Three days later Mr Deacon was advised by the Secretary that members had agreed to send a letter to that effect to all covert owners and was asked to confirm that he would therefore continue for another season.

The original letter, handwritten in black ink with an indecipherable signature on House of Commons paper, is attached neatly inside the Hunt minute book. The missive pulls no punches, explaining that the Hunt is on the cusp of losing one of the most popular and successful Masters in its history due to a scarcity of foxes and the 'growing indisposition of cubhunting in many quarters.' The shortage was said to be most acute in those parts of the Saturday and Monday country that lie beyond the roads leading from Alton to Petersfield and Odiham. Both complaints were directed at a level of game preservation and rearing that 'was almost unknown in Hampshire a few years ago,' accompanied by a heartfelt plea to covert owners and farmers to do everything possible to prevent the further decline of the county's reputation for fox preservation.

Before Henry Deacon had time to respond, events were overtaken by an altogether different tragedy that was the final nail in the coffin of his glorious long innings as Master. In February 1884 a savage fire swept through the stables at Ropley causing considerable damage and the loss of seven valuable horses. It was finally game over for Henry Deacon who put pen to paper on February 27th. 'Gentlemen' he wrote, 'I should have been happy to have acted as Master for next season, but on due consideration I feel I am not justified in rebuilding stabling for

THE HAMPSHIRE HUNT 1749–2022

Feb 1884

Sir,

The Hampshire Hunt Club have met with considerable difficulty in arranging for the management of the hounds after the close of the present season.

Mr Deacon has expressed his disinclination to retain the position of Master, in which he has been so popular and so successful during the last 20 years, in consequence of the scarcity of foxes which prevails in certain portions of the district and, likewise, of the growing indisposition to permit of cub hunting in many quarters.

The scarcity in question exists, for the most part, in that portion of the Saturday's and Monday's country which lies beyond the roads leading from Alton to Petersfield and Odiham respectively, and in the greater part of the Thursday country.

The objections felt to cub hunting appear to be increasing amongst those gentlemen interested in the breeding of pheasants in a way, and to an extent, which was almost unknown in Hampshire a few years ago.

I am requested by the members of the Hunt to ask the serious attention of the owners of Coverts to this subject, and to point out the injury which would be inflicted on the County generally were the old reputation of the H.H. for fox preservation suffered to decline. They have assured Mr Deacon of their anxiety to retain him in his position, & of their conviction that he, if any one, enjoys the support & confidence of the owners & occupiers of land, as well as of those who join him in the field. They

believe that the scarcity complained of is, to a great extent, accidental, and certainly not desired by proprietors or inhabitants in the H. H. country.

They venture therefore to appeal to all persons interested to do what may be in their power to bring about a thoroughly satisfactory state of things before the opening of the next hunting season.

I am Sir,
Yr obt svt —

Appeal to farmers and covert owners to preserve foxes in 1884.

fourteen horses. In addition there would be the expense of purchasing at least eight horses. Under these circumstances I beg to tender my resignation. Thanking you all for the kindness I have met with during my 22 years of Mastership.' On the last day of February 1884 Members accepted Mr Deacon's resignation with gratitude for the courteous and sportsmanlike manner in which he had conducted his Mastership. Under these altered circumstances, the strongly worded letter to covert owners was never sent.

In May 1884 a large and influential company of ladies and gentlemen assembled at the Town Hall, Alresford, for a presentation to the retired Master of a magnificent service of silver and other articles worth £600 from Members and friends of the Hampshire Hunt. Mr Deacon had asked for the presentation to be made privately, but the committee felt obliged to reconsider in light of the very strong feeling throughout Hampshire that he should be accorded a public farewell. A press cutting describing the event noted that 'the enthusiastic gathering of yesterday, demonstrated, if proof were necessary, that by his gentlemanly courtesy he has gained the respect and regard of all classes and of both sexes of society.' The Chairman and son of a former Master, Mr Montague Knight, cast his mind back to 1862 when the Hampshire Hunt had the good fortune to secure the services of Mr Deacon as Master, and noted the impact he had made on the country ever since. 'By his tact, courtesy, and kindliness of heart and manner, by his sympathy with sportsmen of all classes, high or low, rich, or poor, gentle, or simple, Mr Deacon had won the hearts of all with whom he had been brought into contact, and his name is a household word far beyond the length and breadth of the Hampshire Hunt country.'

For such a shy man, Henry Deacon gave a humorous and well received response. He recounted the circumstances that led to his arrival in Hampshire, the very warm welcome he received and his observations on the challenges and rewards of hunting hounds. Mr Deacon admitted that he was a hopeless shot who could not hit an elephant, but he had always sought to reconcile the interests of both sports and could not recollect a single incident when he had spoilt another man's shooting. He recalled to much laughter how he had been advised to swear at miscreants in the hunting field, but that he could not possibly bring himself to do so in the presence of so many lovely ladies. He also revealed that he had never received an unkind word from a farmer and thanked them from the bottom of his heart, explaining that his long Mastership had only been possible because of their support and help. When Mr Baily responded, he complimented the retiring Master on his sportsmanship and the good feeling that existed between farmers and the Hunt. He ended his short address by saying that the greatest difficulty facing Mr Deacon's successor would be having to follow 'an angel in top boots.'

> **PRESENTATION TO H. W. DEACON, ESQ.**
>
> *May 1884*
>
> Yesterday (Friday) afternoon a large and influential company of ladies and gentlemen assembled at the Town Hall, Alresford, to partake of a most *recherché* lunch, and to witness the presentation of a magnificent service of silver and other articles of the value of over £600, subscribed for by 250 members and friends of the Hampshire Hunt, as a token of respect and esteem towards the late master, Mr. H. W. Deacon, on his retirement from that position after 22 years' service. On Mr. Deacon signifying his intention of resigning the mastership it was felt that he could not be permitted to sever his connection with the hunt without some mark of the appreciation in which his services are held being made on the part of the gentry, agriculturists, and others, with whom he had made himself so universally popular. A committee was formed, consisting of Viscount Baring, M.P., and Messrs. M. G. Knight, W. Wickham (hon. sec.), A. H. Wood, F. M. E. Jervoise, W. Greenwood, M. Arnold, F. P. Baily, T. Cordery, J. Barton, G. Langrish, and J. Stratton, and into whose hands subscriptions rapidly flowed, the ladies contributing a very considerable sum. When it was found that the necessary arrangements could not be completed before the end of the hunting season, and that the presentation could not take place at a meet of the hounds, in accordance with the expressed wish of Mr. Deacon, it was intended to make the presentation privately, but so pronounced was the feeling that a public farewell should be accorded him that the committee were compelled to reconsider their plans, and hence the enthusiastic gathering of yesterday, demonstrating, if proof were necessary, that by his gentlemanly courtesy he has gained the respect and regard of all classes and of both sexes of society. Unfortunately a gloom was thrown over the closing days of Mr. Deacon's mastership by the destruction by fire of his stud of horses, and although, by the kindness of friends and others, he was enabled to finish the season, it was a serious loss to him, and, as he himself states, confirmed his wish to relinquish the horn, which he had previously thought of doing. The chair was occupied by Mr. M. G. Knight, himself a son of a former master, and among those present, several ladies gracing the occasion with their presence, were the following :—
>
> Viscount Wolmer, the Right Hon. G. Sclater-Booth, M.P., Mr. W. W. B. Beach, M.P., Mr. and Miss Beach, Mr. W. Wickham, Mr. A. H. Wood, Mr. F. M. E.

Presentation to Henry Deacon in May 1884.

Chapter Five 1884–1909

The Coryton and Jervoise Era

A.H. Wood Esq., 1884–1888, F. Coryton Esq., F.M.E. Jervoise Esq., M. Knight Esq., 1888–1889, F. Coryton Esq., F.M.E. Jervoise Esq., 1889–1895, F. Coryton Esq., Lieutenant Colonel Knox 1895–1899, F. Coryton Esq., A.T.E. Jervoise Esq., 1899–1909.

Arthur Wood becomes Master in 1884, Frederick Coryton, Montague Knight and Francis Jervoise become Joint Masters in 1888, Lt. Colonel Knox joins the Mastership in 1895, railways and barbed wire, shortage of foxes, poultry fund, gamekeepers and find money, hounds poisoned, restricted access to hounds during autumn, sport under Alfred Summers, visit of the Royal Buckhounds and the recapture of Clanwilliam in 1889, boundary disputes with neighbouring hunts, purchase of land and property at Ropley, reinstatement of the HH point-to-point in 1899, formation of the Shire Horse Society in 1891, philanthropy including hospital beds, Ropley school and HSBS, Alfred Summers replaced as huntsman by Albert Guy, followed by Jack Cooper and Harry Payne, resignation of Messrs Coryton and Jervoise.

At the time of the 'Angel In Top Boots' resignation the Hon. Secretary, Arthur Wood, resigned his position to take on the Mastership with a guarantee of £1,600 to hunt the country four days a week with a professional huntsman and two whippers-in.[1] Henry Deacon, who was made an Honorary Member in November, had generously given the bulk of his pack to the Hampshire Hunt Club, but did sell eight couple of young hounds to his successor, who was obliged by the terms of his agreement to leave 51½ couple at the end of his tenure.

Mr Wood's guarantee was increased to £1,800 the following season, but in February 1888 he wrote to resign after four seasons in office. A selection committee

---

1 Some accounts say that Mr Wood hunted the hounds himself but the minutes of a meeting on April 17th 1884 from the HH minute book reveal his terms were to employ a professional huntsman and two whippers-in.

was appointed to secure a replacement but in April they reported a worrying lack of success. One potential candidate had gone elsewhere, another wished to hunt the hounds himself and the third had withdrawn his offer. At this point Arthur Wood offered to resume his Mastership hunting the country only three days a week, but when Members insisted on the full four days, Arthur sent a terse and abrupt reply to the Hon. Secretary. 'My dear Pigott' he responded, 'I am obliged by your letter informing me of the meeting. I can only say I am extremely glad for my own sake that the Members have declined the offer I made to the Hunt and with this letter kindly close all correspondence as far as hunting the country is concerned, Believe me, yours truly A. H. Wood.'

At the annual meeting a few weeks later Members requested that a committee[2] consisting of Frederick Coryton, Montague Knight and Francis Michael Ellis Jervoise 'be requested to carry on the hounds.' Montague Knight only stayed one season, but for the next twenty years Frederick Coryton remained in office, initially with Alfred Summers as his professional huntsman, to guide the fortunes of the Hunt throughout two decades of unprecedented change in the hunting field. Frederick Coryton resided at Liss Place but came from a long established Devon family whose surname is inexorably linked with the Dartmoor Hunt, whilst Francis Jervoise lived at Herriard Park and was descended from Sir Thomas Jervoise who had married the heiress of Sir Richard Powlett in 1601. Mr Coryton was joined by Lt. Colonel Knox from 1895–1899, but with the exception of those four seasons the Mastership included a member of the Jervoise family throughout Frederick Coryton's long innings. Francis Jervoise served seven seasons, whilst his younger brother, Arthur Tristram Ellis Jervoise completed ten years from 1899–1909.

Following on from the first passenger railway linking the cities of Liverpool and Manchester in 1830, an extensive rail network was well established across the Hampshire countryside by the time Frederick Coryton became a Joint Master. The London to Southampton railway had been fully operational since 1840, the Reading to Basingstoke line since 1848, the Basingstoke to Salisbury railway since 1857, and the Mid Hants Railway linking the settlements of Alton, Medstead, Ropley, Alresford, Itchen Abbas, Kings Worthy and Winchester, since 1865. The wider hunting community's initial fear of railways does not appear to be shared by Members of the HH Club, for there are no references to any perceived threats

---

2   Most historians have followed the description written in the minute book of the Joint Masters for the 1888–1889 season as 'A Committee,' however, same or similar terminology is often used to describe a Mastership in early hunt records.

in minute books, only a letter from the Superintendent of the London and South Western Railway, which was read out to Members on March 5th 1894. Mr White kindly agreed to convey servants, horses, and hounds free of charge from Ropley to Bentley and back 'occasionally during the season.' This generous offer was repeated annually up until 1912 when the Club's request was refused by the railway company, and not made again. When the Royal Buckhounds met at Winchester in 1899 a special train was chartered from the same railway company to convey gentlemen, hunt staff, hounds, and stags to Hampshire.

Of much greater concern was barbed wire, a hideous invention from the USA that began to affect hunting in Hampshire during the late nineteenth century, some twenty years after an American farmer, Joseph Glidden, first submitted an application to the US Patent Office for his refined invention in 1873. By 1896 Members were discussing measures that could be taken to induce landowners and farmers to remove wire during the hunting season, which led to the formation of an official Wire Committee following a meeting at Ropley on October 5th 1896. The committee was subdivided into Monday, Tuesday, Thursday, and Saturday districts and asked to report back on which farmers were using barbed wire in each area. The Wire Committee was given authority to collect subscriptions and guaranteed £20 from Hunt funds to get started. When the subject of wire was raised at a later meeting Montague Knight suggested that Members should use their influence to persuade landowners and agents to place a clause in tenants' leases prohibiting the use of wire to repair fences.

It turned out that the increased use of wire to replace or supplement traditional wattle fencing throughout much of the county was an unstoppable tide that almost drove the dependable Frederick Coryton to resign his post. 'I am willing to hunt the HH country for another season,' the MFH wrote in January 1901, 'but if wire goes on increasing as it does at present, I do not see how I can do much longer, to give satisfaction. It is a much more serious question than many consider it to be, and unless some very strenuous efforts are made by all hunting men to induce landowners to take this matter up, hunting must be stopped in some districts before long.' His views were echoed by his Joint Master, Arthur Jervoise, who referred to 'that fearful scourge, barbed wire' when agreeing to continue his Mastership. Three years later Members decided that the Chairman must write to Sir Henry Tichborne pointing out that some dangerous wire had been spotted on his land and requesting permission to remove it, but in common with every other hunt in Britain, the battle against barbed wire was gradually being lost. In the fullness of time the sight of barbed wire in the hunting field ceased to draw comment and came to be accepted as an inconvenience to be lived alongside rather than a blight to be eradicated.

If the quantity of correspondence and time spent discussing the matter at Members' meetings is anything to go by, a shortage of foxes to hunt was of much greater concern. Various measures were introduced to stall a decline in the fox population, which had been contracting since Henry Deacon's time in inverse proportion to the popularity of shooting and high sporting rents during a time of agricultural depression. Gamekeepers were not the only culprits, for almost as many foxes were killed by poultry keepers, who relied on income from egg sales during this era of agricultural decline. Up until the First World War most affluent hunts sought to mitigate the problem by compensating smallholders generously and favourably for their losses. Claims for fox damage were frequently discussed at meetings, leading to the appointment in December 1886 of a subcommittee to consider and settle poultry claims in different parts of the country. They decided that claims must be made within a week of the loss to qualify, and the Hon. Secretary was instructed to place an advertisement to this effect in every paper in Hampshire.

If compensation for fox damage was one way of allowing the vulpine population to survive, another was to reward gamekeepers when a fox or litter of cubs was found by hounds on their beat. When Frederick Coryton drew Members' attention to the scarcity of foxes in 1894 it was decided to increase the reward to ten shillings for every fox found on keepered land, and five years later Members agreed to place £15 at the disposal of the Masters for distribution to keepers at their discretion. If these schemes should fail, there were the determined powers of persuasion from Members of a highly regarded club to fall back on. In February 1887 they passed a resolution authorising the Hon. Secretary to place an advertisement in the *Hampshire Chronicle* expressing hope that 'all owners and occupiers of coverts would assist the master in his earnest endeavours' to show sport by preserving foxes. Despite the three pronged attack on vulpicide, the problem persisted with depressing regularity.

A list of meets advertised in the *Hampshire Chronicle* in November 1888 was preceded by the offer of a £5 reward for information leading to the conviction of anyone laying down poison in the HH country, and in October 1892 Members heard that Lt. Colonel Knox had discovered a dead fox in Willows Green, which he believed had been trapped by Colonel Larkington's keeper. A letter was dispatched to the Colonel requesting that he 'take serious notice of his keeper's conduct.' By

1903 the reward offered to anyone providing information that would convict a fox poisoner had risen to £10, and in April 1895 there were suspicions that hounds had picked up poison out hunting. One of the victims eventually recovered but another hound was never seen again.

The first rumblings of restricted access to shooting coverts during cubhunting began in the early years of Henry Deacon's Mastership, but in the 1880s some landowners and shooting tenants began extending the ban until Christmas or worse. In 1883 Mr Hamilton Fletcher of Brockwood Park requested that the traditional meet at Bramdean Common on the first Tuesday in November be postponed to later in the season. It was decided to write to Mr Fletcher to explain that the HH had met at Bramdean Common on the corresponding date since 1805 and that it 'would be ruinous to the traditions of the hunt to meet at any other place that day, traditions to which all classes, the farmers especially, attach great importance.' Members hoped the recipient could be persuaded to maintain a time honoured convention and thanked him for his longstanding support to the Hunt. Diplomacy prevailed, for Mr Fletcher wrote back confirming his wish to uphold hunting traditions and undertaking to shoot Bramdean on an earlier date in future years. In February 1906 Arthur Jervoise pointed out the great difficulty the Joint Masters had experienced during cubhunting on account of many coverts being closed for shooting, and suggested Members should take this matter in hand. By December it was resolved, 'that the country be sounded as to an appeal being made to the owners and occupiers of coverts to refrain from asking the Masters to stop hounds when running, a practice which is so detrimental in every way to sport.'

Despite these impediments, Alfred Summers, a cheery character with a fine voice but challenging to mount on account of his large frame, provided excellent sport. An extraordinary incident took place during 1888 following a meet at the Corytons' Liss Place, when hounds ran fast on a fox from Blackmoor to ground in the ruins of an old cellar beside the parish church of Hartley Mauditt,[3] where only minutes earlier a fox had been discovered inside the church with a trap attached to its leg. The Rector and gardener succeeded in catching and releasing the animal unharmed – apparently none the worse for its experience – only moments before a different fox pursued by hounds and a large field of nearly a hundred horsemen arrived on the scene. The Saturday country provided a high standard of sport that

---

3   St Leonard's Church in the abandoned village of Hartley Mauditt dates from the 12th century and is around 900 years old.

season, the best run taking place on a fox found in Lord Basing's Pountneys covert that was killed in the open at Itchel Park near Crondall after 75 minutes having run thirteen miles and made an eight-mile point. Since the hounds ended up eighteen miles from home, Mr Jervoise, the Master in charge that day, decided they would not draw again. The *Hampshire Chronicle* correspondent reported that 'it was a treat to see these Hampshire bitches work and twist with their fox, and the way Summers handled them.'

On January 7th 1890 hounds ran so hard and far on a fox from Brownfields that the huntsman's horse collapsed of exhaustion in a ditch, leaving Frederick Coryton to continue with hounds until dark, but one of Summers's greatest runs as a huntsman took place shortly before the end of his final season following the meet at Marsh House, Bentley on February 8th 1896. Hounds found an outlier close to the meet at 11.30am and finally lost their fox 22 miles and nearly four hours later having traversed a huge swathe of country and crossed numerous main roads, the River Wey and a railway line. Summers sustained a nasty fall during this exceptionally long hunt but carried on regardless until the end of the day.

On March 23rd 1889 an estimated crowd of some 7,000 spectators gathered at Manor Farm, Headbourne Worthy, to witness a spectacle reminiscent of the Kempshott Hunt more than a century earlier.[4] The Royal Buckhounds arrived by train at Winchester Station at 11.30am accompanied by the Earl of Coventry, several officers of the Royal Dragoons, huntsman John Harvey wearing scarlet with gold facings, three whippers-in, and second horsemen dressed in the Queen's livery. A full pack of hounds[5] and two stags nicknamed Lords Clanwilliam and Andover were on board the same train. On arrival at Winchester at 11.30am the deer were taken away in a covered van drawn by two horses attended by servants in green livery, whilst guests including Frederick Coryton and the Masters of several neighbouring packs, were entertained to a lavish breakfast of food and wine by John Harvey at Manor Farm. Following this hospitality they adjourned to a meadow nearby where over 400 riders were waiting for the start of the hunt.

At 12.45pm the magnificent Clanwilliam bounded out of a van discreetly concealed between two large haystacks, and after a little hesitancy trotted off northwards into worsening weather. Hounds were laid onto Clanwilliam's line fifteen

---

[4] The Royal Buckhounds had actually met at Popham Lane in 1841, and at The Grange near Northington in 1854.

[5] Since no mention is made of horses travelling by rail for this particular day in contemporary accounts and press cuttings, it cannot be assumed they were on board the specially chartered train with hunt staff and hounds. It is possible the royal visitors rode horses supplied by their hosts.

minutes later, and twice fresh found their quarry before he set off across country in earnest with the buckhounds flying in his wake. By the time they reached Kilmeston Westwood in torrential rain several hours later the stag had established such a long lead that no more could be done, and he was reluctantly given best around 4pm with only twenty odd riders remaining from the enormous field that had set off earlier in the day. Lord Coventry, hounds and hunt staff caught the train home from Winchester, leaving Clanwilliam behind, who over the following days was seen several times in the locality.

The story was not yet over, for the Hampshire Hunt met at Medstead Green a week later and after a busy morning hounds suddenly divided, one half catching their fox attended by the Master, whilst the remainder set off at a blistering pace to Chawton Park, and from there past Medstead Green to the Alresford and Basingstoke turnpike road and on into the village of Preston Candover. By now it must have been clear to all that the quarry was no ordinary fox, but none other than the gallant Clanwilliam, who astounded locals by sailing over a succession of fences dividing Major Aubertin's enclosures before taking refuge in a pond opposite the Purefoy Arms. Dislodged from his temporary sanctuary, Clanwilliam galloped down the village street and straight into an outhouse belonging to the local butcher, who promptly slammed the door shut behind him. Hounds had covered 8½ miles in just 34 minutes without touching a covert or getting a check. Reporting on this extraordinary run in the *Hampshire Chronicle* a few days later, Blackcoat described the 'cross country race of horse, hound and stag' as 'one of the best and fastest bursts ever seen in Hampshire with foxhounds – though illegitimate 'tis true.' A telegram was dispatched to the royal huntsman soon after Clanwilliam's recapture, but what fate befell the true hero of this run was never recorded.

Every Hunt in the county cooperated to facilitate the meet of the Royal Buckhounds in the spring of 1889, but squabbles continued with neighbouring Hunts over boundaries, chiefly with the Chiddingfold and Hambledon. Only two months before the royal meet Mr Pigott had to write and remind the Chiddingfold Master to add the words 'By permission' when advertising a meet in the HH country. In November that year a committee appointed to resolve boundaries with the Chiddingfold Hunt agreed that the eastern boundary of the HH was the high road from Farnham to Liss including the Alice Holt enclosures. The Chiddingfold again omitted to acknowledge permission for a meet at Liphook in April 1895, but a representative from the Hunt quickly wrote back to apologise for the oversight, and the fact that they had killed a heavy vixen.

In March 1893 the HH sought permission to draw parts of the Hambledon country close to Hedge Corner and the Cricketers Arms at Steep, claiming that local fox preservers were disappointed by the lack of hunting in the area. Permission was duly granted, and in 1894 a subcommittee of the HH Club defined the Hunt boundaries, which were printed and circulated amongst Members, with subsequent amendments recorded in ink on the original copy retained for Hunt records. Relationships between the two Hunts remained cordial until 1907 when the Hon. Secretary to the Hambledon Hunt was obliged to write to his new counterpart, Major Pole, objecting to the HH meeting at Hawkley. He claimed this meet was within the Hambledon country as indicated by old maps formerly used by the committee of Boodles. The dispute ended up being referred to the MFHA,[6] whose committee of the great and good of contemporary foxhunting included Earl Bathurst, the Dukes of Buccleuch and Rutland and other hunting luminaries such as Messrs Barclay, Brassey and Straker from the Puckeridge, Heythrop and Zetland Hunts respectively. Their detailed and final resolution of June 27th 1908 defines the exact boundary between the two hunts to this day and is pasted neatly inside the 1884 Hampshire Hunt Letter Book.

When Members became aware of the imminent retirement of Mr Garth in 1902 the Hon. Secretary wrote to take back the country loaned to him personally by the HH Club. The news was received with regret, together with advice that the Hunt would continue to be known as the Garth Hunt, in honour of the man who had reigned over it for half a century. In 1908 a request from Captain Jackson of the 1st Cheshire regiment requesting permission to hunt a pack of harriers around Bordon Camp was rejected on the grounds that there were already sufficient packs in the neighbourhood. He was later granted permission to hunt beagles for one season only provided they avoided all coverts and did not meet the same day or the day before the HH. However it wasn't all friction with neighbouring hunts; during the first decade of the twentieth century the HH and Vyne[7] Hunt jointly hosted several balls at Basingstoke, where partygoers danced into the small hours.

Boundary disputes were just one of many grey areas to be refined as hunts across the land became better organised, and privately maintained packs subsidised by wealthy individuals became increasingly rare. Subscription hunts needed to put their financial houses in order if they were to survive, and those with the

---

6   Masters of Foxhounds Association.

7   Early records refer to the Vyne Hunt, which later came to be known as the Vine until amalgamation with the Craven Farmers in 1968, when the Vine and Craven Hunt was formed.

> Copy
>
> M.F.H. Association,
> Tattersalls,
> London. S.W.
> 27th June 1908
>
> The Committee having carefully considered the case submitted to them by the:–
>
> **Hambledon and Hampshire Hunts**
>
> are of opinion that the Boundary between the two Hunts is from Hedge Corner down the Road to the Cross Roads marked B on Map then up the Road past White Horse Inn, Bakers Farm, Church Farm and following same Road to Cross Roads marked E on Map thence along Buttons Lane to the old Chalk Pit marked A on Map and thence following the Lane to Lower Green, Jolly Robbins Farm and on to Upper Green, then due East following black line on Map by Farewell Farm and following same Road to West Liss.
>
> (signed) Bathurst (chairman)   (signed) E. E. Barclay
>   „ Albert Brassey.   „ Dalkeith.
>   „ J. C. Straker.   „ Manvers.

Boundary between the Hambledon and HH Hunts resolved by the MFHA June 27th 1908.

foresight to acquire their own kennels and stabling would be rewarded for their prudence in perpetuity. In 1889 Mrs Pullinger's cottages at Ropley were added to the Hunt's property portfolio at a cost of £90, and in 1908 a further acre of land was purchased from Miss Hagen for £50 on which to build two more cottages for hunt staff. Being £539 in credit at the end of the 1907–1908 season, the Hunt Club could well afford these judicious one-off investments.

In 1899 it was decided to resurrect point-to-point races last run during Henry Deacon's time, and the inaugural meeting was held at Berry Hill, Farringdon on March 22nd. The afternoon kicked off at 2.30pm with a red coat lightweight race for Members or subscribers over three miles of fair hunting country for a private

THE HAMPSHIRE HUNT 1749–2022

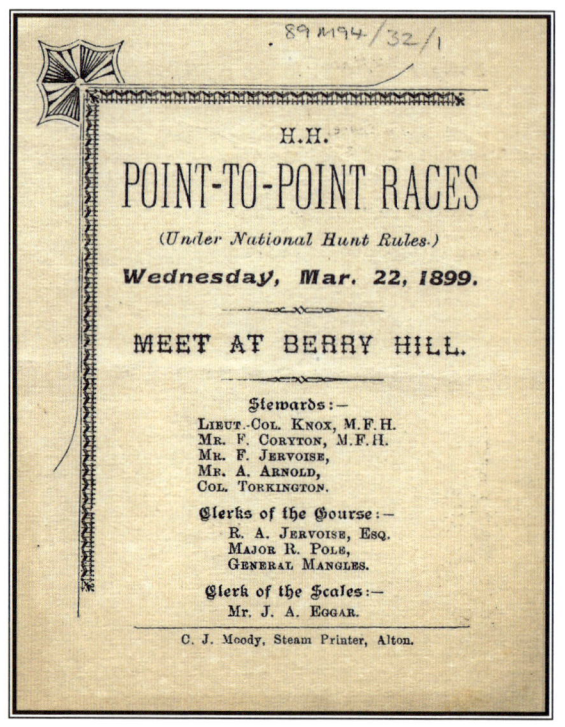

89M94/32/1

H.H.
POINT-TO-POINT RACES
(Under National Hunt Rules.)

Wednesday, Mar. 22, 1899.

MEET AT BERRY HILL.

Stewards:—
Lieut.-Col. Knox, M.F.H.
Mr. F. Coryton, M.F.H.
Mr. F. Jervoise,
Mr. A. Arnold,
Col. Torkington.

Clerks of the Course:—
R. A. Jervoise, Esq.
Major R. Pole,
General Mangles.

Clerk of the Scales:—
Mr. J. A. Eggar.

C. J. Moody, Steam Printer, Alton.

1899 point-to-point race card.

FIRST RACE, 2.30 p.m.

RED COAT LIGHT-WEIGHT RACE.

A Private Sweepstakes of 2 sovs. each, P.P. (if ridden by owner and horses belonging to ladies 1 sov.) for horses the property of Members or Subscribers to the Hunt, that in the opinion of the referees have been fairly hunted with the H.H. Hounds. About three miles over a fair hunting country. Catch weights 12st. and over. To be ridden in hunting costume.

1.—Lieut. Col. Knox's b.g. "Dizzy" Mr. Spencer.
2.—Mrs. F. Baring's b.m. "Miss Bright" Mr. R. Ward.
3.—Mr. A. Seawell's b.g. "Kingfisher" Owner.
4.—Mr. Walmsley's bn.m. "Girton Girl" Mr. Aldridge.
5.—Mr. A. C. Nicholson's bk.g. "Pilot" Owner.
6.—Mr. R. Spicer's bn.g. "Erin" ,,
7.—Mr. R. Nicholson's bn.g. "Roscius" ,,
8.—Mr. F. Bussey's g.g. "Squire" ,,
9.—Mr. H. Dumaresq's ch.m. "Sarah" Owner
10.—Mrs. Waterhouse's "Nautch Girl" Mr. Eyre Lloyd.
11.—Capt. Dougall's Owner.
12.—Mr. Hussey's h.g. "Phelim" Mr. Garlick.
13.—Mr. Montagu Knight's bk.m. "Hazel" Mr. D. Wood.
14.—Miss Torkington's bn m. "Ursula" Mr. Thompson.
15.—Capt. Studdert's ch.m. "Luca" Owner.
16.—Mr. Wilbraham Taylor's bk.m "Iolanthe" Owner.
17.—Mr. Denistoun's ch.m "Pride" ,,
18.—Capt. G. Traver's h.g. "Waterford" ,,
19. Miss Christy's "Tom Thumb" Mr. Mackarness.
20.—Mr. L Clark's "Lady Golightly" Owner.
21.—Mr. Davson's b.m. "Boadicea" ,,
22.—Mr. Barrett's bn.g "Jesse" ,,

SECOND RACE.

FARMERS' RACE.
Entrance Free.

For horses the property of, and to be ridden by, Farmers or their Sons, who reside or occupy land in the H.H. Country, or of any person who has walked one or more puppies for the Masters of the H.H. during the years 1997 and 1898. Catch Weights 13st. and over. About three miles over a fair hunting country

1.—Mr. H. Stratton's ch.m. "Reckless" Owner.
2.—Mr. B. Warner's bn.g. "Limerick" ,,
3.—Mr. Baigent's "Cigarette" Mr. A. Chalcraft.
4.—Mr. Twitchen's "Grasshopper" Mr. G. Langrish.
5.—Mr. Tuckett's b.g. "Prince" Owner.

THIRD RACE.

RED COAT WELTER RACE.

Same conditions as first race. Catch weights 14st. and over.

1.—Capt. R. Stephen's b.g. "Peter" Owner
2.—Mr. Eyre Lloyds ch.m. "Queens Birthday" ,,
3.—Mr. R. Spicer b.g. "Scott" ,,
4.—Capt. Sprot's ch.g. "Scots Fusilier" ,,
5.—Mr. Cole's bn.g. "Swallow" ,,
6.—Mr. Bickford's b.g. "Gambler" ,,

PLEASE NOTICE—Permission to ride over the farms is only granted to those who take part in the Races.

sweepstake of two sovereigns per entrant. Twenty-two amateur riders dressed in full hunting costume took their own line between strategically placed flags. The second race was open to farmers or their sons residing in the HH country and anyone who had walked puppies during the preceding two years, with the third and final welter race restricted to horses carrying more than fourteen stone. The *Hampshire Chronicle* reported that the meeting had been a thorough success.

On February 16th 1891 Mr Coryton told Members he had collected £120 for the acquisition of an entire shire horse for the use of farmers in the Hampshire Hunt country and proposed that a committee be formed to acquire a stallion and arrange its management. In September the Shire Horse Society published a report in the *Hampshire Chronicle* that explained Members of the HH Club wished to acknowledge the courtesy and kindness of those who welcome the Hunt and its followers, even if they do not hunt themselves. Under the chairmanship of Frederick Coryton the Shire Horse Committee attended the 1891 Shire Horse Show at the Agricultural Hall in Islington, London, where they secured an entire seven year old bay named Macbeth for £175. The stallion stood between April 6th and July 15th (Sundays excepted) on alternate weeks at Ropley and Church Farm, Lasham for a subsidised fee 'not to exceed one guinea.'

The Society quickly went from strength to strength, acquiring a second stallion, Prince George, for 83 guineas the following year and extending the list of farms and villages where they would be available to serve mares during the covering season. In 1893 the Shire Horse Society held its inaugural Parade and Show at Ropley on the first Monday in September, where prizes were awarded for the best yearlings and foals sired by their stallions. Macbeth died the same year and was replaced by Shelford Patriot, a four year old who had been bred by Lord Hothfield in Kent and cost a hundred guineas but was insured for £150. At the 1895 show the Ladies' Challenge Cup was awarded for the first time to the tenant farmer exhibiting the best foal, yearling or two year old got by a Society stallion. As the Society continued to expand further stallions were acquired, each one accompanied by a personal groom to supervise the covering of up to 130 mares during the three month season.

The venture was such a success that by November 1900 the Shire Horse Society Committee was able to report that their endeavours during the previous nine years had resulted in a very distinct improvement of the breed of cart horse in the HH country, which was much appreciated by the great majority of tenant farmers. The Society now asked that the HH Club acknowledge financial liability and assume ownership of the stallions, a request that Members agreed to, provided they were furnished with a report in January of each year. In 1904, when the ninth annual show was held at Upton House, Alresford, the *Hampshire Chronicle* commended the success of the Society in raising the standard of cart horse in the county and praised the close relationship the venture had engendered between the Hunt and tenant farmers.

By then the show had expanded to several classes, with catering provided by the Globe Inn from Alresford and a lively programme of music courtesy of the Alresford Town Band. At the prize giving ceremony Mr W.G. Nicholson MP proposed a vote of thanks to the Christy family for hosting the event and his wife presented the Challenge Cup to Mr Atkinson for the best yearling owned by a tenant farmer. Jas Stratton from Chilcomb spoke for the farmers when thanking Mr Coryton warmly for his efforts and perseverance to introduce such splendid shire horses to the county, and called for three resounding cheers, which were heartily given, followed by three more for his Joint Master, Arthur Jervoise. But even as the Shire Horse Society grew in popularity and purpose, contemporary hunting reports were referring to individuals attending meets 'on wheels.' It is unlikely that anyone amongst the merry crowd attending the show at Upton could have foreseen the future of British agriculture, but on that glorious September afternoon the writing was already on the wall for the great English shire horse.

The Hampshire Hunt's philanthropic outlook extended beyond the provision of subsidised stallions to farmers. In December 1899, the British government needed more troops to fight the Second Boer War, which resulted in the issue of a Royal Warrant to create the Imperial Yeomanry. The Hampshire Yeomanry responded by sending the 41st Hampshire Company to South Africa in February 1900, and the 50th Hampshire Company to Mozambique in May. Soon afterwards Members raised a subscription from friends of the Hunt to finance a Hampshire Hunt bed in the field hospital for volunteers from the Hampshire Yeomanry, which raised £75 and was handed over to Lady Baring to administer. In the same year the Club donated £20 to Ropley school, and in 1906 a collection was made for the Hunt Servants' Benefit Society, which had been established in 1872 to support hunt staff who had fallen on hard times. Caps were also taken most seasons in favour of the Royal Agricultural Benevolent Institution, initially established in 1860 to secure a home for, or pension to, the bona fide farmer or widow of a farmer and to maintain and educate the orphan children of farmers.

When Alfred Summers retired in 1896, he was succeeded by his first whipper-in, Albert Guy, who carried the horn with distinction for six seasons. Halfway

THE CORYTON AND JERVOISE ERA 1884–1909

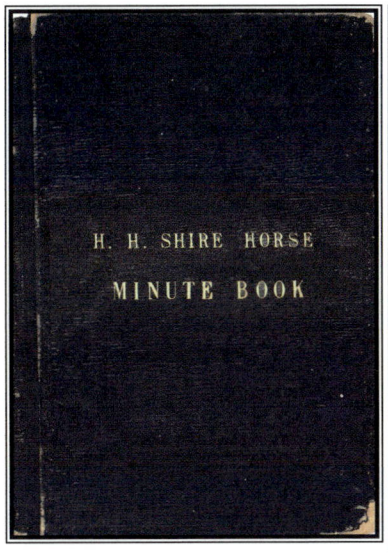

RULES.

1.—"Macbeth" will serve a limited number of Mares, the *bona fide* property of persons farming in the H. H. County, at the fee of £1 1s. inclusive of Groom's fee.

2.—Applications for using "Macbeth" should be made in writing to James Bailey, Stud Groom, Ropley, on or before the 31st day of March next.

3.—All fees to be sent with the application for service, when a printed receipt will be forwarded, and no Mare will be served without the production of such receipt. No person to send more than two Mares.

4.—No Mares will be served on a Sunday.

5.—No Mares will be served after July 15th.

6.—The Committee reserves the right to refuse service to any Mare an unreasonable number of times, or to any Mare that may be considered unfit.

7.—A limited number of applications will be received from persons residing outside the limits of the Hunt, at a fee of Three Guineas.

8.—The Horse will stand alternate weeks at Church Farm, Lasham, and the H. H. Stables, at Ropley, and will travel in these districts.

At a Meeting of the committee held at the Agricultural Hall Islington on Wednesday February 25th 1891

Present F Coryton Chairman M.F.H.
         F. M. E Jervoise M.F.H.
         M. G. Knight
         W. G. Nicholson
         H. W. Deacon
         J. Barton
         J. Godwin
         C. J. Stacey
         J. Alfred Eggar

The above Committee purchased the Shire Horse "Macbeth"
           Description

H. H. SHIRE HORSE "MACBETH."
SEASON 1891.

"MACBETH" (5188), bay, 7 yrs. old; sire, "KENILWORTH" (4497); dam, "POLLY," by "MASTERMAN" (2464).

"Macbeth" was exhibited at the Shire Horse Show held at the Agricultural Hall, Islington, in February last, and was commended by the Judges, receiving a Card of Merit.

For the sum of £175

Top left: Front cover of the Shire Horse Society minute book.

Top right: Rules of the Shire Horse Society.

Left: Macbeth, the Shire Horse Society's first stallion.

H.H. SHIRE HORSE SOCIETY.

Dear Sir,

There can be no question but that this Society is of great benefit to farmers in the H.H. Country; it would only need to be withdrawn to elicit a strong expression of opinion in its favour.

The Society is unable to provide the best Horses at the small fees charged, and pay its way, without a considerable sum of money in the shape of annual subscriptions, which should at least amount to £150.

The subscriptions have greatly fallen off in recent years, and a special effort is being made to increase the amount from those who hunt with the H.H.

The Society was originated by Mr. F. Coryton, who felt that one of the best ways of showing the farmers how much those who hunt with the H.H. appreciate their allowing their land to be hunted over, was by improving the breed of Cart Horses.

It is a recognised fact that the class of horse throughout the country has greatly improved, as is evidenced by the good prices which are made.

The example set by Mr. Coryton has been followed by other Hunts, who have written to the Secretary for full information and particulars, thus proving that farmers in other hunting districts appreciate the value of the work of such a Society.

The Committee hereby make a strong appeal to all those who hunt with the H.H. for subscriptions, in order that the work may be carried on efficiently.

Subscriptions will be received by any Member of the Committee, whose names and addresses are given below.

H.H. Shire Horse Committee for 1909.

Members of Hunt.

Mr. F. Coryton, Manor House, Greatham.
Mr. A. T. E. Jervoise, Herriard Grange.
Mr. Montagu G. Knight, Chawton House.
Mr. A. E. Seawell, Marelands, Farnham.
Col. Lord Basing, C.B., Hoddington House.
Sir R. Rycroft, Bart., Dummer.
Mr. F. H. T. Jervoise, Herriard Park.
Capt. G. D. Jeffreys, Burkham.
Mr. F. Seth Smith, Upton Grey Lodge.
Capt. Holroyd, Ropley Manor.
Major R. E. Pole, Westfields, Wrecclesham.

Non-Members.

Mr. A. Arnold, Bramdean.
Mr. H. Mells, West Liss.
Mr. J. Twitchin, Holybourne.
Mr. J. F. Complin, Holybourne.
Mr. J. Pain, Micheldever.
Mr. T. S. Mitchell, Hartley.
Mr. H. Seaward, Weston Corbett.
Mr. J. Godwin, Tichborne.
Mr. J. Fawcett, West Tisted.
Mr. T. Chalcraft, Amery, Alton.
Mr. J. Alfred Eggar, Farnham.

J. F. COMPLIN, *Hon. Treasurer*,
Holybourne, Alton.

J. ALFRED EGGAR, *Hon. Secretary*,
Farnham, Surrey.

Shire Horse Society committee in 1909.

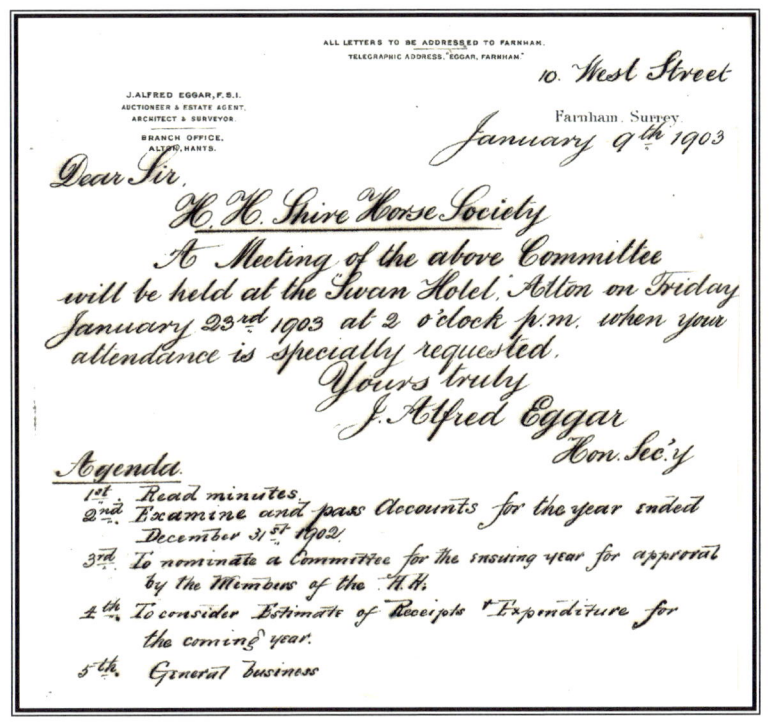

Notice of Shire Horse Society meeting in 1903.

through his penultimate season Queen Victoria died on January 22nd 1901 having been on the throne for an unprecedented 63 years, and the nation fell into mourning. All hunting was cancelled until after her burial on February 4th which was followed by a hard frost that prevented hunting for another week, resulting in ten lost days by the time sport resumed. In 1902 a dashing horseman named Jack Cooper took over the horn. His red letter days included a brilliant late afternoon run following the Opening Meet at Bramdean Common in 1904, when hounds found in Sutton Wood at 3pm after a somewhat steady day. They settled to run fast past Ropley Station, through The Gullet and on past Medstead to Chawton Park where a bold forward cast recovered the line. The hunt continued over the railway line and the Alton turnpike to Farringdon village where the fox was seen dead beat not far in front, but he made his point to Rotherfield Park where a hitherto undiscovered litter of cubs intervened to save his brush after a capital 95 minutes. By the end of that season Cooper could claim the distinction of catching more foxes – 33 ½ brace during 78 days regular hunting – than any other huntsman during the Coryton and Jervoise era. Despite these successes, Jack Cooper's critics claimed that the pack was much diminished by his practice of continually lifting them to hollloas rather than letting them work out the line. He left the Hunt in 1907 and was replaced by Harry Payne, a sick man whose hounds soon became dispirited and slack in drawing the coverts.

Perhaps the pack's rapid deterioration and lack of enthusiasm was in part a consequence of being frequently stopped when running, for in 1908 Messrs Jervoise and Coryton sent in their resignations owing to so many coverts being closed to hounds until late in the season. To the relief of Members they had both written to withdraw their resignations by March, when it was proposed that a letter 'be presented to the owners and occupiers of coverts and land to ask them to be good enough for the sake of sport and for the welfare of the country to open their coverts to hounds and also for cubhunting.' The letter must have fallen on deaf ears for the Joint Masters tended their resignation again early the following year. Frederick Coryton was unequivocal that he was standing down due to the wanton destruction of cubs and denial of access to shooting coverts. 'Under these circumstances,' he wrote, 'I cannot show the sport I have been accustomed to show, so send in my resignation.'

Arthur Jervoise's correspondence from Herriard Grange was equally gloomy, citing the reason for his resignation as 'the scarcity of foxes, including of course litters of cubs in many places, the vast amount of country shut against the hounds from even running into the coverts, as well as wire make it quite impossible for the country to be properly hunted.' He believed a change in Mastership might induce certain covert owners and shooting tenants to modify their restrictions and expressed much regret at having to step down after ten enjoyable seasons as a Joint Master. Members accepted the resignations of these two most popular Masters with the deepest regret and resolved to invite farmers to lunches at Alton and Alresford to discuss the shortage of foxes. However, when Members next met barely a month later, a motion was carried to let the matter drop.

Resolution in 1906 to appeal against hounds being stopped when running.

Chapter Six 1909–1914

Cometh the Hour, Cometh the Man

G.P.E. Evans Esq., 1909–1914.

George Evans becomes Master in 1909, his hunting credentials, drafting and procuring hounds, moderate first season, clay pigeon shoot and puppy show, hunters sold by Tattersalls, superb sport from 1910 onwards, increase in subscriptions, resignation and increased guarantee, HRH King George V, the Prince of Wales, and the HH button, the 1914 point-to-point and closing meet, the outbreak of the First World War.

Following the resignation of a popular Mastership, and Payne's lacklustre approach to hunting hounds, the Club urgently needed someone with the knowledge, skill, and enthusiasm to turn around the fortunes of a much diminished pack. The arrival of George Patrick Elystan Evans was about to do all that, and a great deal more besides, for there could not have been anyone better qualified than the man who was blooded with the Cambridgeshire in 1878 when just five years old. According to the hunting scribe, Sabretache, 'hounds killed in the middle of a big grass field, and young George was out on a leading rein and came out of the wood through a hand gate. The groom let go of the pony, and when he saw hounds kill their fox our young hero promptly galloped up and stood in the middle of the pack, very excited, saying, "I am here first, I get the brush." The quest for the brush was to remain with George Evans for the rest of his life, and within five years of his first recorded presence in the hunting field, he was happily hunting a pack of beagles around his home at Hatley Park in Cambridgeshire.

He gained his first experience of handling a pack of foxhounds on December 20th 1892 when out with the Cambridgeshire, by which time he had already started the hunting diaries he was to maintain throughout his life. 'Fox crossed ride in front of me, Dereck whipped them off,' he wrote, 'Newman was away at the top and having fourteen couple of hounds with me, I told Dereck to put them back on the line again. Away to ground 45 minutes without a check, fox getting to ground in view of hounds thus ended a splendid day. But very unfortunately.' By the following year[1] he was Master of the Cambridgeshire, where he remained until 1903, when he was most unusually without a pack of hounds for a season.

However he put this time to good use, gaining valuable experience by hunting 84 days with twenty different packs, including the famous Pytchley in Northamptonshire, where he condemned a huge field for their lack of interest in venery. 'Bitch pack. I should think 150 ladies and 200 men out not one of them seemed to care anything about hounds and very few even knew which pack was out.' George Evans's next move was to the Tickham in Kent in 1904, where he remained for four seasons before leaving to take the position of agent to Lord Curzon, who had recently taken on the lease of Hackwood Park inside the Hampshire Hunt country. Whilst there George gained valuable experience in managing shooting interests, which would stand him in good stead when organising hunting in a heavily shot country.

In February 1909 he wrote to the HH Club Chairman, Montague Knight, setting out his terms to take the Mastership on a guarantee of £2,400 with the right to draft 35 couple of inadequate hounds. He asked to replace them by spending up to a thousand pounds on new ones and insisted that urgent repairs and improvements were made to stables and kennels. 'I am afraid I shall find it a very hard task following two such popular Masters' he wrote, 'however I am prepared to try.' George had been singularly unimpressed by the existing pack during a morning's cubhunting in September the previous year, when hounds were hunted by Harry Payne. 'Pain (sic) new huntsman' he wrote, 'large pack of hounds out, old and young seemed very fond of riot. Very difficult country to school hounds in as there are few cubs and no end of riot. They had been out nine mornings and killed only a brace, those they dug out. Pain seemed as if he had no heart in him. Poorish show.'

Given his short but illustrious hunting record, it's hardly surprising that Members were determined to secure George Evans's services. Letters between the Chairman, Montague Knight, and the Hon. Secretary, Major Pole, underline this resolve and confirm the inadequacy of the present pack, which the Chairman admits was spoilt by the previous huntsman's wild ways, predicting that, 'it will take some

---

1   According to *Baily's Hunting Directory* George Evans became Master of the Cambridgeshire in 1891, however some hunting historians firmly state 1893. It is clear from this account that George Evans was not hunting hounds in 1892. It is likely that he was a Joint Master in 1892 but did not hunt hounds until the following season.

time to undo the mischief done by Cooper.' By the time he sent a second letter to Major Pole on February 20th, the Chairman's mind was made up. His willingness to embrace the concept of a full time amateur huntsman that would cost the hunt more, but be worth every penny in the long run, was a view that ever more Hunts would adopt as the twentieth century progressed. 'From all I hear of Mr Evans I think he is just the man we want; he knows the difficulties we are surrounded by, and he is prepared to face them. He is evidently a very energetic man and would devote a great part of his time to furthering the interests of the Hunt. He gave great satisfaction with the Cambridgeshire and the Tickham. I believe we can raise the money and if he is successful in improving the sport, I have little doubt the money will come in.'

Members wholeheartedly agreed. Captain George Jeffreys[2] wrote to the Hon. Secretary the same day making his own views very clear. 'I am strongly in favour of George Evans's Mastership, and, in the evil days to which we have descended, I think we shall be very lucky if we get so excellent a hound man and thoroughly experienced MFH to take the pack. It would be a pity to lose a good master for the sake of saving say £50, and therefore it is advisable to carry out the work as Evans wishes.' Two days later Members met at Binsted Wyck to appoint George Evans as sole Master and huntsman on £2,400 a year, with him undertaking to pay all fines for foxes, licences for hounds, taxes, and £25 per annum for the rent of a house and stables at the kennels. A subcommittee was formed to consider the matter of buying and selling hounds, and it was agreed to hold a point-to-point.

On March 23rd 1909 the outgoing Masters met the new incumbent at Ropley, where they agreed to hand over all hounds in the kennels. At a Members' meeting on April 16th permission was granted for Mr Evans to sell the doghounds and any unwanted bitches, provided he return 40 couple of entered hounds and ten couple of puppies at the end of his term. This agreement was to be of major significance a few year later when George Evans was compelled to stand down after the outbreak of the First World War, and was meticulously supervised by the new Hon. Secretary, Captain Edmund Purefoy Ellis Jervoise,[3] who had taken over from Major Pole following the untimely death of his son in November 1909. In 1912 Captain Jervoise, who had spotted an error in Mr Evans's favour relating to hound ownership in *Baily's Hunting Directory*, was congratulated on his diligence by the

---

2   Later General Sir George Jeffreys.

3   Edmund Purefoy Ellis Jervoise was the younger brother of the former Master, Arthur Tristram Ellis Jervoise. He became a Captain in the Royal Navy in 1904 and was subsequently promoted to Rear Admiral in 1915.

"Times" Mar 13 1909

HUNTING.

HAMPSHIRE AS A SPORTING COUNTY.

A well-known veteran of the field, who has lived 36 years in Dorset, is a Cornishman by birth, and has had 50 years' experience of varied sport in all parts of the kingdom, has lately assigned to Hampshire the distinction of being the best all-round sporting county in England. Nor is he the first to have discovered the inherent love of sport of its inhabitants. Some years ago "Cecil" expressed surprise that Hampshire for its size should possess so many packs of hounds, especially as it is far from a first-rate scenting country or ideal from a riding man's point of view. Portions of the county have known the rule of famous masters of hounds, including such celebrities as Mr. Chute, Mr. Villebois, Mr. John Warde, and Mr. Assheton-Smith. Yet foxhunting in Hampshire has not had entirely plain sailing in all places and at all times; for here and there shooting has strong counter-attractions, and it will be remembered that some weeks ago it was felt that a crisis had been reached in the H.H. country when Mr. Frederick Coryton and Mr. A. T. E. Jervoise announced their resignation of the mastership on account of the scarcity of foxes and the closing of coverts to hounds before Christmas.

Fortunately, in choosing Mr. George Elystan Evans to fill the vacant place, the Hampshire Hunt has selected one who has not only the tact but the persistence and determination to put matters on a proper basis, besides the requisite experience of hunting hounds over cold-scenting country to enable him to show sport with the H.H. Mr. Evans's career as a huntsman began at the age of 13, when he took command of a pack of beagles; and he was only 20 when he was appointed Master of the Cambridgeshire. For ten seasons he held office there, his retirement in 1903 being regretted by followers and farmers alike; and then at short notice he went to the Tickham country in Kent, where he was equally fortunate and well-liked. It is to be hoped that in his new country he will be well supported, and that his rule will be long; for with a fair field, even with no favour, he is likely to prove not the least successful of the many notable sportsmen who have hunted hounds in Hampshire.

I saw the Bitch Pack and the Entry of the H.H. Foxhounds in the Kennels at Ropley on Wednesday the 20th October 1909 and beg to report as follows:—

There was shown me:—

6 Seasons	½ Couple
5 "	2 "
4 "	2½ "
3 "	7 "
2 "	7 "
1 "	5½ "
Unentered – only	2½ "
	27 Couples

Of these 10½ Couples of the Entered Hounds were Draft Hounds, bred in other Kennels. The Entered Bitches were very under sized and hardly any suitable for Brood Bitches. Owing to this and the bad reputation they have in their work I do not consider them worth more than **450 Guineas**.

* This with the 241 Guineas for the 22½ couples of Dog Hounds sent to Rugby on the 22nd April would make **691 Guineas** for the Pack of 49½ Couples.

S. Rooke Rawles
Tattersall.

* N.B. There were 22½ couples of Dog Hounds sent to Rugby, of these 19 Couples were sold for 199 Guineas, and one lot of 3½ Couples bought in at 42 gs.

Above: *The Times* announces George Evans's appointment as MFH to the HH in March 1909.

Above right: Valuation of HH hounds in 1909.

Right: Belvoir Weaver '06. By 1933 every hound at Ropley was descended from this doghound.

BELVOIR WEAVER '06
The Duke of Rutland's Hounds

Every hound in HH Kennel descended from this dog. G.E.

A NOTABLE GROUP AT THE BELVOIR KENNELS

The names, reading from left to right, are: Standing—J. Hewitt (whip), C. Wright, T. Butt Miller, — Grosvenor, A. W. Heber Percy, W. de P. Cazenove, P. Wroughton, George Walters (huntsman, Tynedale kennels), Sir H. Langham, Rev. E. A. Milne, Captain W. Peacock, H. Compton, Sir George Bullough, Gerald H. Hardy, W. M. Wroughton, Ben Capell (huntsman, Belvoir Hounds); seated—H. Preston, J. A. Radcliffe, George Evans, John C. Straker

George Evans MFH and others at the Belvoir Hunt kennels in August 1909.

Master. 'What a good Secretary you are' he wrote through gritted teeth, 'you never let anything slip.'

The new Master wasted little time in putting his kennels in order, sending 22½ couple of doghounds to Rugby sales on April 22nd, where they made 241 guineas, leaving 27 couple of bitches at Ropley, which were inspected by a representative of Tattersalls in October. He found the entered bitches 'very undersized and hardly suitable for brood bitches. Owing to this and their bad reputation they have in their work, I do not consider them worth more than 450 guineas.' George Evans's solution was to draft into Ropley the best possible blood that was available. 'When I took over the kennels, I drafted nearly all the hounds as there was no type about them,' he wrote in 1913, 'Belvoir blood is what I go for, with a lot of Grafton Woodman blood through the Puckeridge. For three years I had the Puckeridge draft, getting the blood I wanted from the Belvoir and the Grafton.'

His first season commenced on September 6th 1909, each day recorded in black ink inside a succession of large, leather-bound bespoke hunting journals supplied by the Army and Navy Cooperative Society in London. Columns on the left hand page of each double spread are to record the coverts drawn, the names of gamekeepers and foxes found, killed, and run to ground, leaving ample room on the opposite side for remarks and observations. The pages are interspersed with press cuttings and evocative black and white photographs from an era when turnout in the hunting field was impeccable, but elsewhere tweed caps, soft hats or bare heads were the norm when astride a horse. Hounds went out 83 times that first season, killing 23½ brace but also suffering many days when only one fox – or worse – was found, and too many occasions when the pack had to be stopped in the interests of shooting. 'On the whole not a good season' the Master wrote after it had ended on April 10th, 'the foxes not making good points. Hounds being a scratch lot, they don't make a good cast when left to themselves. Out of my 55 couple have about 30 couple that will do for next season only.'

George Evans was determined to bring about change within the shooting community and instead of a point-to-point in the spring of 1910 his first season ended with a clay pigeon shoot for gamekeepers and a glowing tribute to the new Master in the local press. The *Hampshire Chronicle* correspondent felt assured that gamekeepers within the Hampshire Hunt country would preserve foxes with such enthusiasm as to make a blank day with the Hunt 'practically an impossibility.' Henry Jervoise's keeper, Buckle, won the coveted first prize in the HH Keepers' Championship, which was a hammerless double-barrelled gun by Crutchley valued at £15. The runner-up in this exciting match was Titheridge from Rotherfield Park, who also held the honour of having provided more foxes from his coverts than any other shoot during the previous season. For the first time in many years there was a summer puppy show at Ropley, where the guests sat down to lunch of salmon mayonnaise, lobster salad, quail in aspic, lamb in mint sauce, sirloin of beef, macedoine jellies, fruit tarts, cheese, biscuits, and cake.

George Evans was in the habit of consigning all the hunters in his stables to be sold by Tattersalls at Albert Gate, Knightsbridge[4] at the end of most seasons in order to make room for younger stock, and no doubt reap a healthy profit from horses made by himself and the hunt staff. Given his reputation across country, these sales attracted huge interest from the galloping grass countries in Leicestershire and beyond. At the end of George's first season in Hampshire his entire stud was offered for sale on June 27th 1910, including Silver Cloud, a Leicestershire horse up to fifteen stone, Anchor, a beautiful seventeen stone hunter,

---

4 Tattersalls owned eleven acres in Knightsbridge, which was sold in 1946 as a bomb site after the Second World War, although there had been no horse sales at Knightsbridge Green since 1939. A pub called the Tattersall Tavern was built on the site in 1958 and flourishes to this day.

KELS,
ROPLEY,
HANTS,
March 23rd, 1910.

On Friday, April the 8th, I am giving a Clay Pigeon Match in Mr. Complin's Field, where the Alton Show was held, ten minutes' walk from the Station towards Holybourne. I shall be glad to know if you or your men would care to enter for any of the matches.

Shooting starts at 10.45.

There will be Five Pigeon Matches.

1.—Open to all Keepers, Monday Side. Prizes—1st, £1; 2nd, 15s.; 3rd, 10s.; 4th, 5s.; 5th, 2s. 6d.
2.—Open to all Keepers, Tuesday Side. Prizes—1st, £1; 2nd, 15s.; 3rd, 10s.; 4th, 5s.; 5th, 2s. 6d.
3.—Open to all Keepers, Thursday Side. Prizes—1st, £1; 2nd, 15s.; 3rd, 10s.; 4th, 5s.; 5th, 2s. 6d.
4.—Open to all Keepers, Saturday Side. Prizes—1st, £1; 2nd, 15s.; 3rd, 10s.; 4th, 5s.; 5th, 2s. 6d.

The 5th Match will be open to all Keepers in the H.H. Hunt. 1st Prize, a Gun value £15; 2nd, £2; 3rd, £1; 4th, 10s.; 5th, 5s.: 6th, 2s. 6d.

Entry Form and Rules on enclosed slips.

Lunch at 1 o'clock.

Yours truly,
G. P. EVANS, M.F.H.

HAMPSHIRE HUNT.

RULES.

Keepers to bring their own guns, Mr. Evans finds all cartridges. No Keeper is allowed to load his gun until at the firing point.

Guns must be unloaded before turning from the traps.

No Keeper allowed inside the ropes.

Any Keeper breaking the rules can be disqualified for any of the matches.

The entry form must be filled up and returned by April 1st to

GEORGE EVANS, ESQ., M.F.H.,
The Kennels,
Ropley, Hants.

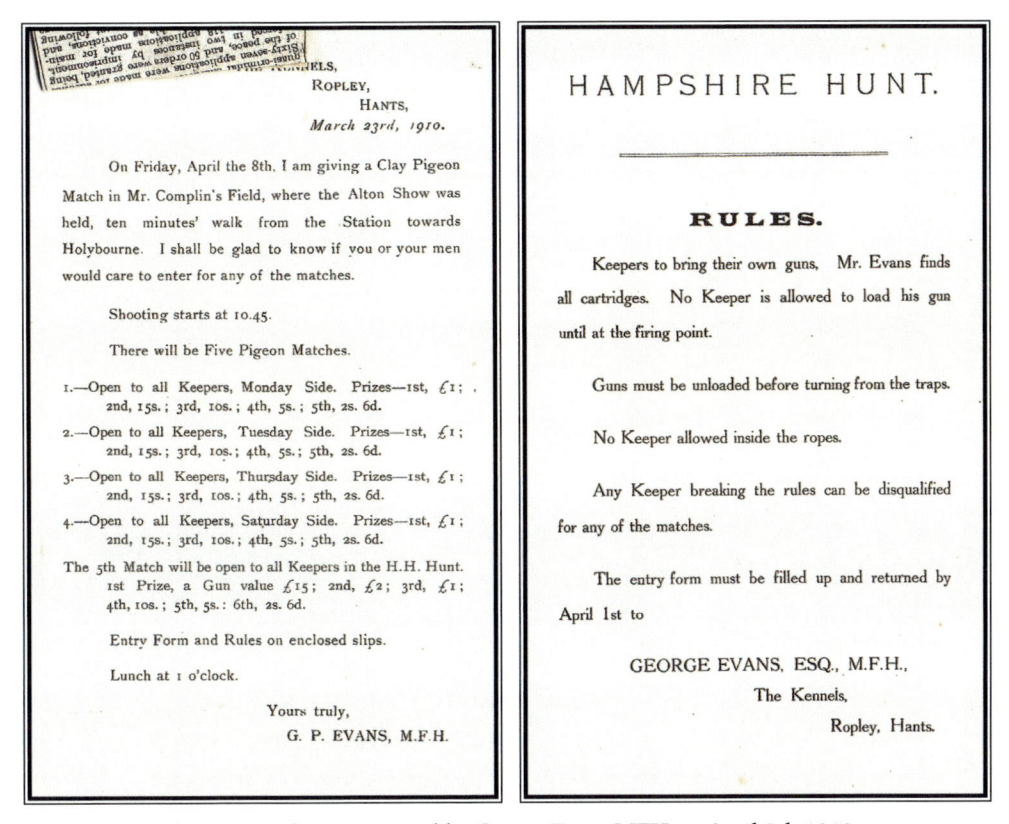

Clay pigeon shoot organised by George Evans MFH on April 8th 1910.

and Rainbow, who looked like 'winning a point-to-point or something better.' Old Bob, a six year old roan up to sixteen stone, made the top price of £175 and was described in the catalogue as a 'Good Hunter, and a real old fashioned, short-legged horse with perfect manners and a wonderful timber jumper.'

There was a much better show of foxes the following season, and after several hounds were drafted on account of running mute, a noticeable improvement in the performance of the pack. The point-to-point resumed at Tom Mitchell's farm at Hartley in April where freezing temperatures and blinding snowstorms failed to dampen racegoers' enthusiasm and the race for officers, government chargers and horses leased from the Aldershot and Southern Command was won by Mr Dobson's Dante. During his speech inside the luncheon tent for some 800 farmers, their wives and friends of the Hampshire Hunt, the Chairman thanked the farmers and landlords for their warm welcome during the previous season and revealed that there was no longer a single covert closed to hounds. Despite the weather, the

MESSRS. TATTERSALLS.
ALBERT GATE, KNIGHTSBRIDGE.
Will Sell
On JUNE 27th, 1910,
At 2.30.

[Auction catalogue listing, annotated with handwritten names and prices:]

1. HATFIELD.—Black Gelding, 6yrs. old, 16 hands. Irish horse. Pedigree unknown. Good hunter; up to 13.7 stone. Nice horse for a lady. Winner of several 1st prizes in show ring last summer.
2. MORGAN.—Black Gelding, 7yrs. old, 16 hands, by Johnny Morgan. Makes a slight whistle; up to 13.7 stone. Wonderful temperate horse. Nice horse for a lady. Winner of prizes.
3. HARD NUT.—Chestnut Gelding, 6yrs. old, 16 hands, by Karacoura, dam by Nutshell. Good hunter; up to 13.7 stone. Very clever over a big country. Real hard horse. Winner of prizes.
4. BURGESS.—Bay Mare, 7yrs. old, 16 hands, by Don Alonza. Good huntress; up to 14 stone. Fast; and gun in show ring, carrying a lady.
5. SWEEP.—Black Gelding, 6yrs. old, 16 hands, by Marioni. Good hunter; up to 13.7 stone. Fast. A perfect wonder over a country. No day too long.
6. SILVER.—Chestnut Mare, 6yrs. old, 16 hands, by Rosens. Good huntress; up to 14 stone. Very quiet mare for old gentleman; also very easy in her paces for a lady.
7. SILVER CLOUD.—Chestnut Gelding, aged, 16 hands, by Sleeve Gallion. Up to 15 stone. Good hunter. Wonderful manners. Carry anyone. Such a good ride.
8. OLD BOB.—Roan Gelding, 6yrs. old, 16 hands, by Chicago, dam by Sunset. Good hunter. Real old-fashioned short-legged horse with perfect manners. Wonderful timber jumper; up to 16 stone.
9. ROOK.—Black Gelding, 6yrs. old, 16 hands, dam by Ascetic. Good hunter; up to 14 stone. Carried the Master all the season without making a mistake. Good wire jumper. Winner of prizes.
10. GREY TICK.—Bay Gelding, 7yrs. old, 16 hands, by Brayhead, dam by Brown Prince. Up to 15 stone. Good hunter, good manners, and suitable for any child to ride. Winner of prizes.
11. SCOTTY.—Bay Gelding, 7yrs. old, 16 hands, by Old Coin. Makes a slight noise; up to 15 stone. Wonderful wire jumper, and no day too long.
12. TAD POLE.—Chestnut Gelding, 6 years old, 16.1 hands; by Matador, dam by York. Good hunter; up to 15 stone. Real hard horse.
13. LEGGS.—Chestnut Gelding, 6 years old, 16.2 hands, by Wonderbar, dam by Brown Prince; up to 15 stone. Good hunter; very fast; and likely to win a point-to-point. Very improving young horse.
14. RAINBOW.—Bay Gelding, 7 years old, 16.1 hands, by St. David. Good hunter; very fast; and likely to win a point-to-point; up to 15 stone.
15. ANCHOR.—Bay Gelding, 6 years old, 16.1 hands, by Anchor, dam by Lothario. Good hunter; very fast; up to 14 stone; very free jumper. Winner of prizes.
16. FIELD.—Bay Gelding, 5 years old, 16.1 hands, by Gold Medalist, dam by Utility. Good hunter; very fast; likely to win point-to-point race. Very nice young horse.
17. CHARGER.—Chestnut Gelding, 5 years old, 16 hands, by Matador. Good hunter and broken charger; fast; and went well at the beginning of the season in the Cottesmore country.
18. Q.C.—Black Gelding, 6 years old, 16 hands, by Don Alonza. Good hunter; quiet in harness, and a real useful slave.
19. PRINCESS ROYAL (3200 stud book).—Chestnut Mare, aged, 15.3 hands, by Henry VIII., dam Royal Lady. Good huntress; very quiet. Suitable for child to ride.
20. JOAN.—Chestnut Mare, 5 years old, 15.3 hands. Good huntress; real short-legged, stuffy sort; very quiet, and would suit a nervous rider.
21. GOLD DUST.—Chestnut Gelding, 5 years old, 15.3 hands, by Comfrey. Good hunter; fast; good timber jumper. Winner of prizes in show ring.
22. KID.—Bay Gelding, 5 years old, 15.2 hands, by Merry Matchmaker. Good hunter; very fast. Nice, improving young horse.

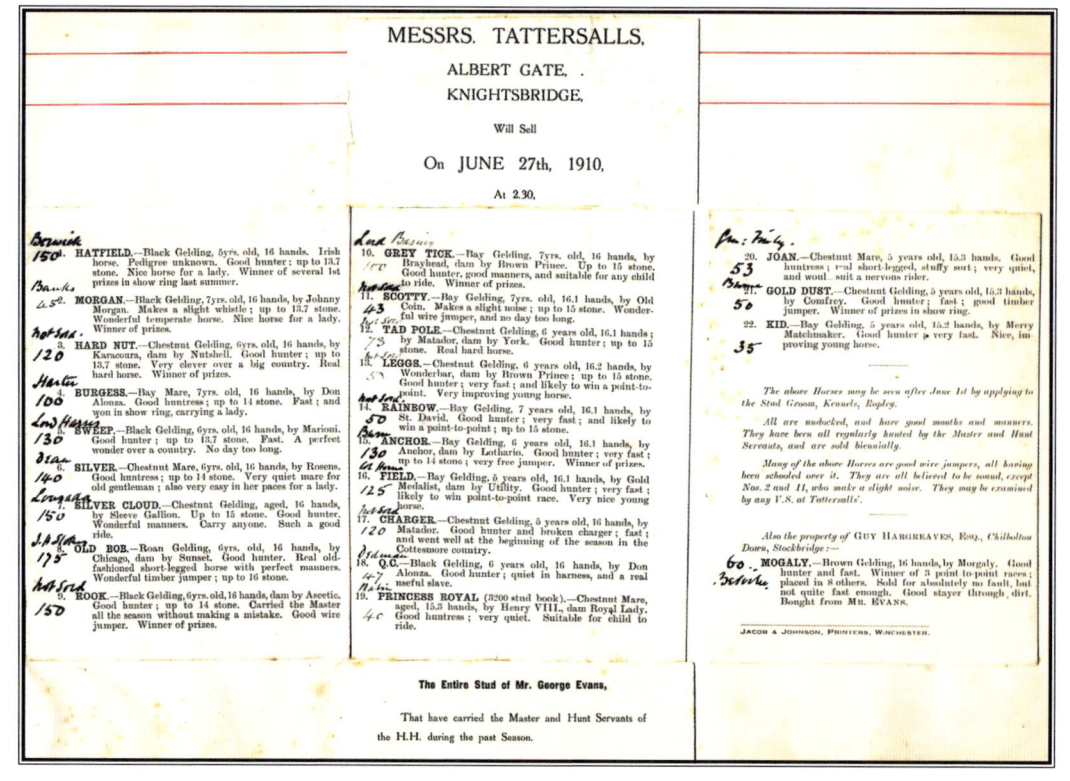

The above Horses may be seen after June 1st by applying to the Stud Groom, Kennels, Ropley.

All are unshocked, and have good mouths and manners. They have been all regularly hunted by the Master and Hunt Servants, and are sold biennially.

Many of the above Horses are good wire jumpers, all having been schooled over it. They are all believed to be sound, except Nos. 2 and 11, who make a slight noise. They may be examined by any V.S. at Tattersalls'.

Also the property of GUY HARGREAVES, Esq., Chilbolton Down, Stockbridge:—

23. MOGALY.—Brown Gelding, 16 hands, by Morgaly. Good hunter and fast. Winner of 5 point to point races; placed in 8 others. Sold for absolutely no fault, but not quite fast enough. Good stayer through; dirt. Bought from Mr. EVANS.

JACOB & JOHNSON, PRINTERS, WINCHESTER.

The Entire Stud of Mr. George Evans,
That have carried the Master and Hunt Servants of the H.H. during the past Season.

George Evans MFH consignment to Tattersalls sales in June 1910 at the end of his first season.

1911 point-to-point was an outstanding success. It had taken George Evans just two seasons to restore the feelgood factor to the Hunt and vindicate Montague Knight's determination to secure his services.

George Evans described himself as an expensive luxury, and Members soon learnt that such a Master would leave no stone unturned in his quest for excellence on and off the hunting field. When fire destroyed part of the kennels in April 1911, the Master insisted that a hospital for sick hounds be included in the renovations, and that claims for poultry and damages were settled promptly and generously. However it was agreed that Mr Dawes's optimistic claim for 48 dead pheasants in 1912 should be settled with a token gesture only as the Hunt did not compensate for loss of gamebirds to foxes. In order to finance increased spending the minimum subscription for Members rose to £25, and for everyone else, to £10 per horse. This was communicated in a strongly worded letter from Edmund Jervoise in September 1910, although the rate was later reduced to £5 for those living beyond the Hunt boundaries and hunting less than ten times a season.

The Master's endeavours to improve all aspects of the Hunt resulted in prolonged good sport. On February 2nd 1912 there was a six-mile point from Thorny Down to Bull's Bushes near Steventon in the Vine country following the meet at The Lunways Inn, and another six-mile point at Preston Candover when hounds ran from Ellisfield to Bushy Warren having crossed the London to Basingstoke road and swum the Basingstoke Canal. During the 1911–1912 season hounds went out 118 times including cubhunting, killing a total of 23½ brace, with Will Orvis now the first whipper-in and Tom Payne as second. According to their huntsman, 'Hounds much improved, good season and plenty of foxes.' That summer the puppy show judges, Messrs Cazenove and Barclay, were shown a superb young entry, which for the first time in many years were entirely homebred. Arthur Jervoise proposed the final toast, praising the persuasive qualities of a Master who 'had managed to get on the right side of everyone and thoroughly understood all things about hunting and also understood everything about shooting.'

The tally had risen to 28 brace – plus a brace of badgers – by the end of the 1912–1913 season, which included a seven-mile point following the meet at Abbotstone in April. October 20th 1913 was quite the best scenting day George Evans had ever seen in Hampshire, which began with a fast hunt from Brockwood Dean to kill at Bishops Sutton. Hounds quickly found again in Brockwood Copse, but a fresh fox intervened just as the huntsman was expecting to handle his fox after a blistering 60 minutes. The original quarry was so dead beat that a local farmer was able to pick the fox up and give it to the Master's chauffeur – described in his diary as 'my driving man' – to be brought on by car. By the time he arrived hounds had caught their second fox of the day, and George Evans insisted the captured one be released unharmed. More than 150 mounted followers turned out for the Opening Meet at the Chairman's Chawton House, and in January 1914 hounds produced the run of the season on a fox from Wield Wood, running via Abbotstone, Preston Candover and Moundsmere to catch their fox near Ellisfield at 5.15pm after a two-hour hunt, seven-mile point and twice that as they ran, with only a dozen left at the finish. The Tuesday country provided a superb day from the Matterley Gate meet in February, where the pack caught their first fox in the middle of a stubble field after a fast 75 minutes and then went on to make a six-mile point from Durdens to Marwell Hall in just over an hour during the afternoon.

George Evans makes no reference to his own performance in his diaries, however, like many successful huntsmen he was known to be a doggy man who enjoyed a close rapport with his hounds. This intuition was said to extend to all animals, including piglets at the kennels which he taught to sit up and beg like a dog. Although sympathetic and communicative with gamekeepers and countrymen of all persuasions, he was not beyond letting fly with some choice words if the mounted field compromised sport. 'Until I hunted with the Cambridgeshire,' Isaac Bell wrote in his famous work, *The Huntsman's Log Book*, 'I thought Lord Willoughby de Broke had good flow of language, but I soon discovered that compared to George Evans, his was basic English.' In common with his celebrated predecessor, Henry Deacon, George was often at loggerheads with Members when it came to agreeing the size of his guarantee. Halfway through his second season the Hon. Secretary wrote to him explaining there was no prospect of Members being able to guarantee more than £2,100 for the 1911–1912 season but expressing sincere hope that a way may be found for him to continue. George Evans responded by resigning his Mastership on account of it being 'absolutely impossible' for him to accept a reduction in the guarantee. The resignation was withdrawn after Members offered to make up the difference at the end of the season should funds permit, and by 1913 the guarantee had risen to £2,700.

During this time Members were also occupied with ensuring that they would be allowed to continue wearing the Prince of Wales's ostrich plumes on their hunt buttons, a cherished privilege first granted by the Prince of Wales[5] in the late eighteenth century. They had presented a petition to the future King Edward VII's representatives in 1863 praying to be allowed to continue the privilege, which was graciously accorded. They sent another formal request to his son, the future King George V, soon after he had been created Prince of Wales in 1901, writing to his Private Secretary, Sir Arthur Bigge, and signing off 'we have the honour to be Sir, Your Obedient Servants,' above a list of current Members. Sir Arthur responded four days later stating that His Royal Highness was 'much pleased to allow the continued use of his crest on the Hunt Button, in accordance with the ancient usage of more than a hundred years.'

The Hon. Secretary, Captain Edmund Jervoise RN wrote to Sir Arthur again in the summer of 1910, soon after King George V had ascended to the throne, requesting the honour of the King's continued involvement as an Honorary Member of the HH Club. Sir Arthur explained that His Majesty would be unable to remain an Honorary Member but was very glad to renew permission for use of the royal crest. When King George V's son, the future King Edward VIII, came of

---

5   Later King George IV.

COMETH THE HOUR, COMETH THE MAN 1909–1914

Marlborough House,
Pall Mall, S.W.

Royal Pavilion,
Aldershot Camp.

12th July, 1910.

Dear Sir,

In reply to your letter of the 8th instant, I regret that it is not possible for the King to continue to be an Honorary Member of the Hampshire Hunt.

His Majesty is very glad to give permission to the Members of the Hunt to wear the crest of the Prince of Wales on their Hunt button. As soon as His Royal Highness comes of age the question of his becoming an Honorary Member of the Hunt will be considered, if you will kindly make a note to bring the matter up again at that time.

Yours very faithfully,

Arthur Bigge

Captain Edmund Jervoise, R.N.
Hon: Secretary,
Hampshire Hunt.

Please Note.—Permission to ride over the Farms is only granted to those who take part in the Races. No Dogs allowed in the vicinity of the Course.

MARCH 12th, 1914.

H.H.
POINT-TO-POINT STEEPLECHASES

(Run under N. H. Rules (Appendix C) 5 and 167 to 168 inclusive, as regards Corrupt and Fraudulent Practices),

At FARRINGDON,
NEAR ALTON, HANTS
(By kind permission of the Landowners and Occupiers).

Stewards:
ALL THE MEMBERS OF THE H.H.
LIEUT.-COL. H. A. L. TAGART, D.S.O., 15th Hussars, and
MR. F. CORYTON, *Judges.*
MR. A. T. E. JERVOISE, *Starter.*

Committee:
MR. GEORGE EVANS, M.F.H.
CAPT. A. COURAGE, 15th Hussars.
MR. T. S. MITCHELL.   CAPT. E. JERVOISE, R.N.
MAJOR R. E. CECIL, *Clerk of the Course.*
MR. J. F. COMPLIN, *Clerk of the Scales.*
MR. A. E. SEAWELL (*Hon. Sec.*).

SIXPENCE

The last HH point-to-point in March 1914 prior to the outbreak of war.

10, BUCKINGHAM GATE,
S.W.

14th March, 1914.

Captain Edmund Jervoise, R.N.,
Medstead Manor,
Alton, Hants.

Dear Sir,

I have had the honour of laying your letter of the 2nd instant before The Prince of Wales, and I am directed to say that His Royal Highness will be very pleased to permit the Plume of Ostrich Feathers to be continued to be used on the Hampshire Hunt Button, and that it will give His Royal Highness much pleasure to become an honorary member of this old and famous Hunt.

I am,
Yours faithfully,

Walter Peacock
Treasurer to His Royal Highness

Top left: King George V granting permission in 1910 for Members to wear the Prince of Wales's crest on their hunt buttons.

HRH The Prince of Wales accepting membership of the HH Club in 1914.

– 79 –

age in 1914 he accepted the offer to become an Honorary Member with pleasure and also granted permission for the continued use of his ostrich feathers on the Hampshire Hunt button. Encouraged by the response, Edmund Jervoise sent the Prince a set of HH buttons as a present from the Members, together with an open invitation to join them in the field for a day's sport. The Prince's Treasurer, Sir Walter Peacock, wrote back to say that 'His Royal Highness will bear in mind the last paragraph of your letter, but it is impossible to make any promise with reference thereto.' Any ambitions the Prince may have harboured to enjoy a day with the Hampshire Hunt would soon be overtaken by a tumultuous turn of events, and Members would have to wait another 65 years before a Prince of Wales honoured them with his presence in the hunting field.

The 1914 point-to-point was held on March 12th a month before the closing meet, but there had already been enough sport to assure the success of another glorious season. Lord Basing proposed the toast to Foxhunting at the customary farmers' luncheon and told his audience that although he had followed the Hampshire Hunt for more than 40 years, hunting had never been more popular during its entire history than at the present time. There was not a tenant farmer or covert owner who did not welcome the Hunt, and there was no scarcity of foxes. Without a trace of irony, Lord Basing went on to quote R. S. Surtees's famous words describing hunting as 'the image of war without its guilt but only five-and-twenty percent of its danger,' and stated his view that it was the finest school in the world for soldiers and officers. Few of those present could have predicted that seven long years would elapse before there would be another Hampshire Hunt point-to-point meeting.

The season ended with a busy day from Windmill Hill on Easter Monday, and the Master's customary succinct summary inside his hunting diary. 'Very good season' he wrote, 'killed 33½ brace and a badger, 33 brace to ground. Young hounds did very well.' The affairs of the Hampshire Hunt could hardly have been more settled or in better heart than in the spring of 1914, but on June 28th a Serbian patriot murdered Archduke Franz Ferdinand, the heir to the Austro-Hungarian Empire, thousands of miles away in Sarajevo, a city unknown to most of the inhabitants of Hampshire. But within a month the Austrian army had invaded Serbia, and the First World War had begun.

Chapter Seven 1914–1918

The Great War

G.P.E. Evans Esq., 1914–1915,
F. Coryton Esq., (Chairman of a committee) 1915–1919

Start of First World War, MFHA direction to hunts, controlling foxes during the War, summary of the 1914–1915 season, George Evans's departure to France in October 1915, Frederick Coryton and a committee appointed to manage the Hunt, Hon. Secretary changes, disputes between Members and George Evans, hound ownership resolved by MFHA, demise of the Shire Horse Society, food rationing for hunters, further MFHA directions and fox control, end of the War.

Seven weeks after the War broke out, the Masters of Foxhounds Association sent out their resolutions for hunting during the conflict to all Masters. Whilst recognising the impossibility of regular hunting under the wartime conditions, the Committee considered that it would be prejudicial to the country in general if hunting were allowed to lapse altogether and stressed the importance of killing as many foxes as possible, with the proviso that hunting should not be regarded as a sporting activity until the war is over. The Association also urged subscribers to continue supporting their local hunt in order to avoid a very serious state of affairs, and to appreciate that the partial suspension of hunting in some countries was a consequence of many hunt horses being freely and willingly handed over to the service of the country. The MFHA despatched a second letter on September 12th 1914 to reiterate the importance of reducing the fox population, which stated, 'owing to the fact that all foreign supplies of eggs and poultry will be very much curtailed on account of the War, thereby endangering the national food supply, it is imperative that all Masters of Hounds should make special endeavours to reduce the number of foxes below the normal.'

Those who did not agree with the MFHA's robust stance included Rosalind, Countess of Carlisle, who took great offence that hunting was carrying on in the Malton district of North Yorkshire. A press cutting amongst the Hampshire Hunt

> M. F. H. Association.
> Tattersalls.
> London, S.W.
>
> *August 21st, 1914.*
>
> DEAR SIR,
>
> A Meeting of the Committee of the Masters of Foxhounds Association was held at Tattersalls, on Monday, the 17th inst., for the purpose of considering the possibility and advisability of Hunting this coming season. There were present:—
>
> DUKE OF BEAUFORT,   J. C. STRAKER,
> LORD LECONFIELD,   E. CURRE,
> G. W. FITZWILLIAM,   W. H. WHARTON,
> and the Hon. Sec., J. R. RAWLENCE.
>
> The following resolution was passed unanimously, and a copy of same ordered to be sent to all Masters of Hounds, Hunt Secretaries, and to the Press.
>
> I remain,
> Yours faithfully,
> BEAUFORT,
> *Chairman.*
>
> [RESOLUTION.]
>
> "While quite recognising the fact that, under the present circumstances, regular hunting will be impossible, the Committee of the Masters of Foxhounds Association consider that it would be most prejudicial to the country in general if it were allowed to lapse altogether.
>
> "They would, therefore, recommend that cub-hunting should take place, and continue as long as necessary, in order to kill as many foxes as possible in the various countries and enter the young hounds, but that hunting should not be looked upon from a sporting point of view until the War is over.
>
> "Where it is not possible to hunt the full number of days, the Committee strongly recommend Masters of Hounds to take measures to reduce the number of foxes in proportion to the amount of hunting days they think they will be able to manage.
>
> "They would also urge that people, having the interests of hunting at heart, should continue to subscribe, as far as their means permit, to the various packs, as otherwise a very serious state of things may arise.
>
> "The Committee ask the general public to recognise that this partial suspension of hunting is in a great measure caused by the fact that the horses of the various Hunting Establishments have been freely and willingly handed over to the service of the Country."

MFHA advice to hunts on the outbreak of war, August 1914.

archives reveals that foxes were not preserved, nor coverts drawn during the War years by the Middleton Hunt on her Castle Howard estate. 'The injury to the poultry industry due to the preserving of foxes is always deplorable' she wrote, 'but the evil is greatly intensified when food prices are high, and waste is a national danger.' It seems the Countess had confused the new policy of ruthless fox control with the pre-war one of maintaining a stable population and had also overlooked the enormous sacrifice made by hunting establishments nationwide in handing over their esteemed hunters for harrowing service on the front line in Europe.

Back in Hampshire Members decided in August 1914 that cubhunting would continue until Christmas at the discretion of the Master, who agreed to remain at the helm until that time provided he was paid the next instalment of his guarantee by the end of September. 'I am dreadfully hard hit,' he explained in a letter to the Chairman at the end of August, 'not only not getting any private money coming in, but over all my shootings. I shall lose over £600 over them.'[1] At the same meeting it was decided that poultry claims should be settled at the discretion of the Poultry Committee and Mr Complin offered to assist the Hon. Secretary, Captain Jervoise, for the duration of the War. Sir Richard Rycroft offered to take in some of the hounds after Christmas.

However storm clouds were not only gathering in Europe, but much closer to home. Edmund Jervoise wrote to the new Chairman, Frederick Coryton, who had recently replaced Montague Knight after his death earlier in the year, to voice concerns over the Club's agreement with the Master. The Hon. Secretary questioned the wisdom of paying Mr Evans the next instalment of his guarantee against a backdrop of much reduced hunting. 'I imagine he will have but a few horses to feed and of course less stablemen, and in spite of this we are to pay him exactly the same as when he was doing the thing the proper way. With no money likely to come in beyond the Members' minimum subscriptions this will be an impossibility.' Captain Jervoise also described the difficulties he faced in being able to get away from the Royal Naval College at Greenwich to discharge his duties as Secretary but signed off apologising for such a despondent letter. He put pen to paper again a few days later and concluded that even if hunting were possible, it would not be seemly to participate 'as most of us will have relations and many friends at the front and few will have the heart to go out and enjoy it.' In October Mr Frere was appointed as temporary Secretary to the Hunt Club during the absence of Captain Jervoise on military duty.

Despite the gloom, the 1914 season got underway on the last day of August at Windmill Hill where there was a poor show of cubs. 'Young hounds worked well, poor scent and very dull with no one out,' was the Master's summary. For the first time since his diaries began, there are no newspaper cuttings to complement George Evans's handwritten remarks, and from the Opening Meet onwards, no comments at all except to record a blank day from the Golden Pot in November after all the coverts had been shot the previous week. The last entry is for Lower Froyle on December 12th, by which time hounds had killed only eight brace. No hounds were put down during the first year of war, and it must be assumed that hounds, huntsman, and a reduced retinue of hunt staff completed the season, although there are no records of where they hunted or what was achieved.

---

1   In order to preserve foxes George Evans had rented the shooting of several coverts in the HH country at his own expense but expected to recoup this cost by inviting friends and supporters to enjoy the sport and contribute to the expense. Recouping this large rental outlay would not be possible once war had broken out.

In April 1915 George Evans undertook to hunt the country for a further season on a reduced guarantee of £1,800, however within three months he had sailed for France to join the war effort as a Staff Captain, leaving William Orvis in charge of the hounds and appointing Mr Stuart Smith to run hunt affairs on his behalf. His departure at short notice was not well received, and whilst war raged on the western front, George Evans and Members of the Hunt Club fought their own unfortunate battle in a series of tersely worded missives. Major Evans wrote to Mr Frere in July shortly before his departure to France requesting the next instalment of his guarantee and signing off with a request to be addressed as Major in future correspondence. He had not anticipated an aggressive response from the temporary Hon. Secretary, who conveyed Members' very strong feelings at the lack of courtesy shown by his sudden departure. 'It appears to the Hunt Club that if you are away, it is impossible for you to fulfil your agreement, and if you are not hunting hounds yourself, they feel without your presence and personality it will be impossible to get all the subscriptions which they had anticipated and consequently they cannot meet the guarantee arranged.'

Clearly nettled, the Master replied on July 24th whilst being shelled at a clandestine location in France to repeat the current impossibility of discharging his role as huntsman, and cynically apologising for the inconvenience. 'I will apologise for lack of courtesy on the War Office's part in not giving me more notice and very much regret that Members left at home should think that I have failed to do my duty to them and my country,' he wrote. 'It is very difficult for me to arrange my affairs from here, but if you are willing to take over the hounds please do so and

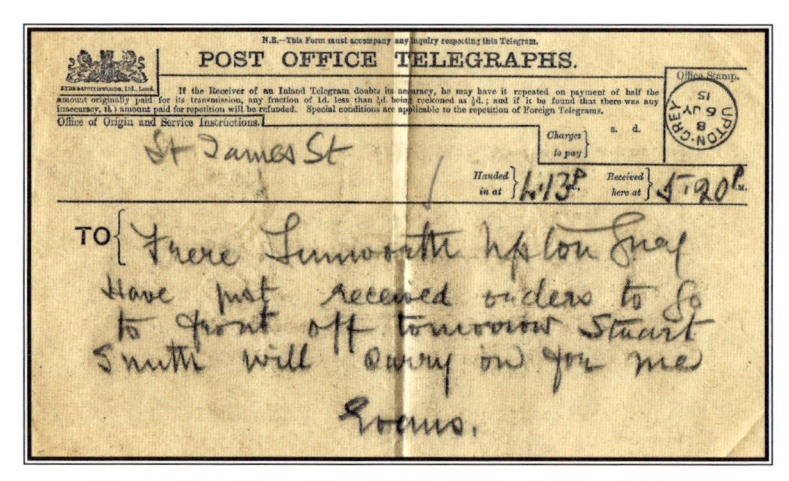

Telegram from George Evans MFH advising the Hon. Secretary that he is leaving for the front in July 1915.

let me know about the valuation.' Mr Frere conveyed Members' sympathy for their Master's patriotic desire to go abroad but insisted that he should have taken them into his confidence first and asked if he was prepared to complete the season by deputy for the sum of £1,000.

The offer of a reduced guarantee was unacceptable to Major Evans, who sent in his formal resignation on August 7th, protesting that he had never made a secret of wishing to support the war effort and that he had given no undertaking to personally hunt hounds when arrangements were confirmed for the current season. 'I wrote to all the keepers before leaving and told them there was a possibility of my not being able to handle the hounds myself, and that I hoped they would support me in the same way as if I were there. I had some very nice letters back from them.' He asked if the Hunt Club would purchase his saddlery and effects, and for how long he would be allowed to retain his house at the kennels. Major Evans's resignation was accepted with regret, and it was unanimously agreed that Frederick Coryton take over the management of the Hunt without financial liability. The Chairman selected a small committee consisting of Messrs Naylor, Complin, Seth Smith and the Reverend Lionel Corbett[2] to assist him in the task. Frederick Coryton and his team were to remain at the helm of the Hampshire Hunt throughout the war years and beyond, up until 1919. One of their first decisions was to retain William Orvis as huntsman after he left George Evans's employ on September 1st.

William Orvis, huntsman during the Great War, (second from left) and the Rev. Lionel Corbett, member of Frederick Coryton's wartime committee (on far right).

Since Mr Frere had found it impossible to discharge his secretarial duties, George Evans now took up the baton with his replacement, John Complin. He offered to sell all his horses to the Hunt Club for a straight £80 each and all his

---

2   These are the names of Frederick Coryton's War Committee recorded on page 45 of the 1912 minute book, however when Mr Complin (himself a member of the War Committee) thanked those who had assisted him during the War at a public meeting in October 1919, Mr Stuart Smith had been added to the list.

other effects including saddlery, coal, oats, hay, spades, shovels, and buckets at valuation. He also claimed ownership of ten couple of hounds which he offered for sale at £250, although he believed their real worth to be twice that sum. He pointed out that the pack he inherited had been valued at only £650[3] but were now worth at least £2000 thanks to his judicious breeding policies and the considerable improvement in their work. He asked if he could retain his house at the kennels for £20 per year because he needed somewhere to store his furniture and 'when I return home, I would like somewhere to put my head to rest.' Members declined to purchase the hunt horses but agreed to rent George Evans the huntsman's cottage for £20 a year and asked for the stables to be vacated as soon as possible.

Members disputed George Evans's claim to hound ownership, and according to the Hon. Secretary there was no reference to any valuation in the minute book, however he must have overlooked the Tattersalls summary attached to page 240 of the 1888 minute book following their visit to Ropley in October 1909. Meanwhile the former Master became increasingly frustrated by protracted correspondence regarding his effects and the Club's apparent refusal to agree a professional valuation. 'What do the Hunt Club want?' he asked in exasperation, 'I really have not the time to give my attention to business in England. I have done what I thought was best for foxhunting which many of the Members approved of. Yours in haste.' Despite the friction there are conciliatory gestures from both sides in correspondence; Major Evans offered the use of his house for hunt meetings, and the Hon. Secretary asked if William Orvis should look after his former employer's retriever gundogs during his absence.

By September George Evans had appointed Captain Stanwick to negotiate with the Hunt Club on his behalf, but the issue of hound ownership refused to go away. When John Complin was tipped off that Lord Lonsdale's huntsman intended to visit Ropley and collect the disputed ten couple,[4] he forbade William Orvis to allow any hounds to be removed and immediately wrote to propose that the matter be resolved by the MFHA. George was back in the UK on leave by October, but instead of a return to Hampshire he went to Gaick in the Scottish Highlands for

---

3 This figure is the rounded down valuation reached by combining the proceeds of selling 22½ couple of doghounds for 241 guineas at auction on April 22nd 1909, plus the Tattersalls valuation the same year of the bitches left in kennels at 450 guineas.

4 George Evans claimed 10 couple as his own property, since the pack was reduced soon after his appointment as Master from 65 to 55 couple, and that he believed he must leave 45 couple as per his agreement. In 1909 he actually agreed to hand over 40 couple of entered hounds and 10 couple of puppies on giving up the Mastership.

a well-deserved sporting break. Between stalking and salmon fishing he found time to write to the Hon. Secretary expressing anger and frustration with the Club, particularly their reluctance to compensate him for forage, coal, and other items he had paid for, but left behind at the kennels. 'Will they take everything off me at the kennels or not?' he asked, 'I took everything off the late Masters, as is the usual thing to do. I really think the way the Hunt Club have treated me is absolutely disgraceful. To start with they go back on their guarantee. Then they go back on their conversation about the number of hounds, simply because my military duties prevented me from hearing the minutes read. Then I have heard from farmers that I have put the country in a hole by resigning.' He finished his letter by offering to waive his right to the hounds in exchange for a one off settlement of £500.

Members eventually agreed to meet the former Master at The Swan Hotel in Alton on November 22nd so that he could explain the reasons for his sudden departure. During a conciliatory meeting George Evans stated that the Club had always treated him well and that he hoped to be free of any accusation of discourtesy, but when asked if he wished to resume Mastership, the answer was an emphatic No. To the relief of both parties a motion that the Club accept Mr Evans's explanation and record their regret for any misunderstanding was carried unanimously; the proposal was swiftly followed by his election as an Honorary Member for the current season. The controversy over hound ownership was finally decided by the MFHA under the chairmanship of Lord Southampton the following year, who upheld the original agreement that the retiring Master should leave 40 couple of entered hounds and 10 couple of puppies at the end of his term.

The Shire Horse Society, which had done so much to improve the quality of cart horses throughout the county since its inception 25 years earlier, was a sad casualty of the Great War. When the Society's founder, Frederick Coryton, proposed that it be dissolved in January 1916 an optimistic motion for its continued existence found no seconders, and it was decided to enter the Society's two stallions for sale at the London Show in February. Mr Coryton thanked the secretaries, Messrs Complin and Eggar, for all their hard work and with those words a great institution slipped permanently away. Since 1891, 27 different stallions had covered 6,286 mares, but by the 1920s the British Shire horse was already on the way to being superseded by the mechanical tractor.

In April 1917 all previous resolutions as to the number of hounds maintained by the Club were rescinded, and the pack was reduced to 27 couple in line with

HAMPSHIRE HUNT.

LIST OF MEMBERS,
NOVEMBER, 1915.

Names	When Elected	Postal Address
H.R.H. The Prince of Wales (Hon. Member)	14th March, 1914	...
Right Hon. Earl of Northbrook	8th February, 1871	Stratton Park, Micheldever.
H. Dutton, Esq.	8th February, 1871	Hinton House, Alresford.
W. G. Nicholson, Esq., M.P.	10th February, 1880	Basing Park, Alton.
Right Hon. Earl of Selborne	13th April, 1882	Blackmoor, Liss.
A. C. Nicholson, Esq.	16th January, 1886	2, South Audley Street, W.
F. Coryton, Esq.	22nd April, 1886	The Manor House, Greatham, Liss.
Brig.-General Right Hon. Lord Basing, C.B.	7th March, 1887	Hoddington House, Winchfield.
Spencer Charrington, Esq.	2nd February, 1888	Winchfield Lodge, Winchfield.
R. Nicholson, Esq.	13th November, 1888	Basing Park, Alton.
Colonel Torkington (re-elected 1897)	15th November, 1890	Willey, Farnham.
F. Seth Smith, Esq.	7th April, 1891	The Lodge, Upton Grey, Winchfield.
Heath Harrison, Esq.	12th November, 1894	Le Court, Liss.
Major R. E. Pole (Hon. Member)	24th February, 1896	Chandos Lodge, Anstey, Alton.
A. T. E. Jervoise, Esq.	29th November, 1897	Herriard Grange, Basingstoke.
A. E. Seawell, Esq.	9th January, 1899	Marelands, Bentley, Farnham.
Eyre Lloyd, Esq.	9th January, 1899	North Hall, Preston Candover, Basingstoke.
A. E. Scott, Esq.	18th November, 1899	Rotherfield Park, Alton.
C. F. G. R. Schwerdt, Esq.	29th January, 1900	Longwood House, Winchester.
C. T. Naylor, Esq.	11th April, 1901	Dean House, Kilmeston, Alresford.
Sir Richard Rycroft, Bart.	24th January, 1902	Dummer House, Basingstoke.
Brig.-General G. D. Jeffreys	3rd November, 1902	Burkham House, Alton.
Major M. C. C. Pinching	7th April, 1903	Willems Barracks, Aldershot.
F. H. T. Jervoise, Esq.	2nd November, 1903	Herriard Park, Basingstoke.
Major P. Holroyd	4th April, 1907	Ropley Manor, Alresford.
E. V. Frere, Esq.	18th November, 1907	Tunworth, Basingstoke.
H. Hoare, Esq.	18th November, 1907	Ellisfield Manor, Basingstoke.
G. W. Harrap, Esq.	2nd November, 1908	Marsh House, Bentley, Farnham.
G. Evans, Esq. (Hon. Member)	16th April, 1909	Ropley, Alresford.
Rt. Hon. Earl Curzon of Kedleston	1st November, 1909	Hackwood Park, Basingstoke.
Major H. Rostron	1st November, 1909	South Warnborough Manor, Winchfield.
Stuart Smith, Esq.	20th November, 1909	Hall Place, Ropley, Alresford.
Sir Joseph H. B. Tichborne, Bart.	13th January, 1911	Tichborne Park, Alresford.
Roland Orred, Esq.	26th January, 1911	Sheldon Manor, Chippenham.
John F. Complin, Esq.	26th January, 1911	Holybourne, Alton.
F. Summers, Esq.	11th March, 1911	Froyle Place, Alton.
Colonel A. Bibby	12th April, 1911	The Wakes, Selborne, Alton.
R. Elliott Cooper, Esq.	6th November, 1911	Bentworth Hall, Alton.
Rev. L. Corbett	4th November, 1912	Hockley House, Alresford.
C. W. Laird, Esq.	9th April, 1914	Malt House, Ropley, Alresford.
General Sir A. Hunter (Hon. Member during period of Command)		Aldershot.

Hampshire Herald, Alton.

Members of the HH Club in November 1915.

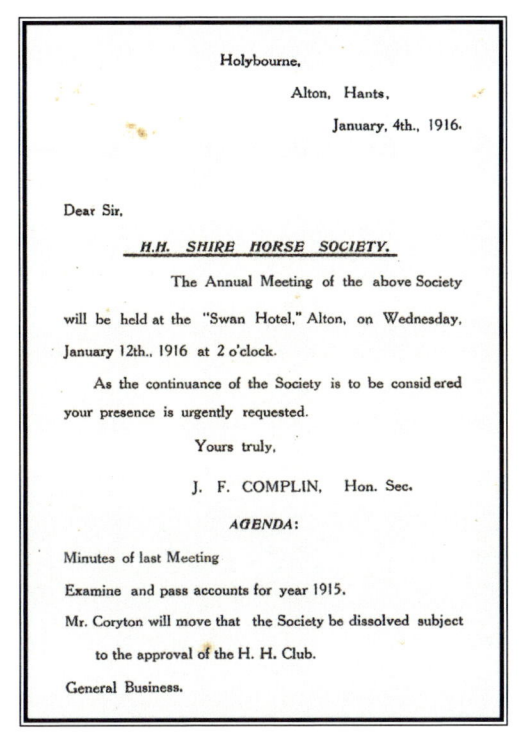

> Holybourne,
> Alton, Hants,
> January, 4th., 1916.
>
> Dear Sir,
>
> **H.H. SHIRE HORSE SOCIETY.**
>
> The Annual Meeting of the above Society will be held at the "Swan Hotel," Alton, on Wednesday, January 12th., 1916 at 2 o'clock.
>
> As the continuance of the Society is to be considered your presence is urgently requested.
>
> Yours truly,
>
> J. F. COMPLIN, Hon. Sec.
>
> *AGENDA:*
>
> Minutes of last Meeting
>
> Examine and pass accounts for year 1915.
>
> Mr. Coryton will move that the Society be dissolved subject to the approval of the H. H. Club.
>
> General Business.

Notice for the last ever meeting of the Shire Horse Society on January 12th 1916.

recent MFHA recommendations to keep only enough hounds to hunt twice a week. Members agreed to continue hunting twice weekly with the occasional bye day provided there were no contradictory orders from the government, and to reward gamekeepers for litters and finds in their coverts during the previous season. This policy was somewhat at odds with public opinion at the time, including Lord Selborne, who suggested that poison could be used to control foxes. When Members met to consider his letter, their response was that 'the destruction of foxes by any other means than hunting is outside the control of the Hunt and should be left to the landowners to act as they may think best having in view the future of hunting.' Mr Robinson also warned Members that the Crown Authorities intended reducing the number of foxes in Alice Holt woods and the Hon. Secretary was instructed to express regret that such steps should be taken and request that a fair stock of foxes be left.

In July Owen Llewellyn from the Ministry of Food wrote to the Chairman of the MFHA to ration feed to hunt horses and those belonging to recognised followers to 6lbs of oats a day up until November 1st, and 10lbs thereafter. He explained that the concession during a time of nationwide food rationing was intended to nurture a reliable source of remounts for the Western Front. 'The reason for this diminution is that at present hunting is not to be looked on as a sport, but simply as an aid to the supply of fit remounts for the army. As your Secretary has been notified, it must be understood that hunters are rationed as army remounts to be kept in good condition by their owners.' Rations were only available to horses fit for military purpose, later clarified as being from four to twelve years old and suitable for service as an Officer's Charger, Cavalry Troop Horse or Artillery Riding Horse. Masters were obliged to keep a list of qualifying hunt horses, together with those belonging to subscribers and followers. 'Horses so registered' the Ministry warned, 'are liable to be called up by the Army Remount Department at any moment.'

The 1917–1918 season commenced on October 2nd and finished earlier than usual on March 18th following recommendations from the MFHA. At the start of the season Lord Leconfield wrote to all Masters urging them not to advertise more than the permitted number of days in the local press, as to be seen hunting three or four times a week could provoke a public outcry at a time when everyone was feeling the pinch of food rationing. There are no detailed hunting records for the Hampshire Hunt beyond December 1914 for the duration of the War, but hounds went out twice a week with the hunt staff mounted on borrowed horses from the 1915 season onwards, and there was no food rationing for hounds until the final year of hostilities. Most Members maintained their subscriptions and when the First World War ended with Germany signing an armistice agreement with the Allies on November 11th 1918, Members of the Hampshire Hunt Club could boast a decent, but much reduced, pack of hounds.

M.F.H. Association.
Tattersalls.
Knightsbridge.
London. S.W.1.

September 20th, 1917.

DEAR SIR,
    The Rationing of Horses has been transferred to the Committee on the Utilization and Feeding of Horses, and I append a copy of a letter received from that Committee which slightly modifies the arrangements set out in my last letter of August 15th. You will observe that Masters and Acting Masters are now required to register their own and servants' horses, and those of their followers and subscribers in a book, a copy of which will be sent you by the Hon. Sec., Mr. Rawlence, free of charge. The Counterfoil of this book will be the Master's list, and of the two certificates attached to each form, one will be returned by you to the owner and will be his authority for rationing his horses, and the other you must send to the Secretary of the above Committee at 7, Whitehall Gardens, London, S.W.1.

    The form of License sent to you by Captain Llewellyn authorising you to keep a specified number of hunt horses is cancelled, and you will be entitled now to put on your list as many as you require for yourself and your hunt servants.

I remain,
Yours faithfully,
LECONFIELD,
Chairman.

MINISTRY OF FOOD,
COMMITTEE ON THE UTILIZATION AND FEEDING OF HORSES.
7, WHITEHALL GARDENS, LONDON, S.W.1

September 14th, 1917.

MY LORD,
    I am directed by the Minister of Food to say that it is intended to allow an oats ration of:—

        6lbs per day until the 31st of October, and
        10lbs per day for the rest of the Season,

for hunting horses of Subscribers and Followers, under the following conditions, viz.:—
    The horses must be between the ages of 4 and 12 years (both inclusive), regularly hunted, sound and suitable for military service as *(a)* Officers' chargers, *(b)* Cavalry troop horses, or *(c)* Artillery riding horses; such horses being the property of (1) The Master or Committee of a recognised pack of hounds or (2) recognised Followers subscribing to or living within the limits of the Hunt.

    It will not of course be in order for a Subscriber or Follower to place his horses on the list of more than one Master.

    The Horses must be registered by the Master or his authorised deputy, who shall notify the owners of the horses and the Committee on the Utilization and Feeding of Horses, 7, Whitehall Gardens, London, S.W.1, of such registration.

    The method of registration could very properly take the form of a book, containing a counterfoil and two certificates, one to be sent to the owner and the other to my Committee. It is understood that horses so registered are liable to be called up by the Army Remount Department at any moment.

    Proper records must be kept by the owner, of the oats, maize, beans, and peas, or other cereal foodstuffs fed to such horses. These records are at all reasonable times to be open to the inspection of an Officer of Police, or any person authorised by the Food Controller.

    I shall be glad to hear from you as soon as possible as to what horses it is desired to hunt with your pack under these conditions, together with the names and addresses of their owners.

    Hunt Horses or those belonging to the Master shall be permitted to have a 6lbs ration up to October 1st, and a 10lbs ration afterwards as previously arranged, and will of course be registered.

    This letter modifies slightly but does not alter the effective operation of the arrangements set out in your letter of 15th August last.

I am, my Lord,

MFHA advice on food rationing for hunt horses season 1917–1918.

M.F.H. Association,
Tattersalls,
Knightsbridge,
London. S.W.1.

October 20th, 1917.

DEAR SIR,

A Meeting of the Committee of the Masters of Foxhounds Association was held at Tattersalls, on Thursday, the 11th inst., for the purpose of considering the advisability of not advertising the Meets in the Papers more than two days a week during the coming season. There were present :—

  DUKE OF BEAUFORT,   G. FITZWILLIAM,
  LORD LECONFIELD,   H. STRAKER,
  LORD GALWAY,   E. E. BARCLAY,
  SIR WATKIN WYNN,   H. O. LORD,
      J. S. H. FULLERTON,
   and the Hon. Sec. J. R. RAWLENCE.

The following recommendations were unanimously agreed to, and a copy of same ordered to be sent to all Masters of Hounds and Hunt Secretaries, with the request that it be kept private, and not communicated to the Press.

            I remain,
            Yours faithfully,
              LECONFIELD,
               Chairman.

"The Committee of the Masters of Foxhounds Association are desirous of bringing the following point to your notice, as they consider it of special importance for the continuance of Hunting.

"It will be remembered that, in the arrangement made with the Food Controller last spring, it was agreed that packs should be reduced in the numbers of Hounds and Horses to the level of two days a week, and on this understanding Hunting was to go on and food was allowed for Hounds and Hunt horses. Prominence was given to this reduction both in Parliament and in the Press.

"In all the large towns, especially in the Midlands and the North, the Provincial Daily Paper is read by all, and if during this winter a long list of Hounds advertised to meet three and four days a week appears every day in the paper, the readers will refuse to believe in the truth of these reductions. When, too, the demand is made upon them, as it probably will be, to further reduce their own rations of bread and food, it would not be difficult for those who are opposed to Hunting to persuade the inhabitants of the towns that they have a grievance owing to the arrangements with the Food Controller being disregarded, and consequently a very serious outcry against Hunting being allowed to continue at all might be raised.

"Under these circumstances the Committee would strongly urge that, in the interests of Hunting in the future, every M.F.H. should <u>only advertise the agreed two days a week</u>, but in large countries where three or even four days a week are considered to be an absolute necessity to kill the foxes, it is hoped that the extra days will be given as <u>unadvertised 'Bye-days'</u> with a small pack and notice given by card, which might also be sent to all local markets and hotels where market dinners are held."

MFHA advice to hunts in October 1917.

Chapter Eight 1919–1926

An Uphill Road

A.P. Robinson Esq., 1919–1921, Major A.C. Bovill DSO, MC 1921-1923, Lieutenant Colonel Mangles 1923–1924, Lieutenant Colonel Mangles, Captain Orred 1924–1925, Lieutenant Colonel Mangles, Captain J.B. Scott 1925–1926.

A. P. Robinson becomes Master and huntsman in 1919, General Meeting and the mood of the country post the Great War, purchase of extra hounds, farmers and the Hampshire Hunt Club, Major Bovill becomes Master in 1921, Mrs Hobart hunting row, MFHA resolution re Chiddingfold Hunt, Lt. Colonel Mangles becomes Master in 1923, formation of covert and management committees, Captain Orred joins the Mastership in 1924, resumption of the Hampshire Hunt point-to-point races, miscellaneous damage claims, Captain Scott joins the Mastership in 1925, George Evans joins the Mastership for second time in 1926.

A meeting of the Hampshire Hunt Club was called in January 1919 to consider the appointment of a new Master to replace Frederick Coryton and his committee, who were ready to stand down having done a superb job in keeping the Hunt going through the War. After General Jeffreys withdrew his offer to hunt the country due to military duties, advertisements for the Mastership in *The Field* and *Horse & Hound* magazines attracted six applicants. These included Mr Robinson, a businessman from Norwich, who agreed to hunt hounds three days a week on a guarantee of £1,500.

In order to facilitate the revival of hunting after the War it was decided to hold a special meeting for Members, subscribers, landowners, and farmers at the Assembly Rooms in Alton on October 14th 1919. This was the first time the Hunt Club had held an open meeting of this nature, which was called to give all interested parties, but especially the farmers, an opportunity for a friendly discussion about the Hunt as it emerged from four years of obscurity. In the absence of the Earls of Northbrook and Selborne, Frederick Coryton took the chair and began by paying tribute to the farmers who had held their own meeting on how best to support the

> To the:-
>
> Covert Owners & Shooting Tenants in the H.H. Country.
>
> We, the undersigned Farmers, wish to call your attention to the material damage that has been done to hunting by the wholesale destruction of Fox Cubs and in some instances of old Foxes that has taken place in some parts of the H.H. Country, and ask your assistance in remedying the same.
>
> We, as Farmers, fully appreciate the benefits derived by having an established pack of Fox Hounds in our midst; which, in addition to circulating money in the neighbourhood, provides us with a market for young horses, corn, hay and straw.
>
> We, on our part, are always pleased to see hounds and shooting tenants, and do ask all owners of coverts and shooting tenants to consider the interest of hunting by preserving foxes.
>
> Many of those who used to hunt with the H.H. have been serving their Country, and we feel that it is up to everyone, now that the War is over, to see that they can return and find that they are still able to enjoy hunting as before.
>
> (signed)

H. ALLEN	W. ATKINSON	W. ALLAM	W. ABRAHAMS
E. A. BROCK	W. BROOK	P. BOWTELL	W. P. BUTLER
J. E. BAIGENT	F. BOWTELL	G. PENFORD	A. BESLEY
T. BISHOP	N. AUSTEN CHALCRAFT	THOS. A. CHALCRAFT	J. COX

(see over)

(Farmers' Appeal re H.H. - continuation of signatures)

H. L. Chalcraft	G. G. Chalcraft	A. Copper	J. F. Dingle
F. Downs	H. Edgar	W. A. Earwaker	John Fawcett
J. S. Gray	J. Gould	Fleet Goldsmith	J. R. W. Godwin
A. E. Harris	W. J. Haydon	Thos. Hutton	W. Holmes
C. Higgens	C. Harnett	J. N. Heal	W. Knight
George King	R. Lee	William E. Legg	E. J. Longman
G. Langrish	T. S. Mitchell	Joseph H. Mills	John T. Mills
A. Munday	G. Penn	F. N. Padwick	John Pain
F. J. Pitkin	F. R. Rook	F. A. Retallack	H. Silvester
J. Stockdale	Percy W. Seward	W. Stratton	P. B. Shelley
Fred N. Taylor	W. C. Twitchin	R. K. Twitchin	J. V. C. Talbot
R. P. Tuckett	D. F. Terrill	E. Morris Wells	B. Warner
D. G. Whistler	I. Wren	Hy. Waters	J. Westbrook
H. R. Wake			

Open letter from HH farmers in 1919 to covert owners and shooting tenants.

Hampshire Hunt earlier in the year. The result had been an open letter in the press signed by 69 of them calling for an end to the wholesale destruction of foxes in the HH country and expressing their strong wish that those who have been serving their country abroad should be able to enjoy hunting again on their return to England. The Chairman reminded everyone present that the farmers' letter had achieved widespread publicity throughout Hampshire and beyond and pointed out that many of his friends had passed favourable comment on the sentiments it expressed.

Mr Coryton then summarised the difficulties of keeping the Hunt going during the War, when food for hounds and horses had been rationed and the pack reduced to just 27 couple. By the end of the war the only meal available to feed the hounds on was so bad that it was hardly fit for a pig, and several nearly died as a consequence. He paid tribute to the huntsman, William Orvis, who had coped admirably with very difficult conditions and frequently went hunting alone with no one to turn hounds. The Chairman read out a recently published letter in *The Field* magazine from Lord Bathurst, which highlighted the enormous contribution made by the hunting community to the war effort and ended with a plea to all farmers to welcome hounds and remove wire, so that the 'reconstructed England will still be Merrie England and that farming and foxhunting will flourish side by side for many a long day.' As the ovation subsided Frederick Coryton introduced the new Master to further warm applause, describing him as a very plucky man to come into fresh country. Mr Robinson pledged every endeavour to provide good sport during the coming season but reported that there were only 22½ couple in kennels. Hounds had already been out on fifteen mornings and accounted for 5½ brace, although they were currently prohibited from hunting part of the Saturday country due to a muzzling order[1] from the Board of Agriculture. Alfred Eggar responded to Mr Robinson on behalf of the farmers by pledging their support and noting, to further warm applause, that hunting beat shooting hollow as a sport. He recalled Henry Deacon's kindness during the golden age of hunting in Hampshire and hoped the new Master would restore the same standards of excellence.

When the meeting was thrown open to the floor several of the farmers present were able to have their say. Tom Mitchell appealed to shooting tenants, explaining the destruction of foxes improved sport for a few, but ruined it for many, and proposed a resolution that everyone present support the new Master

---

1   The case for keeping the Muzzling Act in force in other districts until the 1920s, was due to soldiers bringing home dogs and puppies from the front at the end of the First World War. It was discovered that some of these strays had become infected with the rabies virus.

Appeal to purchase additional hounds in 1920.

HOLYBOURNE,
ALTON, HANTS.

February 3rd, 1920.

DEAR

At a Meeting of the Members of the H.H., held on January 22nd, it was decided to issue an appeal to the Members of and Subscribers to the H.H. for a Special Fund to purchase at least fifteen couples of hounds, at a probable cost of £400.

Owing to the compulsory reduction of hounds in 1917, and the difficulty in obtaining drafts since, the Pack is now barely sufficient for two days a week; and when this season is over there will not be enough hounds for even two days a week next season. Under these circumstances the Members feel that, in fairness to the Master, an effort should be made to restore the Pack to twenty-five couples: hence this appeal.

The Master himself will find additional hounds to enable him to hunt three days a week.

The following donations were promised at the Meeting:—

	£	s	d
General Jeffreys, C.B.	30	0	0
Major Rostron	20	0	0
Lieut.-Colonel Knight	10	0	0
Mr. F. Coryton	10	0	0
Mr. Seth Smith	10	0	0
Mr. Stuart Smith	10	0	0
Rev. Corbett	10	0	0
Mr. C. W. Laird	10	0	0
Captain Peto	10	0	0
Captain A. Coryton	10	0	0
Major F. Jervoise	10	0	0
J. F. Complin	10	0	0

May I ask you to send me a donation?

Yours truly,

J. F. COMPLIN,
Hon. Secretary, H.H.

1920's cartoon celebrating the HH's new mechanical hound van.

in carrying on foxhunting in the Hampshire Hunt country. Mr Chalcraft asserted the importance of involving the whole community in hunting, a theme that was taken up by Mr Eggar who recalled a visit to Devon when everyone from people on donkeys to the driver of a baker's cart joined in the fun of the hunt. He was sure that if everyone pulled together in the same fashion, they would find that foxhunting was not only a fine sport but an activity that benefited farmers through the sale of corn and hay. The Hon. Secretary, Mr Complin, dispelled rumours that the meeting had been called because the Hunt was in disarray, and spoke optimistically about the future, pointing out there was only one covert currently closed to hounds. He said hunting must be kept going 'for Englishmen who had risked their lives to keep up the glory of old England' and thanked all those who had worked so hard to make this possible, especially Mr Coryton and his committee of Messrs Stuart Smith, Seth Smith, Naylor, and the Rev. Corbett.

Following the drastic reduction of hounds in kennels in 1917, it was going to take much time and effort to restore the pack to the former high standard attained by George Evans prior to the War. In January 1920, Members and subscribers were invited to contribute to a fund established to purchase at least fifteen couple of hounds for an estimated £400, without which there would be insufficient to hunt more than twice a week. The benefactors included General Jeffreys who donated £30, but on June 1st the purchasing committee appointed to invest the proceeds reported a fruitless visit to Rugby hound sales and Mr Robinson informed the Club he would be unable to hunt more than two days a week until he had more hounds.

There are few records of sport provided by Mr Robinson during his first season, but a second general meeting for all connected with the hunt was held at Alton on October 12th 1920, with the Earl of Northbrook in the chair. The tone was little different from the previous year, with most of the meeting given over to a discussion on how farmers could be given a greater role in the management of the Hunt. Tom Mitchell spoke passionately in favour of their representation on the committee, however Lord Northbrook explained there was no committee to co-opt farmers onto, as the management of the Hunt had always been the sole responsibility of Members, currently 43 individuals each subscribing a minimum of £25 a year. General Jeffreys pointed out that far from being a modern establishment, the Hampshire Hunt was a very old fashioned one indeed, which throughout its long history had never appointed a management committee. He explained that Members were not only responsible for conducting the affairs of the Hunt but also for financing it, and if necessary, making good a shortfall out of their own pockets. He confirmed that temporary subcommittees were formed from time to time to address important issues such as the appointment of a new Master, but that any such organisation dissolved once its function had been discharged.

The Chairman suggested that representatives from the farming community should be invited to the next meeting of the Hampshire Hunt Club to discuss the issues in greater detail, after which General Jeffreys proposed a hearty vote of thanks to Lord Northbrook, whose well-foxed coverts were always open to hounds. The General was certain that if shooting tenants would only realise that hounds running through large Hampshire woodlands, 'made pheasants fly instead of flapping along there would not be a quarter of the difficultly there was about meets.' A subcommittee of Members met Mr Mitchell and other farmers later the same year and agreed to form a joint committee of reference consisting of no more than six Members and six farmers to meet at least twice a year to discuss the affairs of the hunt. But it was all in vain, for in February 1921 Tom Mitchell had to advise Members that whilst they had the best interests of hunting in the district at heart, his farming colleagues had decided little good would come of the proposal. For the time being, the matter of farmers being officially represented at Members' meetings was allowed to drop.

AN UPHILL ROAD 1919–1926

THREE POPULAR HUNT SECRETARIES

**A.F. Coryton, Major R. E. Pole and J.F. Complin
all served as Hon. Secretaries to the HH Club.**

Unlike the previous year when there had been fulsome praise for the new Master, there was remarkably little reference to either current sport or Mr Robinson in October 1921. By then it was almost certainly public knowledge that a meeting had been called three months earlier to discuss the many letters received by the Secretary complaining that the Master owed money all over the county. Mr Robinson's offer to resign if the Hunt considered he was not acting in their best interest, or showing good sport, had been read out, however Members instead sent a small delegation to meet the Master and examine his financial affairs. Mr Robinson gave an assurance that all his debts had been settled, and also agreed to send his receipts to the Hon. Secretaries[2] and to open a separate banking account for Hunt business only. However his financial situation continued to deteriorate, and when Mr Robinson's second offer of resignation was accepted in December 1920, Members were compelled to withhold £350 from the guarantee until he had submitted his accounts to the Club. There followed a succession of heated exchanges between the Club and Mr Robinson, who was said to have been a hard rider and effective huntsman in the field. To the regret of all, a Mastership that had been so warmly

---

2   From 1920 onwards Augustus Coryton (son of the former Master and Hunt Chairman, Frederick) appeared to share secretarial duties with the existing Hon. Secretary, Mr Complin.

and optimistically embraced at the outset ended in acrimony after only two seasons.

Major Anthony Bovill, DSO, MC, was appointed to replace Mr Robinson as Master and huntsman for the 1921–1922 season, on the understanding that the Club would pay for all hunt expenses, limiting Major Bovill's financial responsibilities to his personal costs only. It was also resolved to reward gamekeepers £1 for every litter found and hunted, and a further fifteen shillings for each adult fox found, although either bonus could be reduced by five shillings if a fox found sanctuary in a recognised earth on the relevant keeper's beat. There were still only enough hounds to hunt twice a week with the occasional bye day, but six couple were purchased in June for the price of £216, and the new regime got off to a flying start by scoring a brilliant nine-mile point from Alresford Pond to Chawton Park across blind country on a blazing hot cubhunting morning in October. In April the following year Major Bovill was authorised to spend a further £250 on another fifteen couple.

Shortly after Major Bovill's first Opening Meet an unfortunate accident in the hunting field ignited a major incident that consumed Members throughout November 1921. At a Members' meeting on November 11th letters were read out protesting the foul language used in the hunting field by Mrs Kathleen Hobart from Bordon Camp to another lady subscriber, Mrs Richardson. Instead of taking the matter up with Mrs Hobart direct, the Hon. Secretary was instructed to write to her husband's Commandant at Bordon, General Daly, to ask if he would be kind enough to ascertain whether Mrs Hobart had apologised, or if she had any explanation to offer the Hunt for her behaviour. Mrs Hobart took exception to this intervention and wrote to Mr Complin asking the Hon. Secretary to clarify exactly what she was supposed to be apologising for, and who had reported her behaviour. She made her position clear by writing, 'I am quite unable to forward either an apology or an explanation without knowing exactly on what ground the Members of the committee passed the resolution which was handed to me by my husband who received it from General Daly to whom apparently it had been addressed. Yours Truly, Kathleen Stanley Hobart.'

Mr Complin wrote back promptly to disclose that the matter was brought before the Hunt by General Jeffreys and explained, 'that the Hunt were informed that you had spoken to Mrs Richardson in a manner and had used language which was not to be expected from a lady hunting with the HH and in consequence the Members feel that an apology or explanation is due from you to them.' The Hon.

Meets of the HH at Hoddington House (top) and South Warnborough during the Mastership of Major Bovill 1921–1923.

Secretary's letter drew an immediate and robust response from Mrs Hobart, who began by setting down exactly what had taken place. 'I was galloping down a lane in front of my husband when I heard a bang behind me, turning round, I saw that my husband had been badly kicked,' she wrote. 'I pulled up and galloping back to him, jumping off my cob and holding onto him and his cob. I was certain from the noise I had heard and the awful pain he was in that his leg was broken, and in my furious rage I used language for which afterwards I was sorry. My husband went up to Mrs Richardson and apologised on my behalf, which she accepted and said the apologies were all due from her, and that she had not heard anything that was said.' Kathleen Hobart criticised the Club for condemning her without investigating the matter properly or giving her the opportunity to defend herself. However her greatest ire was reserved for the Club's decision to contact her husband's military superior about her behaviour. 'Colonel Commandant C. A. Daly is commanding the garrison,' Mrs Hobart reminded Members in writing, 'but he does not (underlined twice) command me.' The unfortunate scandal was put to bed by Mr Complin tactfully conveying Members' satisfaction with Mrs Hobart's letter, to which he added his own approval and the hope that he would soon see Major and Mrs Hobart out hunting again.

The 1894 letter book also contains much correspondence between the Hampshire and Chiddingfold Hunts in relation to the hunting of Woolmer Forest, particularly the latter's frequent omission to insert the words By Permission when advertising meets in country loaned to them by the Hampshire Hunt. In his letters Mr Complin refers to agreements reached between the two hunts in 1893 and 1897, however the matter was not clarified until December 1st 1921 when the MFHA committee ruled that if the Chiddingfold apply to the HH for leave to hunt the country south of the Petersfield and Liss Roads it is necessary for them to place the words By Permission when advertising meets in that district.

At the end of his first season Major Bovill agreed to continue as Master but expressed great disappointment that the Saturday country surrounding the kennels was so short of foxes. Members hoped for an improvement, but it did not come, and by January 1923 Major Bovill had resigned in favour of a move to the Isle of Wight Hunt. He had succeeded in building up the pack during his short Mastership, which was also noteworthy for the first reference to artificial jumping places in the hunt records. Lieutenant Colonel Frank Mangles, MC, late of the 20th Hussars and a man who had lived and hunted in Hampshire since childhood, was appointed to take over as Master and continue the amateur tradition of carrying the horn. Members were anxious to ensure there were sufficient foxes for him to hunt, and during the Lt. Colonel's first season a concept first mooted in 1898 came back into play when Colonel Knox proposed the formation of a covert committee for the

Lt Colonel Mangles MFH and huntsman 1923–1926 (on left) and Captain Orred MFH 1924–1925. From a frieze in the possession of Major Mangles's grandson.

purpose of renting and subletting shooting coverts for the benefit of the Hunt. This initiative, which was financed privately by participating Members, resulted in a three-year lease being agreed for the rental of the Old Down shooting at £64 per annum. The woodland extended to more than a hundred acres with a further 400 acres of rough scrubland, which became the domain of a gamekeeper instructed to preserve foxes. The covert committee also recommended that the Club pay £400 to secure Sutton Wood for posterity; their advice was not acted upon, although the covert was eventually purchased by the Hunt nearly forty years later.

In September 1923 Lt. Colonel Mangles proposed the formation of a Management Committee, which speakers at the general meeting six years earlier had gone to some lengths to explain did not exist within the Hampshire Hunt Club. The establishment of this subcommittee of six individuals, including the Master and Hon. Secretaries, took the Club a step closer to the contemporary system of running a hunt. In November the new committee defined their duties as the ordinary management of the Club, the upkeep of Hunt property and general financial business, with the mandate to respond to any question that may arise between the hunt and other third parties. They undertook to submit a report to Members at least twice a year, however the transition from a Hunt run in its entirety by Members to one managed by a committee was not altogether straightforward. Further rules were proposed and agreed to in subsequent years, and the management committee's expenditure was restricted to £200 for any one item without Members' approval. In 1925 they were authorised to offer £20 an acre for the field adjoining the kennels at Ropley, which was successfully purchased for £287.

By 1924, when Lt. Colonel Mangles agreed to continue with Captain Orred as his Joint Master on a guarantee of £2,000 per annum, there were enough hounds

Price—ONE SHILLING

Please Note.—Permission to ride over the Farms is only granted to those who take part in the Races. No one on horseback allowed on the Course. No Dogs allowed in the vicinity of the Course.

APRIL 2nd,   1921.

HAMPSHIRE HUNT
Point-to-Point Steeplechases

This Meeting is to be subject to the Rules and Regulations of the M.F.H. Association and to the National Hunt Rules, 5 and 164 to 168 (disqualifications of persons and corrupt practices.)

At LASHAM,
Near ALTON, HANTS
(By kind permission of the Landowners and Occupiers)

Stewards

Mr. F. H. T. JERVOISE.	Major-Gen. G. D. JEFFREYS, C.B.
Capt. LORD BASING.	Col. G. C. R. OVERTON.
Major H. ROSTRON.	Major C. H. FURNEAUX, D.S.O.
Mr. G. PETO.	~~Mr. W. SAVILLE.~~
Mr. A. F. CORYTON.	~~Mr. A. P. ROBINSON, M.F.H.~~

Judge : Mr. F. CORYTON. *Major A Bovill M.F.H.*
Starter : Mr. A. P. ROBINSON, M.F.H. *T. A. Chalcraft*
Clerk of Course : Major H. ROSTRON. *T. S. Mitchell*
Clerk of Scales : Major FURNEAUX, D.S.O. *G. F. Complin*
Hon. Secretary : Mr. A. F. CORYTON.

The Band of the 3rd Battalion Royal Fusiliers
(By kind permission of Lieut.-Colonel E. B. NORTH, C.M.G., D.S.O., and Officers of the Regiment)
Will play the following Selection of Music.

1.—March—"The King's Herald"	...	Fulton
2.—Selection—"Carmen"	...	Bizet
3.—Valse—"Destiny"	...	Baynes
4.—Selection on Sullivan's Operas	...	Arr. Winterbottom
5.—One Step—"Swanee"	...	Gershwin
6.—Selection—"Gaiety Echoes"	...	Godfrey
7.—Song—Land of Hope and Glory	...	Elgar
8.—Selection—"Smile"	...	Chappelle
9.—Fox-Trot—Indianola	...	Onivas
10.—Galop—John Peel	...	Hunt

GOD SAVE THE KING.
Conductor, Mr. E. WRIGHT, Bandmaster.

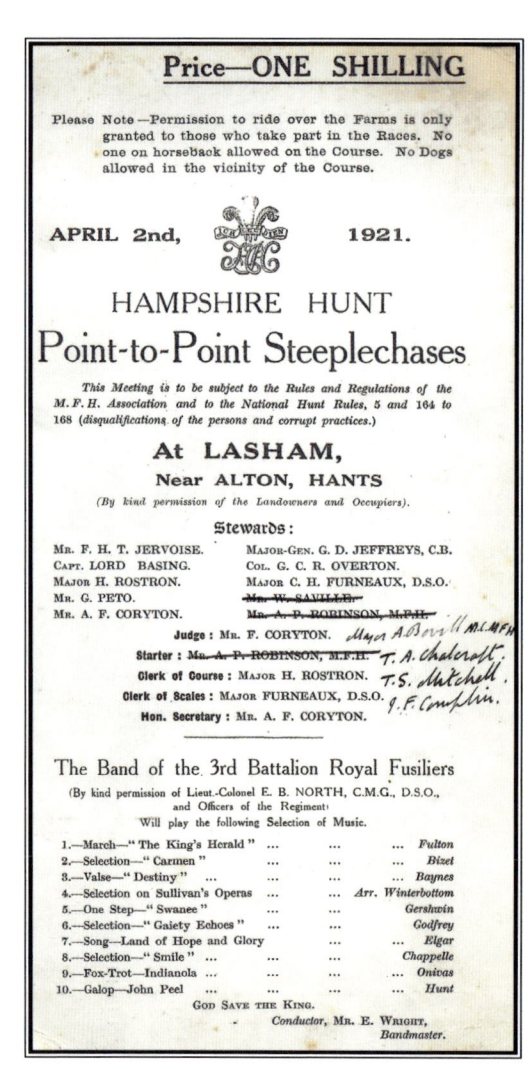

H. H. Point-to-Point
Entertainment of Farmers

It is desired to bring to the notice of Farmers living in the country hunted by the Hampshire Hounds that the Masters and Members of the Hunt Club wish to entertain them on the day of the Point-to-Point Steeplechases in a somewhat different manner to that which has been the custom since the war.

The Masters and Members of the Hunt Club will have pleasure in inviting those Farmers who farm an area of not less than 50 acres to a sit-down luncheon on the Course, and them and their wives to tea. They also wish to invite Farmers who farm a lesser acreage than the above and their wives to tea. Although it is the earnest desire of the Masters and Members of the Hunt to endeavour, to the best of their ability, to show their appreciation of the sporting spirit evinced by all Farmers in allowing them to follow hounds over their land, it is hoped it will be realised that the limited amount of accommodation and funds at their disposal render a limitation of the number of invitations issued for the sit-down luncheon inevitable.

The Hon. Secretary will, in due course, issue invitations.

C. G. MANGLES, M.F.H.
R. ORRED, M.F.H.
February, 1925.

Above: Joint Masters' invitation to a farmers' lunch at the 1925 point-to-point.

Left: First HH point-to-point after the War 1921.

Below: Mr Thomas, terrierman to the HH during Lt. Colonel Mangles's Mastership in the 1920s.

in the kennels for the new Mastership to hunt three days a week and commit to handing over 40 couple at the end of their term. There had been no Hunt races since the March 1914 meeting at Hartley, but the HH Point-to-Point Steeplechases resumed at Lasham on April 2nd 1921, when the five races included one for farmers and a military contest for horses or chargers from the Aldershot or Southern Commands. Racegoers were entertained by the band of the 3rd Battalion Royal Fusiliers during an afternoon when nearly all of the entrants were ridden by their sporting owners and £50 was raised for hunt funds. The following year the point-to-point returned to Tom Mitchell's land at Hartley, and the profit was increased to £200. In 1925 the Joint Masters resumed the hospitality offered to farmers in the pre-war years, inviting all who occupied more than 50 acres to a sit-down luncheon on the course, but those farming less had to make do with tea.

It was perhaps just as well that a revitalised point-to-point was able to make significant contributions to the Hampshire Hunt Club every year, for in addition to the usual expenses of running a hunt there were often significant claims for damage. These ranged from an optimistic claim for tame rabbits killed by a fox at Binsted to a claim for fourteen slipped lambs after hound puppies at walk with Joan Miller from Dummer Grange chased Mr Best's pregnant ewes at North Waltham in the spring of 1923. The Hon. Secretaries examined the rabbits and 'were perfectly satisfied that the mischief was done by dogs and not foxes' but agreed compensation of £48 for the aborted lambs. At the time of the incident the Hunt could certainly afford to compensate the farmer generously, for the Club accounts showed a balance in hand of £516[3] and even the Poultry Fund showed a surplus of £45. Given the healthy state of finances, Members agreed to spend £450 on the purchase of a further 15 couple of hounds.

In December 1924 the Joint Masters tendered their resignation at the Swan Hotel, Alton after a partnership that had lasted just one season, citing a shortage of foxes in the Saturday and Tuesday countries. After the committee vowed to tackle the problem, the Joint Masters agreed to reconsider their resignations by the end of the year. Captain Orred let his stand, but Lt. Colonel Mangles committed to another year on a £2,000 guarantee provided Members supported him in the preservation of foxes and the walking of puppies. He also asked that Captain Jervoise Bolitho Scott from Rotherfield Park replace Captain Orred as his Joint Master, which was something of an inspired choice. A former officer of the 7th Hussars, Captain Scott

---

3   The value of £516 in 1923 is approximately £30,000 in 2022.

was one of the largest landowners in the HH country who loved a good hunt and went well on quality horses.

Despite the boost such a man must have provided, Lt. Colonel Mangles stood down at the end of the season, but Captain Scott offered Members a choice between hunting the country three days a week with a professional carrying the horn or four days a week with George Evans as his Joint master and huntsman. On February 10th 1926 Members were in unanimous agreement to reappoint Mr Evans to his former role. After eleven years in the wilderness the man who transformed the pack in the years leading up to the First World War was back at the helm. Since hostilities ended hounds had been hunted by three different amateurs in just six seasons, during which time hounds had become slack and the fox population had dwindled accordingly. The only thread of continuity had been provided by the faithful William Orvis, who had struggled on manfully during the war years as professional huntsman, only to step back in 1920 to whip-in to a succession of amateurs. In the spring of 1926 the question on everyone's lips was the same. Could George Evans once more transform a moderate pack of hounds into a brilliant one?

Chapter Nine 1926–1939

The Magician's Wand

Captain J.B. Scott, G.P.E. Evans Esq., 1926–1929, G.P.E. Evans Esq., 1929–1932, G.P.E. Evans Esq., J.M. Hastings Esq., 1932–1933, G.P.E. Evans Esq., J.M. Hastings Esq., B. Hamilton Esq., 1933–1934, G.P.E. Evans Esq., B. Hamilton Esq., 1934–1935, G.P.E. Evans Esq., Mrs G.P.E. Evans 1935–1937, G.P.E. Evans Esq., Lieutenant Colonel M.R.F. Courage, DSO, 1937–1939.

George Evans's successful return to hunting hounds, hounds catch a fox with two brushes, George Evans's marriage to Diana Stuart Smith in April 1929, ladies, hunt buttons and evening dress, Selborne Common and the National Trust, John Hastings joins the Mastership, a vulpicide tenant at Newton Valence, Mr Hamilton joins the Mastership, Mrs Evans joins the Mastership, success at Peterborough and Aldershot hound shows, bus accident, George Evans stands down as huntsman in favour of Will Scott, George Evans's retirement and farewells.

On August 26th 1926 George Evans and his first whipper-in, Will Scott, took 35 couple of hounds to Dogford Wood for the first morning of the new season. There was a good show of cubs, and although the huntsman confided in his diaries that he should really have caught a brace, he also wrote that he was satisfied with the new pack, which in recent years had been reduced by catastrophic outbreaks of distemper. Largely thanks to the generosity of his Joint Master, Captain Scott, the 30 couple George Evans inherited on May 1st had since been bolstered by drafts from the Badsworth, Belvoir, Carmarthen, North Shropshire, Puckeridge, South & West Wilts, and Taunton Vale Hunts, but not all of them lived up to expectations. 6½ couple of newly arrived drafts from Ikey Bell in Wiltshire disappointed in early November, especially Gretna, who rioted so badly 'after her own shadow' that she had to be shut away for the second half of the day.

However by Christmas it was clear to all that the old magic had returned, and there was a succession of good days during the latter part of the season, including a corker on February 26th when Will Scott hunted hounds for the first time. On

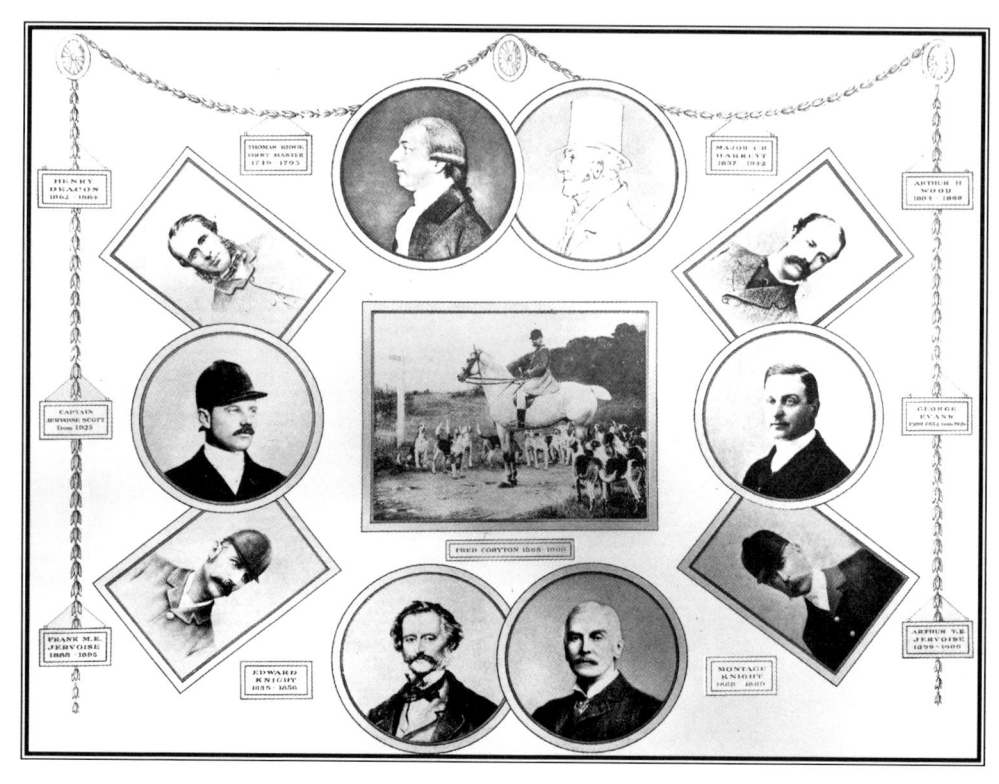

Masters of the HH from 1749–1926.

March 29th 1927 hounds bowled their fox over in the open after a brilliant seven-mile point from Hawkley, and a month later George Evans resumed the end of season summary in his hunting diaries by noting that, 'considering the hounds had to be made, it was quite a fair season. Very short of foxes in the Saturday country but managed not to have any blank days. I like the Welsh cross very much indeed. Killed 47 foxes and ran 65 to ground. Sold all the horses.' As so few puppies had been sent out to walk the previous summer there was no puppy show in 1927, but Members, subscribers, farmers, and friends of the Hunt were invited to an open day at the kennels, which by then housed an impressive 66 couple. During the afternoon Tom Mitchell was presented with a fine piece of Waterford crystal to thank him for providing the venue for the point-to-point races on his farm at Hartley, and for his long-standing duties as Clerk of the Course there.

Hounds returned to the reliable Dogford Wood at 5.30am on August 29th for the first day of the 1927–1928 season, where they caught two brace after a busy morning. The following week the stud groom and stable staff were astonished when a mare named Eiderdown produced an unexpected and healthy foal; had she not

Eiderdown and her unexpected foal in September 1927. From a sketch inside George Evans's hunting diaries.

banged a leg, the mare had been due to carry Will Scott the previous day. Eiderdown did not wax up prior to foaling and carried her foal so high that no one suspected she was pregnant. A full page colour sketch to commemorate this unusual event is pasted into George Evans's hunting diaries. In November the doghounds enjoyed a superb hunt from Lasham Station and caught their fox above ground for the tenth consecutive day, and at the end of January there was a seven-mile point from Blackmoor Wood to Stoner Hill, grass all the way.

That fine hunt was surpassed on February 16th when hounds found a straight-necked[1] fox near Woodridden and ran hard to Gaston Wood. The pack crossed the Bentworth road to Burkham and continued through Herriard Common to Fryingdown Copse and on over the Basingstoke road into Hen Wood where they were stopped at 5.45pm in the gloaming having run twenty miles and scored a nine-mile point. On February 20th a privately chartered train brought soldiers to hunt from Aldershot, and on March 6th barbed wire 'strong enough to hold a herd of wild elephants' caused a lengthy detour. The front cover of the 1928 point-to-point programme, which was run before the end of the season on March 31st at Hartley, lists the race officials and the command in bold red capital letters along the

---

1   A straight-necked fox is one that runs across country in a straight line when pursued. Such foxes are responsible for long points.

bottom: *LADIES – DO NOT WEAR FOX SKINS*. Geoffrey Peto proposed the toast of foxhunting at the farmers' lunch and described the Master and huntsman – to much laughter and applause – as the perennial and perpetual vermin killer of Hampshire. The Joint Master, Captain Scott, paid glowing tribute to the Chairman, General Jeffreys, praising his resolute commitment to the chase and observing that he never went home before hounds. The hunting correspondent, Forrard On, noted that the 1927–1928 season had been the best since the end of the Great War, and complimented the hunting qualities and drive of the Hampshire Hunt pack, which their Joint Master and huntsman, 'has evolved, as if by waving a magic wand, in two short seasons.'

On November 1st 1928 hounds caught a fox with two brushes after a fast 70 minute hunt from Abbotstone Down to Wield Wood, which was mounted inside a glass case by the taxidermists, Rowland Ward. The event was also commemorated by a silver replica, which years later came into the possession of Sir Newton Rycroft and occupied pride of place on his sideboard.[2] Thereafter the 1928–1929 season was plagued with such bad weather that 29 days were lost to frost and the Hon. Secretary had to write to the RABI, the HSBS,[3] the Distemper Fund and the Earl Haig Fund expressing regret that the Hampshire Hunt had been unable to take the usual cap to support their charities. Halfway through the season Captain Scott tendered his resignation on account of being posted abroad, much to the regret of Members who expressed their sincere wish that he could find some way to continue.

However a frustrating season ended gloriously and uniquely in warm spring sunshine on April 25th 1929 with the marriage of George Evans to local hunting lady, Diana Stuart Smith, at Ropley Church. Shortly before midday the groom rode up to the church gates dressed in scarlet accompanied by his hounds and hunt staff; he left Will Scott in charge of the pack and went into the church on foot, pausing every so often to chat with familiar faces amongst the throng of well-wishers that had come to witness the greatest spectacle in the history of Ropley village. An official count put the crowd at 5,047 strong; over 250 arrived mounted on horses whose manes and tails had been decorated with white rosettes, others came in horse drawn carriages and by car and more still arrived by motorcycle, push bike or on foot. On the stroke of noon Miss Stuart Smith of Hall Place, Ropley

---

[2] The silver replica was left to Sir Newton Rycroft by George Evans in his will. In 2021 the memento was offered for sale by the auctioneers Woolley and Wallis in Salisbury and was purchased by a Member of the Hampshire Hunt Club.

[3] Royal Agricultural Benevolent Institution and the Hunt Servants' Benevolent Society.

THE MAGICIAN'S WAND 1926–1939

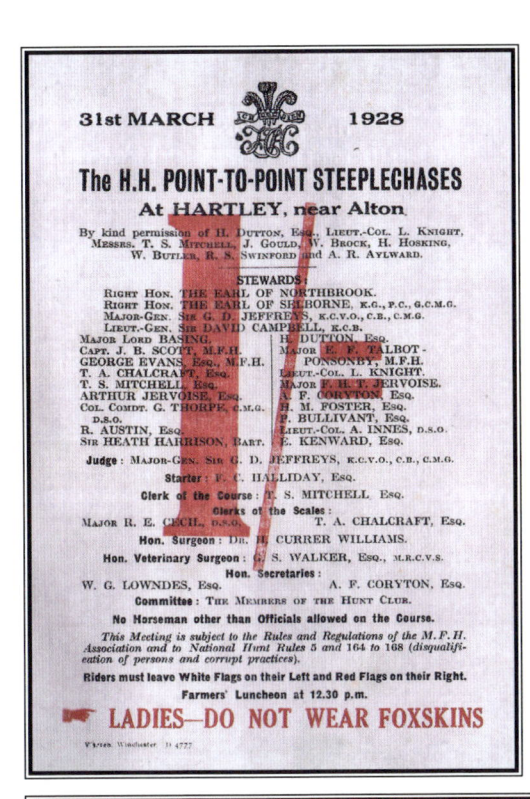

Above left: Racecard for the 1928 point-to-point.

Above right: Fox with two brushes killed by George Evans MFH and the HH hounds on November 1st 1928.

Above: Silver model of fox with two brushes.

Left: Sample of Royal Household blue cloth worn as HH evening dress attached to the inside back cover of the 1888 minute book.

appeared riding side saddle accompanied by her father, much to the delight of some 50 members of the press on hand to record the unique event for posterity. Quite overcome by the magnificence of the occasion, one reporter described the wedding as 'a demonstration of public interest and goodwill unprecedented in the annals of private weddings in this county.'

After the ceremony the newly wedded couple left the church beneath an arch of hunting whips formed by Members of the Club whilst being showered with rice, rose petals and confetti. Mr Evans had not progressed more than a few yards before the Rotherfield head gamekeeper, Mr Healey, stepped forward and presented him with a silver hunting horn on behalf of all the gamekeepers in the Hampshire Hunt country. The bride and groom mounted their waiting hunters and rode the short distance to Hall Place for the reception where waiters dispensed cake and champagne and Mr Austen Chalcraft presented the couple with an engraved silver tray and a hunting whip on behalf of the farmers. Members of the Hampshire Hunt and friends of the Orleans Club gave the newly-weds a cheque for the purchase of a 16 horsepower Austin saloon car, the officers of the Aldershot Command sent a silver fox; even the Ropley Tennis Club gave a table and ashtray. By one o'clock it was time to go hunting and an exceptionally large mounted field saw hounds find a brace in Old Down, one of which was marked to ground in Chawton Park. Finding again in Kitcombe Wood, hounds ran across Rotherfield Park before defeat close to Tisted Station to conclude a busy afternoon's sport, after which the couple left immediately for their honeymoon. In his diary George Evans devotes just ten words to the momentous occasion; 'Met Ropley Church got married 5,000 people came to see it.'

Earlier that year Members had met for dinner at The Swan Hotel in Alton where the sumptuous menu included caviar, mock turtle soup, turbot with lobster sauce, saddle of mutton, roast turkey, marrons glacés, mince pies, and angels on horseback. Since ladies were debarred from membership the evening was for the exclusive benefit of gentlemen, but dilemmas involving the fairer sex had been gathering momentum since the start of the twentieth century. The question of ladies being allowed to wear the hunt button had first been raised in April 1902, but then lay dormant for a further 22 years until the Hon. Secretary, Frederick Coryton, proposed that they be granted permission. General Jeffreys disagreed strongly, explaining that it would be difficult to obtain the consent of the Prince of Wales and Mr Coryton's proposal was defeated by seven votes to four. A solution was next put forward by the Master elect, George Evans, in April 1926, who proposed

Diana Stuart Smith and her father on the morning of her wedding April 25th 1929.

George and Diana Evans leaving Ropley church after their marriage.

The bride and groom greeted by well-wishers following their marriage.

Silver salver presented to George Evans MFH by the HH farmers
on the occasion of his marriage April 25th 1929.

Bride and groom leaving the meet following their marriage.

that lady subscribers be nominated by ballot for the privilege of wearing a button that did not include the Prince of Wales's ostrich plumes. Members finally agreed to this concession nearly a quarter of a century after the subject had first been raised, which led to lady subscribers of £15 or more being invited to wear a blue collar livery on a dark grey, black, or dark blue habit. On December 18th 1928 the first 25 ladies were granted this annually renewable privilege, but they had to wait until 1951 before being allowed to wear velvet caps in the hunting field.

Members were often preoccupied with the subject of their own dress, and after Lieutenant Colonel Hope observed in 1931 that Members looked 'rather a motley crew, with different shades of royal blue,' at hunt dinners, the Hon. Secretary was instructed to write to Frederick Scholte of Savile Row, informing him that the colour of the Hunt evening coat should be exactly the same as the blue worn by officers of the Royal Household. This had been reconfirmed back in 1911 when a sample of the rich blue cloth was pasted into the back of the 1888–1912 minute book. It was agreed that evening dress should be worn throughout the year, and not confined to the hunting season as was the custom elsewhere, but the question of gilt buckles on knee breeks and shoes was left to individual discretion. The importance attached to evening dress was reiterated in 1938 when Members attending a dinner at Rotherfield Park were given special dispensation to wear ordinary dress 'for this occasion only' subject to a fine of 10/6d to accrue to the Poultry Fund.

The 1929–1930 season was marred from the outset by the tragic death of Diana Evans following an operation at Winchester Nursing Home after only a few months of marriage. George Evans's diaries reveal a shortage of foxes from December onwards, however when the quarry obliged sport was as good as ever and 27 brace were brought to hand. Frustrated by the scarcity of raw material, and no doubt devastated by the loss of his bride, the Master tendered his resignation in January, but relented a month later and accepted a guarantee of £3,500 to continue for another season. Sport of the highest order followed; a six-mile point from Ropley in December 1930, and a staggering 30-mile, 5½-hour hunt that included another six-mile point from the meet at Herriard Church on March 2nd 1931, with only the Master, hunt staff and one follower up with hounds when they caught their fox in High Wood.

Hounds met at Harkers Crossroads on April 13th 1930 and scored an eight-mile point on a fox found in Selborne Common to Ellen Wood in the Hambledon country. The 246-acre Selborne Common has not been ploughed since the Middle Ages and consists of ancient beech interspersed with scrub, grassy clearings and gorse that was a reliable find throughout most of the Hampshire Hunt's long history but is best known for its association with the pioneering eighteenth century naturalist, the Rev. Gilbert White, who lived close by at The Wakes.[4] The Common was still owned by Magdalen College when one of its vulpine residents provided George Evans with an eight-mile point in 1930, but two years later the land was donated to the National Trust, which in those days was well disposed to hunting. In 1933 the Hunt took a special cap on behalf of the Trust to assist with cutting out rides on the Common, and the Hon. Secretary, Frederick Coryton, was put forward to serve on the local National Trust committee. The following June Mr Coryton resigned as the Hunt's Hon. Secretary after fourteen years in office, during which time he had discharged his duties with distinction and fronted the committee that had kept the Hunt going throughout the First World War. In 1928 he had been granted a £10 annual allowance for clerical assistance, which had increased to £50 by the time of his resignation.

---

[4] The Rev. Gilbert White is best known for his book, *The Natural History and Antiquities of Selborne*, which was published in 1789.

THE MAGICIAN'S WAND 1926–1939

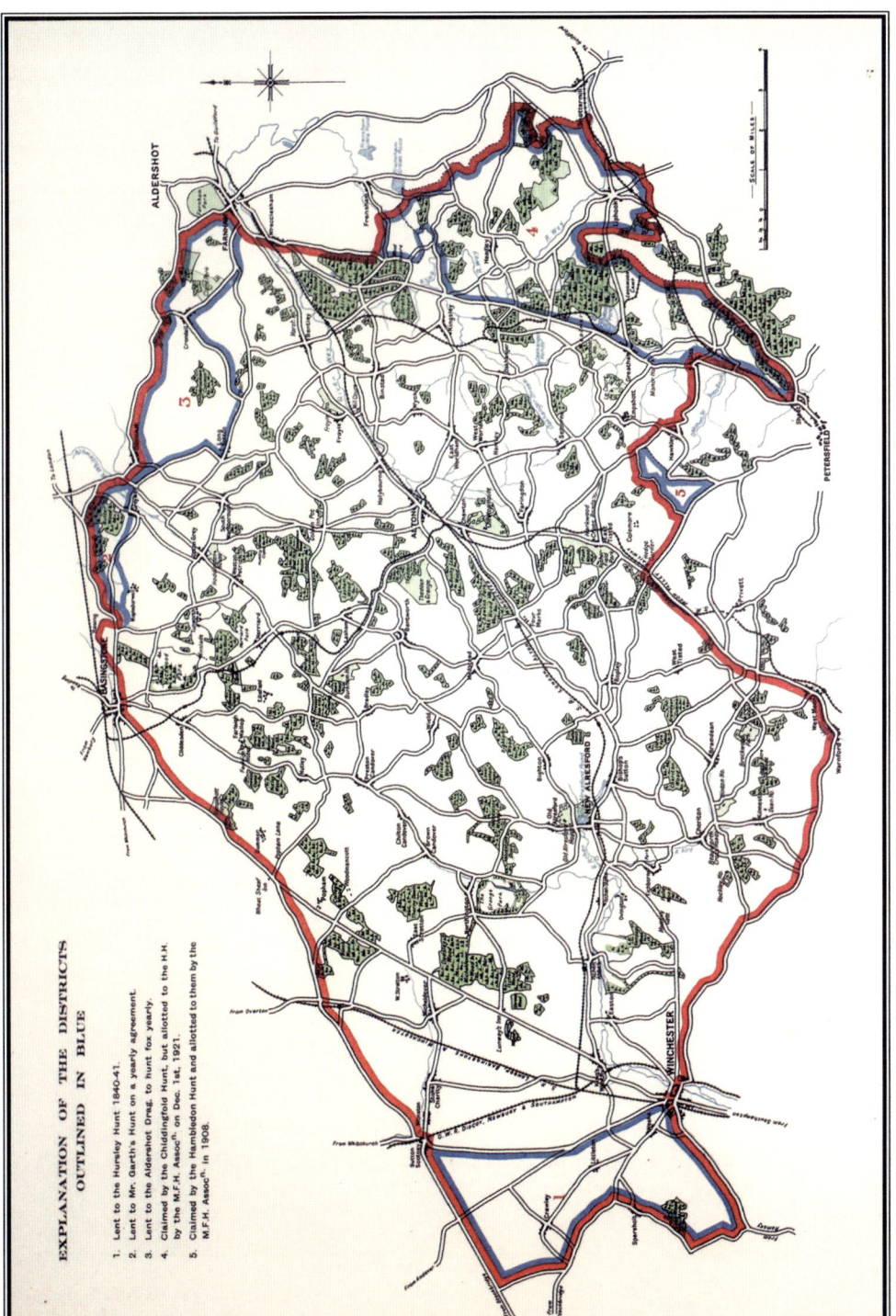

Map of the HH country in 1929.

The children's meet at Farleigh House in 1931.

George Evans with his piglets after hound exercise during the freeze up in December 1933.

Financial pressures led to George Evans taking John Hastings, formerly of the Vyne Hunt, as a Joint Master for the 1932–1933 season, under an arrangement whereby they shared hunting the hounds,[5] during a season when sixteen days were lost to frost. Their request that Mr Hamilton join them in the Mastership for the 1933–1934 season was overwhelmingly rejected at a heated meeting during which George Evans walked out before Captain Jervoise Scott could finish explaining the Hunt's offer. A proposal that the Chairman take on the country was received with great applause, but Captain Scott replied that it was impossible for him to do so for many reasons. The owner of Rotherfield Park wrote to resign his membership a month later, which was viewed as a most serious blow for the Hampshire Hunt and foxhunting in general. A subcommittee appointed to persuade him to change his mind must have been successful, for Captain Scott was present at the next meeting, however the Joint Masters' wish for Mr Hamilton to join them prevailed.

The 1933–1934 season was the very worst on record according to George Evans's diaries, with frost preventing hunting throughout December. After the end of the season in May an extraordinary incident took place that provides a fascinating insight into how strongly farmers and local people supported the Hunt. The story begins with the arrival of a new tenant at Nore Hall,[6] Newton Valence on the Rotherfield estate in June 1931. Mr Chalmers had been in occupation for less than a year before things started to turn sour between him and his landlord, Captain Jervoise Scott. Mr Chalmers's frequent complaints about fencing and the landlord's failure to provide a promised water supply led to him withholding the rent, which was only recovered by the serving of a writ. During the second year of his tenancy Mr Chalmers submitted a claim to the Hampshire Hunt for loss of poultry to foxes, which was settled promptly, but a further claim for the loss of 170 fowls, turkeys, and lambs in 1934 was met with scepticism and remained unresolved.

Against this backdrop, the tenant farmer became increasingly hostile towards the Hunt and began destroying foxes on his farm, even though he was prohibited from doing so by the terms of his lease. Two unsavoury former convicts, said to be desperate men, were also recruited to assist Mr Chalmers with his gruesome vendetta against the Hunt and his landlord, who was a former Master. But it did not stop there. Mr Chalmers took to attaching the brushes of dead foxes to his car

---

5 George Evans hunted the doghounds and John Hastings the bitch pack.
6 Nore Hall is taken from a press cutting describing the abduction and subsequent court hearing, however the modern spelling is Noar.

radiator for all to see, and erected crude notices around his farm encouraging the slaughter of foxes and offering to purchase pelts from anyone wishing to sell them. On a number of occasions he was alleged to have left dead foxes on the property of hunt supporters and also admitted the illegal use of strychnine to poison foxes on his own land. On May 11th 1934 a lorry driver employed by Captain Scott offered to sell Mr Chalmers a fox skin and agreed to meet him for the exchange at Hedge Corner later that evening. When the tenant farmer saw that the skin was shrivelled up and valueless, he turned towards his car but was confronted by a number of masked men wielding sticks. There are different interpretations of events that followed, but no disputing the fact that Mr Chalmers ended up some eighteen miles away on Harting Hill in the dead of night having been bound, gagged, and doused in beer. He finally made it back to Nore Hall at 5am having been driven home by a member of the Sussex Constabulary.

The press described the subsequent court case at the Hampshire Assizes as 'bristling with amazing and dramatic evidence' that must have captivated the whole county. During his summing up, the Judge conveyed the defendants' view that the plaintiff was a despicable person who was a nuisance to everybody. After a short interlude the jury stated they had found judgment with costs for Captain Scott, who had maintained his innocence and ignorance of events throughout. However £100 damages were awarded against the other six defendants, being Henry Warner from Hawkley, Henry Morris, Edward Gamblin, Frank Reynard and George Turnbull from East Tisted, and Frank Mitchell from Selborne. Mr Chalmers was ordered to pay the full costs of the special jury convened for the hearing and half of all general costs of the case from August 11th onwards. The repercussions of the dispute are not known, but a hunting correspondent reporting on a day from Newton Valence five years later noted that two foxes got to ground in quick succession and observed, 'it is most disappointing that keepers will not stop these earths in this part of the country.'

Early in 1935 Mr Hamilton was deemed to have relinquished his Mastership on account of his absence from England since July the previous year, and the resignation of John Hastings drew to a close three years of turbulence at the helm of the Hunt. George Evans agreed to continue on a guarantee of £3,000 provided his new wife, whom he had married the previous year, could join him in the Mastership. The husband and wife team got off to a flying start when the Duke of Beaufort and Viscount Knutsford awarded Rarity '33 the supreme bitch championship at Peterborough that summer. The daughter of Tiverton Simon '26

The meet on Monday was at Old Alresford House, and the first draw was Alresford Pond, which was blank. Finding a brace of foxes in Sutton Wood, hounds hunted right round here and adjoining coverts for two hours, and neither of the foxes could be persuaded to leave far, and eventually after great perseverance they killed a large dog fox. Going on then to Old Down another fox was found, but was soon lost among houses in Ropley village. Then followed a great hunt from Dogford. Putting in at the top end at 4.50, hounds found a good fox in the Brambles, and going away by Kitwood and Fillies Common turned back through Carters Copse and into Winchester Wood. Hunting very nicely through here, they ran on through Stoney Brow and by Hedge Corner into Basing Park. Continuing well through here they ran on towards Froxfield, where the first check occurred owing to cattle foil, but the Master putting them right they hunted on again over Bydean Farm and Wheelers Farm into Strawberry Hanger. Still running fast they ran along the Hanger to Stoner Hill, where they were stopped at 6.20, as it was getting dark. This was a 6½ mile point, and hounds would no doubt have killed their fox had there been sufficient light.

After the meet at Hawkley on Tuesday hounds moved off to Standfast coverts, and a fox was marked to ground almost at once in the Hanger. While hounds were marking this fox to ground another one was viewed, but unfortunately hounds ran heel away and the fox was given a good start. However, they hunted him slowly to Le Court and then to Noar Hill, where he was lost. Going on to Colborne Hill, some time was spent in this large covert, but there did not seem enough scent to push a fox outside. Hounds then went on to Mary-lane. Finding at the top end, they ran back through Kitcombe into Woodside, making a big circle round here back to Mary-lane.

Some great hunting runs during the 1930s and the Hedge Corner abduction in 1934.

GREAT HAMPSHIRE HUNT
Of 30 Miles in 5½ Hours with a Mask to Finish

Wonderful sport was shown by the H.H. from their Herriard Church fixture on Monday, the bitch pack, hunting continuously, with hardly a check, for over 5½ hours. Starting from Henwood they ran nicely through Fryingdown Copse, past Ellisfield to the Oak Hills, through Down Wood, and on to Bradley Wood.

Going away by Ashley Farm to College Wood they ran hard to Barton Copse and on to Wield Wood, this being a point of just on seven miles. Swinging back past Wield village they went through Gaston Wood and the Wilderness, past Lower Wield to Park Copse, and thence over Preston Downs to Preston Candover village. Running on through Southhall Park and the garden of Preston Grange they bore left-handed to Lower Wield Spinney, where the beaten fox was viewed close at hand.

Unluckily hounds were holloa'd on to a fresh fox, and they ran on by Bradley Wood, Down Wood, and High Wood to Farley Great Wood, and thence back by Parkfield and the Oak Hills to end a great day by catching their fox in High Wood. The furthest point made was nearly six miles, the total distance covered being over 30 miles, only the Master, the Hunt Staff, with one follower, lasting out to the end.

Those who met the H.H. at Dummer Grange on Thursday came in for the best run of the season with this pack. Finding in the Home Covert, Hogsdown, hounds ran very fast by Nutley Wood, on past the Gobley Hole to Farleigh Great Wood, and thence by High Wood, Parkfield, Allwood and Frying Down to Henwood. Changing foxes here the pack ran on through Honey Leaze to Weston Common. After a turn up and down the Common and Herriard High Wood they went away by Great Park on through Hambly Grove and Little Park, turning back past Weston Patrick through Greens and Puddings to put their fox to ground in Sheetland, only a hundred yards in front of them after a great hunt of just on three hours with a point of over seven miles.

AN EPISODE (in Rhyme).

Nigh Selborne—on the old Nore Hill,
There dwells a man who'd foxes kill,
  By shooting—trapping—poison, he
  Declared he would the country free.
And so the sport of hunting men
Prevent—for he had lost a hen!
  He also offered for to buy
  Fox skins from any fool or guy!
Their carcases 'tis said he'd throw
In gardens of the men he'd know
  Would much resent this attitude!
  Now three young men, with aptitude
Decided on a course to take,
Entice this Nore Hill man to make
  A journey to Hedge Corner—there
  To buy a skin beyond compare.
The bait was swallowed—he with glee
Set forth this fox skin for to see—
  Arriving there—soon "smelt a rat,"
  For in the bushes saw a hat!
Decided then 'twas time to flee,
Not quite so fast! the gallant three
  With praps another mate or two,
  Determined this would never do!
So tripped him up—wrap't in a sheet,
Then bound his arms, and legs, and feet,
  And placed him in a nearby car,
  A joy ride then some miles afar
To lonesome spot on Harting Hill,
Where he could contemplate at will,
  And reckon up the skins he'd sell
  When he got home quite sound and well
So here with cords and sheet unbound,
He sat with comfort on the ground,
  And talked of cabbages and crops,
  Of beverages with malt and hops!
With kindly thought and happy cheer,
They offered him to drink—some beer
  (May be 'twas only said in jest
  But he did think " the t'other's best ")
They held the bottle tight withal
Lest he might dare to drink it all;
  Then left him there and homeward went,
  Indulging in much merriment.
He seemingly was not amused,
Their gallantry he much abused!
  Then in the Courts did seek redress,
  With chivalry they did confess
Their bit of fun—was just a joke,
No thought had they 'twould ire provoke!
  But damages the jury found!
  The Nore Hill man—with promise bound,
No foxes would he kill again;
From jokes the three would now refrain!
  May be there's nothing else to tell,
  So "All is well that endeth well."
When next he wants some foxes killed,
Our M.F.H.—is very skilled;
  His pack of hounds beyond compare,
  Will hunt their fox from any lair,
Give followers and huntsmen fun,
And fox and hounds a sporting run!
                      RURAL RIDER.

Hounds at Rotherfield Park in 1933 with Calender '31 to the fore.

Results of the 1932 Aldershot Hound Show with key to prominent hounds in photograph above.

was not only a beautifully balanced bitch but also a brilliant hunter with the ability to own the line down a tarmac road. Rarity had won the same accolade the previous year as an unentered bitch at the Aldershot Hound Show, where she regained the brood bitch class in 1935, but Rarity's sporting owner declined to put her forward to contest the championship for a second time.

THE MAGICIAN'S WAND 1926–1939

By 1935 Aldershot had become something of a Mecca for the Hampshire Hunt, whose hounds were shown to perfection by Will Scott. In 1932 they won the best couple of entered dogs, best stallion hound with Whipcord '28, and the doghound championship with Calender '31,[7] together with the best couple of unentered bitches and reserve champion bitch with Ringdove '28 in the afternoon. However impressive on the flags, George Evans's hounds were first and foremost a pack bred to catch foxes in style. This was achieved by the judicious and avant-garde blending of Welsh blood with the best English strains from packs such as the Belvoir,[8] FitzHardinge, and Puckeridge. The Welsh infusion came principally from Sir Edward Curre's pack at Itton Court, but also from the Carmarthen via Dalesman '22 and Vulcan '24. By 1932 Curre Workman '26 was the sire of eighteen couple at Ropley, and the Welsh outcross had such an invigorating effect that in 1933 their breeder was quoted in *Country Life* as saying he could have killed another twenty brace a season before the War with his current Welsh infused pack.

If winning the bitch championship at Peterborough was a high point during the first year of the Evanses' Mastership, the low point was a tragic accident in December when a bus belonging to the Aldershot Traction Company ran into the pack at Trinity Hill and killed or maimed several hounds, including Nimrod '33. 'Amongst those killed was Nimrod, a super two-season dog,' his huntsman noted, 'I missed him very much indeed and it made a great difference to the pack.' The bus company settled for £380, which was allocated to the Wire Fund after the deduction of costs. Apart from this one dark shadow the 1935–1936 season was a huge improvement on the previous one, with a good show of foxes and 52 killed above ground. However the huntsman was now 63 years of age and noticeably thicker around the girth, which perhaps led to him being persuaded to allow Will Scott to hunt the doghounds twice a week the following season. The best days included a six-mile point from Aston Wood to Kilmeston following the meet at West Tisted church in February and a terrific Monday from Old Alresford House in March when hounds found in Dogford Wood at 4.50pm and were stopped 90 minutes later at Stoner Wood having made another six-mile point.

With these fine hunts yet to take place, on January 27th 1937 the Chairman informed Members that at 'an informal meeting of hunting Members' all were

---

7   Calender is the spelling used by George Evans MFH.

8   At one stage during George Evans's Mastership every hound in the kennels could be traced back to the influential Belvoir Weaver '09.

THE HAMPSHIRE HUNT 1749–2022

HAMPSHIRE HUNT SUCCESSES

The Hampshire Hunt did uncommonly well with their hounds at the Aldershot show yesterday. Here are some of their successes: Foxhounds.—Couples of unentered dog hounds.—1, Handful and Handwell. Entered couples. — 1, Calendar and Sender. Best stallion hound, sire of living puppies.—1, Calendar. Best dog hound in the show.—1, Calendar. Bitches. — Couples of unentered bitches. — 1, Rally and Rarity. Entered couples.—Res., Beeswing and Blenurb. Best Two entered couples.—2, Casket, Canoe, Daffodil and Dabchick. Best bitch in the show (Challenge Cup).—Rarity

Above: Calender '31 champion doghound at the 1932 Aldershot Hound Show.
Below: Watercolour of Rarity '33 from George Evans's hunting diaries.

H. H. ENTRY. 1932.

NAME	SIRE	DAM	DATE	WALKED BY
Bagshot Bailiff Baltimore Bandit Banker Barbara Bargain	Workman 26	Bangl 27	Feb. 17th	Mr. Sprackling Mr. Stanley Mr. Ward Mr. Nixon Mr. Burgess Miss Sutton Mr. Young
Bardolph Barmaid Beeswing	Baker 30	Welwon 29	March 24th	Col. Innes Mrs. Parsons Col. Innes
Blemish Bluebell	Badger 30	Radiant 29	May 31st	Mr. Coryton Mr. Trimmer
Calabar Casket	Workman 26	Taunton Vale, Chantress 25	March 20th	Mr. Inges Mr. Rowland
Dancer Danish	Puckeridge Dolphin 26	Trywell 29	March 1st	Mr. Holmes Mr. Holmes
Glasgow	Baker 30	Gaylass 29	June 4th	Mr. Harris
Nestor	Workman 26	Hambledon Nora 27	Feb. 24th	Mr. Warner
Ruffler Randy Rapid	Noble 28	Rachel 29	May 12th	Miss Harrap Miss Wickfield Miss Harrap
Recall Raceway	Noble 28	Rocket 29	May 2nd	Mrs. Abraham Mr. Bullivant
Rashness	Workman 26	Croome Rescue 24	June 20th	Captain Scott
Topmast Topknot Torment Traffic Tranquil	Ludlow Tufter 25	Wopsy 28	Jan. 1st	Miss Bishop Miss Bishop Mr. Godwin Gen. Sir G. Jeffreys Sir Nelson Rycroft
Warrener Warwick Waterman Wishful	Whipcord 28	Calumny 27	Jan. 10th	Mr. Broad Mr. Bullivant Gen. Sir G. Jeffreys Capt. Cundy Cooper
Wellington Warsong Wayward Waspish	Workman 26	Woodbine 28	March 2nd	Mr. Harding Miss Saunders Mrs. Talbot Lord Basing
Woodcock	Workman 26	Warmley 26	May 9th	Mr. Simpson
Witsbury Walton Witless	Workman 26	Wedlock 28	Jan. 3rd	Mr. Soper Mr. Harris Capt. Cundy Cooper
Wealthy	Puckeridge Wilfred 25	Ringdove 28	April 24th	Col. Cullum

HH 1932 young entry.

Hampshire Hunt Success

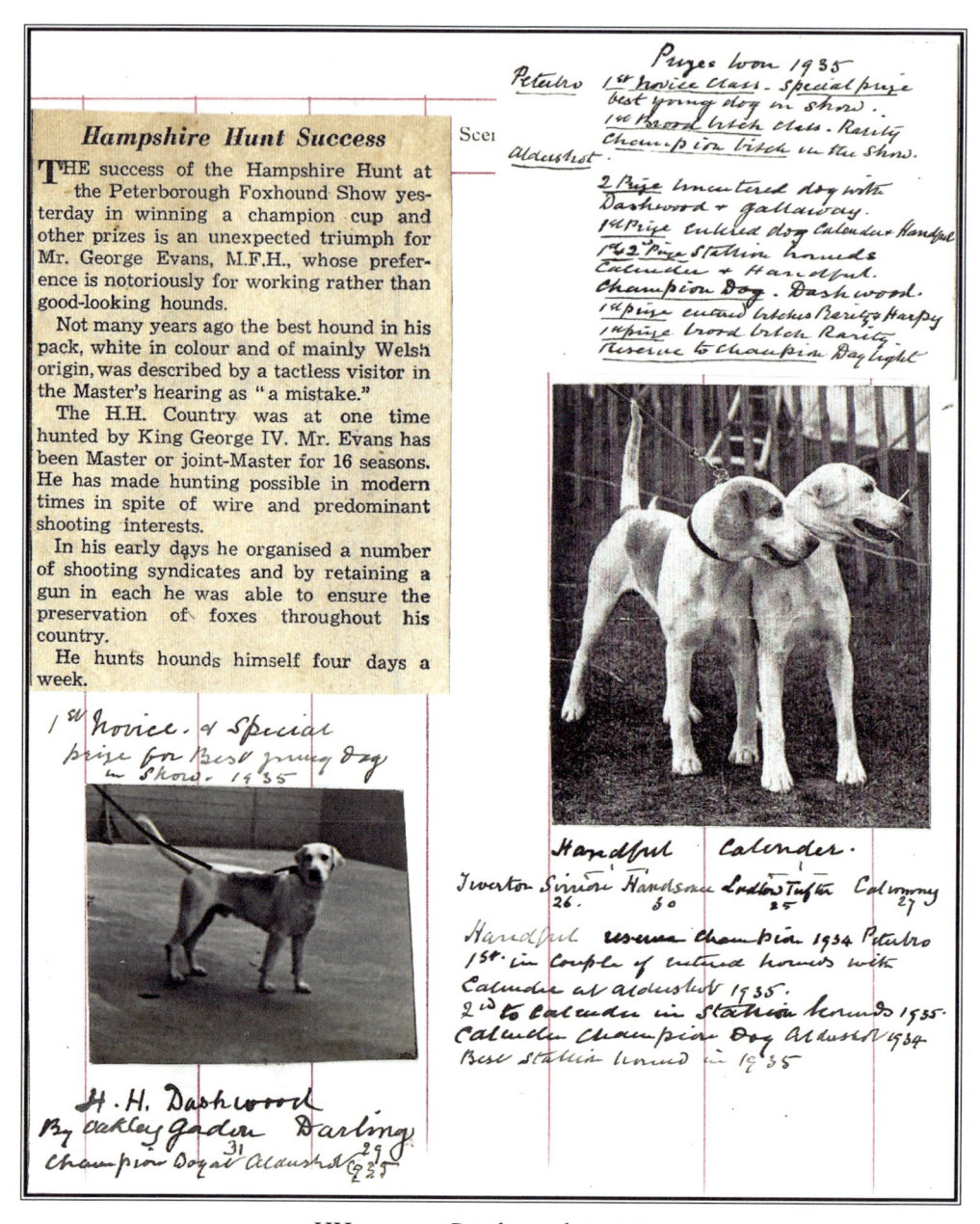

THE success of the Hampshire Hunt at the Peterborough Foxhound Show yesterday in winning a champion cup and other prizes is an unexpected triumph for Mr. George Evans, M.F.H., whose preference is notoriously for working rather than good-looking hounds.

Not many years ago the best hound in his pack, white in colour and of mainly Welsh origin, was described by a tactless visitor in the Master's hearing as "a mistake."

The H.H. Country was at one time hunted by King George IV. Mr. Evans has been Master or joint-Master for 16 seasons. He has made hunting possible in modern times in spite of wire and predominant shooting interests.

In his early days he organised a number of shooting syndicates and by retaining a gun in each he was able to ensure the preservation of foxes throughout his country.

He hunts hounds himself four days a week.

HH success at Peterborough in 1935.

George Evans MFH addressing the Pony Club in 1932.

unanimously in favour of a professional hunting hounds full time with Mr Evans continuing as Master. George wrote to express regret that he was no longer required to hunt the hounds and refused the offer of a £2,750 guarantee. Members were so keen to retain his organisation skills that they offered to keep two horses for him at Ropley, employ Will Scott and assume responsibility for all financial arrangements, but after due consideration Mr Evans decided he would not feel happy working with a committee. Instead he accepted a guarantee of £2,800 and took on former Gunner, keen polo player, and all-round sportsman, Lieutenant Colonel Miles Courage of Preston House, to replace his wife in the Mastership with Will Scott carrying the horn full time.

In addition to the many other responsibilities that are the MFH's lot, the Masters agreed to become joint presidents of the recently resurrected Hampshire Hunt branch of the Pony Club, which had been founded in 1931 only to close down five years later due to lack of support. In 1938 under the guidance and enthusiasm of Mrs Oney Goschen as District Commissioner, the Pony Club quickly expanded during its first year to 172 members, including Joyce Kemp, who later founded a riding school at Mounters Farm, and as Miss Kemp became an inspirational teacher

MEET OF THE HAMPSHIRE AT THEDDON LODGE
Lady Lymington and her son, the Hon. Oliver Wallop. Lady Cantelupe, Lord Templemore, and General Sir George Jeffreys

Above: The meet at Theddon Lodge 1932.

Right: HH Club dinner menu.

Below right: Point-to-point luncheon menu 1939.

Below: Opening Meet 1935.

HUNT CLUB DINNER
FEBRUARY 4th, 1939.

Menu

Consommé Profiteroles
Sole Souchet
Poulet Reine Elizabeth

Longe de Mouton Rôti

Soufflé de Vanille
aux Mille Fruits

Laitance d'Hareng
au Lard

BURKHAM HOUSE,
ALTON.

Nov 4 1935.
Opening meet Chawton House

My wife & myself!
Joint masters
1935 - 1936.

AN "H.H." GROUP, INCLUDING THE FAMOUS M.F.H.
Lt.-General Sir George Jeffreys and Mr. and Mrs. George Evans, joint Masters of the "H.H." at their recent fixture at Chawton House near Alton. The senior Master has unfortunately been in the wars recently, but, as usual, is quite undefeated. Sir George Jeffreys has only just come home from India.

Menu

HAMPSHIRE HUNT
POINT-TO-POINT RACES, 1939

Salmon Mayonnaise

Roast Chicken and Wiltshire Ham
Roast Beef
Roast Lamb and Mint Sauce
Veal, Ham and Egg Pies

Hot Potatoes—Green Salad
Potatoes and Vegetable Salad

Fresh Fruit Salad and Cream
Wine Trifles

Cheese (Cheddar or Gorgonzola)
Rolls, Butter, Biscuits

Chairman: Captain J. B. SCOTT, J.P., C.C.

Teas will be provided from 3.30 p.m.

and mentor to generations of pony mad children. Her handwritten memories recall a rural childhood from the 1930s and make reference to a little boy turning up to Pony Club rallies on a donkey.

It cannot have been easy for George Evans to watch another man hunt his beloved hounds, but for the next two seasons he did exactly that, taking comfort from the fact that Will Scott had been his right-hand man throughout the past decade. With such a mentor, it is hardly surprising that the tough Northumbrian quickly established a reputation for excellence. The new huntsman also inherited a carefully bred pack that had been handled in an exemplary fashion by their long-standing amateur, which no doubt contributed to an impressive tally of 41½ brace for Scott's first season as sole huntsman. George Evans finally gave up the Mastership on May 1st 1939 having provided twelve seasons of superb sport and judiciously built the Hampshire Hunt pack up to being one of the best in the land. Immensely popular with people from all walks of life, he had also elevated the Hunt to the highest of standings amongst the local community. There was considerable regret at his decision to retire, and real concern over who would maintain the Hunt's excellent relationship with the farmers. A suggestion that Mr Evans be allowed to remain in his house at the kennels and be given some work with the hounds, was given short shrift by Captain Scott, who pointed out that no huntsman would stand for that. The outgoing Master stated that he would relinquish breeding the hounds at the end of the season and hoped that Colonel Courage would be able to find a young man to help out financially, learn the country and eventually become an MFH. Miles Courage agreed to go on alone with Will Scott as his huntsman.

At the farmers' lunch prior to the 1939 point-to-point races at Farringdon, Leslie Aylward presented George Evans with a cheque for £35 on behalf of the farmers, and a book with the names of 200 contributors inscribed inside. He paid tribute to 'a great sportsman and a friend of every farmer in the Hampshire Hunt country, who has done more to promote the interests of foxhunting and create that feeling of goodwill that exists amongst farmers today than any master that has gone before him. He has not made one single bad friend amongst the farming community,' before wishing him 'a long life and happiness before being marked to ground.' In responding, George Evans thanked the farmers from the bottom of his heart and cast his mind back 30 years to his first point-to-point luncheon at Tisted where the fare was beer and sandwiches. He had felt that the menu needed to be improved and the following year introduced 'a tremendous luncheon such as this,' by which he meant the extravagant feast the farmers had just enjoyed. Instead of sandwiches they had dined on salmon mayonnaise, roast chicken and Wiltshire ham, roast beef, veal, ham and egg pies followed by fresh fruit salad with cream, wine trifles, and cheese.

On July 1st 1939 General Jeffreys and Viscountess Cantelupe gave a sherry party for Members, subscribers, and friends of the Hunt at Burkham House to mark George Evans's retirement, where he was presented with a silver statue of his beloved Rarity, a motor car, and a substantial cheque. The General reminded guests in his speech that George Evans had twice built up the Hampshire Hunt from being a moderate pack to one of the best in the country, and he was confident that the Hunt would continue to benefit from his wise counsel in the years ahead. George Evans remained a Member of the Hampshire Hunt Club and despite offering to step back from any involvement with the hounds, continued to assist and advise on a regular basis. With the outbreak of the Second World War just months away, his timely retirement also marked the end of a halcyon era between the wars after which hunting in both Hampshire and the entire United Kingdom would never be the same again. George Evans was finally run to ground in a motor accident in 1956, when he was said by the hunting correspondent, Daphne Moore, to be 'still a young man in his outlook and zest for life.' At the Hampshire Hunt Club AGM on July 20th 1956 Members stood in silence in his memory.

Statue of Rarity '33 presented to George Evans on his retirement from the Mastership in 1939.

Chapter Ten 1939–1953

A Time of Gifts

Lieutenant Colonel M.R.F. Courage, DSO, 1939–1944,
H.A. Andreae Esq., 1944–1952, Sir Arthur Blakiston, 1952–1953.

Outbreak of World War Two, Colonel Courage MFH continues hunting five days a fortnight, rural life during the war, financial challenges, farmer Members and Will Ings, Herman Andreae becomes Master in 1944, problems with accommodation at Ropley, end of the war and gradual return to normality, fox population post-war, resumption of the point-to-point at Farringdon, Gerald Barnes and family, Brigadier Selby Lowndes becomes amateur huntsman, bi-centenary dinner in 1949, dinner to honour Herman Andreae MFH, threat to hunting at Westminster and the BFSS, Sir Arthur Blakiston becomes Master and huntsman in 1952.

On September 1st 1939, just as Colonel Courage and his huntsman, Will Scott, were about to start a new cubhunting season, the German invasion of Poland precipitated the start of the Second World War and marked the end of a golden era for foxhunting that would never return. Within a week of the United Kingdom and France declaring war on Germany, Members of the Hampshire Hunt Club convened at Courage & Co's office in Alton and unanimously agreed to keep hunting going through the war if at all possible. It was decided to hunt five days a fortnight at the discretion of the Master, whose guarantee was cut to £2,000, and to immediately reduce the pack from 55 to 40 couple. The hound committee was given the grim task of deciding which hounds were to be destroyed, and which were allowed to live. At the next meeting in November it was reported that the response from Members and subscribers to a circular requesting subscriptions and donations had been sufficiently positive to anticipate raising the full sum of the guarantee, but the Hunt ball was cancelled.

In May 1940 Colonel Courage agreed to continue hunting the country as effectively as possible on a guarantee of £1,400, and the pack were further reduced to just 25 couple. According to the minutes, the Club did not meet again until May 1941 when the Master undertook to 'hunt as much of the country as possible' for

Special Meeting of the Hampshire Hunt Club held at Messrs. Courage & Co's Office Alton on September 11th, 1939 at 5-30 p.m.

General Sir George Jeffreys Chairman.

Colonel Courage M.F.H.	Mr. H.K.Andreae.
Mr. J.W. Harrap.	Mr. G. Evans.
Colonel Middleton.	Mr. S. Smith.
Captain Petre.	H.M. Foster
Colonel Savill	Colonel Lord Basing.
Colonel Lord Templemore	Mr. Aylward.

General Sir George Jeffreys appologised for the shortness of notice of the meeting but stated that it was essential to decide at once how many days a week to hunt and also number of hounds to be kept at the kennels. He proposed that the Hunt should be carried on during the war and this was carried unanimously.

Mr.G. Evans said that during the last war no hounds were destroyed during the first year and that food for hounds was not rationed till the third year of war. The Hunt Club gave him £1800 a year.

Mr.S. Smith said after the first year of war hounds hunted two days a week for four years, horses were borrowed. Members subscriptions were kept up well, outside subscriptions were light, however they managed to carry on without getting into debt and had quite a good pack of hounds at the end of the war.

The Master Colonel Courage thought that hounds should hunt two days a week with an occasional bye day, working out about five days a fortnight, this was agreed to unanimously.

It was agreed to unanimously to reduce the number of hounds for which the Master is responsible from fifty-five couples of hounds to forty couples of hounds. It was agreed that the hound committee should meet and decide which hounds are to be kept.

The Secretary was instructed to circularise Members and Subscribers and to inform them of the decision of the meeting and ask them to continue their subscriptions.

Mr. Aylward suggested that extra food might be got for hounds from waste at Bordon Camp also that Hunt servants should help the farmers to get in the harvest.

General Sir George, Jeffreys said that these were matters for the Master. Colonel Courage said that he would do what he could about it.

Colonel Courage raised the question of a reduction of the guarentee. He informed the committee that the Hunt cost £3600 a year. The question of the guarentee was deferred until after the result of the circular letter was known, but it was decided informally to aim at a guarentee of £2000.

It was left to the Master to decide on which days of the week the hounds went out.

It was decided to cancel the Hunt Ball.

Meeting held on September 11th 1939 to consider hunting during the War.

28.11.39.

just £800 per year. There are no records of sport during the war years, however Charles James replaced Will Scott as professional huntsman in 1941 and was said to be less successful than his hard riding and determined predecessor. Another whole year passed in the grim fog of war before Members reconvened at Courage & Co's office in May 1942 and decided that any landowner in the Hampshire Hunt country could join the Hampshire Hunt Club during the war years in return for a £10 subscription. Colonel Courage was given a unanimous vote of thanks for all he was doing to keep the Hunt going; in response the Master asked Members to help obtain more flesh for the kennels.

As the effects of food and petrol rationing were felt across the county, life became very different during the war years for those at home in rural Hampshire. With every suitable acre of farmland needed to bolster the war effort and help feed the country there was precious little fodder and forage for horses, and few were bred during hostilities. Many horses and ponies were sold for meat, others were broken to harness and taught to pull old traps that had been gathering dust for decades. The clatter of hooves on country lanes replaced noisy petrol engines but given the close proximity of Aldershot and Bordon the appearance of huge tanks was always a possibility. As petrol was strictly rationed hunt staff had to hack long distances to meets, which were held earlier than normal so that hounds and horses could return to kennels before the nightly blackout rules[1] came into force at dusk. Although the Second World War is remembered as a mechanical conflict with tanks and armoured vehicles replacing the cavalry of old, some horses were still required for military use. However they were no longer compulsorily requisitioned, and only a small fraction of the vast numbers enlisted into service during the First World War left England's shores. Joyce Kemp wrote poignantly of riding her pony, Mike, along the road to Guildford Station with other Pony Club members to hand over their mounts to waiting soldiers, who she noted were both kind and caring. 'We did hear from some of these soldiers later on that our horses were with them in the Middle East,' she wrote, 'we had left notes about them on their headcollars, but of course I never saw Mike again.'

Another twelve months elapsed before the next meeting on May 28th 1943, when Colonel Courage was obliged to inform Members that running the Hunt was now costing him £300 a year out of his own pocket. Despite this personal

---

1   Blackout regulations required that all windows and doors should be covered at night with suitable material such as heavy curtains, cardboard, or paint, to prevent the escape of any glimmer of light that might identify a target for enemy aircraft.

The following Farmer Members were elected 96

		Proposed by	Seconded by
✓	Mr. G. B. Barnes, Hall Farm, Bentworth	Gen. Sir George Jeffreys, M.P.	H. A. Andreae. Esq., M.F.H.
	Mr. R. P. Blackadder, Norton Farm, Sutton Scotney	Capt. H. J. M. Holmes	Mr. A. R. L. Aylward
✓	Mr. F. Butler, Lees Farm, South Warnborough	H. A. Andreae, Esq., M.F.H.	George Evans, Esq.
✓	Mr. B. Butler, ditto	Ditto	Ditto
	Mr. K. Clarence Smith, Beech Farm, Four Marks	Mr. J. Highmoor	Mr. A. R. L. Aylward
✓	Mr. H. F. Eames, Wyck, Alton	Capt. H. J. M. Holmes	Ditto
	Mr. H. Edgar, Old Place Farm, East Tisted	Mr. A. R. L. Aylward	Mr. J. Highmoor
	Mr. F. D. Faulkner, Norton Farm, Selborne	Ditto	Capt. H. J. M. Holmes
✓	Mr. John Gray, Graces Farm, Martyr Worthy	H. A. Andreae. Esq., M.F.H.	Mr. A. R. L. Aylward
✓	Mr. D. G. Hunt, Herriard	Mr. A. R. L. Aylward	Capt. H. J. M. Holmes
✓	Mr. W. H. Ings, Bonniesfield Farm, West Tisted	Ditto	Mr. J. Highmoor
✓	Mr. J. N. McClean, Flexcombe Farm, Liss	George Evans, Esq.	Capt. H. J. M. Holmes
	Mr. R. J. Newman, Manor Farm, Holybourne	Mr. A. R. L. Aylward	Ditto
✓	Mr. John Rowsell, Stoke Farm, Sutton Scotney	Capt. H. J. M. Holmes	Mr. A. R. L. Aylward
✓	Mr. H. Warner, Champlers Farm, Hawkley	H. A. Andreae, Esq., M.F.H.	Ditto

A list of the first farmer Members elected in 1944.

expense, the Colonel was prepared to commit to another season on a guarantee of £800 but could not continue for a penny less. After three years of hostilities during which there were no fundraising initiatives such as the point-to-point, and caps and subscriptions were much diminished, the Hunt coffers were seriously depleted. Mr Stuart Smith's proposal that the Master be offered £500 infuriated Colonel Courage, who pointed out that the suggestion was tantamount to expecting him to find £600 of his own to keep the Hunt afloat. He explained the great difficulties of running the Hunt during the war, especially finding the necessary labour, and revealed that his huntsman was now a farm worker. He was especially indebted to Mr Aylward, who had been his right-hand man throughout the previous season. When the Master left the room Leslie Aylward said he thought Members were approaching this the wrong way and that they should find the money and not reduce the guarantee, which was agreed to in principle. Capping at half a crown each day in aid of the Wire and

Poultry Funds had first been introduced in 1933,[2] but had lapsed after the outbreak of war, and it was now decided to reintroduce the practice for the following season. As Messrs Aylward and Andreae were the two Members who hunted most frequently, they were asked to help with collection; Leslie Aylward happily agreed, however Herman Andreae declined on the grounds that he did not want to be made a ticket collector.

The question of farmers being granted greater involvement in the affairs of the Hunt Club had been given a proper airing at a general meeting during the first year of Mr Robinson's ill-fated Mastership back in 1921, but nothing had come of it. In 1943 Leslie Aylward suggested that it was now time to invite farmers to become Members and allow them to contribute to the management and decision making within the Hunt Club. After a long discussion it was decided to accept farmers of more than 200 acres for a reduced subscription of £10, or £5 for those with a smaller acreage, but Members drew the line at allowing them to wear the Prince of Wales's ostrich plumes on the Hunt button, or from balloting new Members. Instead farmers were permitted to wear the same hunt button as ladies.

Will Ings, who came to live at Hobbs Farm in the Hampshire Hunt country when five years old in 1895, was one of the early Farmer Members. Will moved to Brick Kiln Farm after getting married, where he thought nothing of hacking up to sixteen miles across country to meets. On November 1st 1977 Sir James Scott presented the 87 year old farmer, who was riding his twenty year old mare, Paddy, with a tankard at Moundsmere to commemorate his sixtieth consecutive Opening Meet. Will was still riding to hounds in his nineties but nominated a run from Lower Lanham covert in the 1930s, when Will Scott was carrying the horn, as the best hunt he ever witnessed. Hounds ran to ground at dusk and Will did not get home until 8.30pm.

By January 1944 the Hunt bank account was so overdrawn that Members could not offer Colonel Courage more than £200 for the following season. The Master felt that he could not continue under such onerous terms, at which point the future of the Hampshire Hunt appeared as bleak as it had been back in May 1862 when no replacement could be found following the resignation of Mr Tredcroft. Members urgently needed another guardian angel in the mould of Henry Deacon, who had moved from Devon to rescue them eight decades earlier, but in 1944

---

2   On June 21st 1933 Members agreed that a cap of half a crown be taken every hunting day for the Wire and Poultry Funds, but that Members and subscribers could compound this at £2 each for the season.

the saviour lived much closer to home. In the 1920s Herman Andreae had served as senior partner of Kleinwort Sons and Company[3] and moved with his family to the New Forest where he took up hunting. Herman was also an active racing helmsman on board his own yacht, Candida, which was built in 1928 and named after his wife, and competed against HM The King's Britannia, and other America's Cup challengers during the 1930s. In 1934 Herman purchased Moundsmere Manor near Preston Candover, an imposing red-brick manor house at the end of a mile-long drive, and after moving in with his family became actively involved in the Hampshire Hunt during the height of George Evans's second, glorious Mastership. He was elected a Member of the Hunt Club in 1939 and appointed sole Master for the 1944–1945 season on a meagre guarantee of just £200, generously agreeing to take on the Club's 22 couple of hounds at a valuation of £3,000. Herman Andreae's many business and sporting commitments frequently took him away from Hampshire, so he recruited George Evans to supervise the kennels in his absence and allowed him to continue living at his cottage in Ropley. Charles James stayed on to hunt hounds as professional huntsman.

An injection of working capital into the Hunt accounts was not only long overdue, but accommodation for hunt staff at Ropley had also been allowed to deteriorate into a sorry state. The absence of a bathroom in the huntsman's house had first been discussed in 1936, but when the incumbent huntsman, Will Scott, refused the cheapest solution, Captain Scott proposed spending more money to build a proper bathroom. Members were equally divided over committing to the extra expense, but the Chairman cast his vote for the cheaper option, which was to install a bath inside an already cramped kitchen. In 1938 three or four stablemen shared a single room above the stables and ate their meals in the kitchen of a small cottage occupied by one of the grooms whose wife catered for the men. Captain Scott had generously contributed £100 towards the £900 cost of renovations to rectify this, which he regarded as a Coronation gift to the Hunt,[4] and Colonel Courage MFH, offered to loan the balance if required. Members inspected progress in November 1937, but the project was not completed until May the following year, albeit nearly £200 over budget.

The consequences of settling for an inadequate solution to the huntsman's

---

3   Kleinwort Sons and Company (later Kleinwort Benson) was a City Acceptance House which had been founded by Herman Andreae's grandfather, Alexander Kleinwort.

4   The coronation of George VI and his wife Elizabeth as King and Queen of the United Kingdom took place at Westminster Abbey, London, on May 12th 1937.

bathroom before the Second World War came back to bite Members when Will Scott's successor, Charles James, also expressed dissatisfaction with his accommodation. He pointed out that having a bath in the kitchen made it impossible to bathe and cook at the same time, and that a bucket closet[5] across the yard instead of a flushing lavatory inside the house made life very awkward for his family. Following a site visit by the Management Committee the Hon. Secretary was asked to obtain quotes for extending the cottage to make space for a proper bathroom, and the first steps were taken to provide the kennels with a mains water supply, which was eventually connected by the Wey Valley Water Company in 1947. Up until then all water for hunt staff, horses and hounds was either drawn from a 68-foot deep well at the kennels or transported onto site and stored in large holding tanks at considerable expense.

The Second World War ended with the armistice on August 14th 1945, but it would take the Hunt years to fully recover from its deprivations, and for the time being, hounds continued to meet only twice weekly. Messrs Aylward and Warner, who had provided horses for the hunt staff to ride during the war, continued to do so, and by December thirty subscribers had returned to the hunting field, prompting another intervention from Members regarding the correct dress and turnout. The Hon. Secretary wrote to advise Members and subscribers that it was incorrect for anyone other than farmers, their wives and families or children of school age to wear a hunt cap without permission. The Pony Club were approached to establish what could be done about collecting a contribution from children who came out hunting; by 1953 any child subscribing £2.20 for the season and paying the half-crown Wire Fund cap each day was allowed to wear a gilt button engraved with the HH initials. In 1947 the instruction, 'Please Shut Gates' was included on meet cards, and the Club agreed to a request from the National Farmers Union to hold a hunter trial in aid of the Agricultural Disaster Fund.

A reduction in organised shooting during the war years had resulted in such an explosion of the local fox population that Colonel Courage felt obliged to write to the Hon. Secretary in 1946 imploring the Hunt to kill more foxes because there were far too many for good sport. George Evans's suggestion of shooting them on bye days was not agreed to, but it was decided to adopt cubhunting methods for the

---

5 The bucket closet was a small outhouse or privy which contained a seat, underneath which a portable receptacle was placed for the capture of human waste. This bucket was removed and emptied by the local authority on a regular basis.

rest of the 1946–1947 season and hold foxes up whenever possible. Leslie Aylward pointed out that the Hunt did not possess any useful terriers, so the Hon. Secretary was asked to try and procure some. The fox population continued to expand, and in 1952 Godfrey Nicholson MP forwarded a letter to the Club from a lady complaining of 'the enormous destruction foxes were doing in the Farnham area.' Upon closer investigation the problem was found to be outside the Hampshire Hunt country.

Mr Andreae agreed to continue his Mastership for the 1946–1947 season, with Jack Kealy replacing Charles James as his professional huntsman. The Master insisted on accepting a guarantee of just £200 even though the Chairman, General Jeffreys, had offered to more than treble the sum to £700. Members were reminded that they would never find anyone else to run the Hunt under such favourable terms and there was unanimous agreement to record in the minutes a vote of thanks to Mr Andreae and Colonel Courage for their 'distinguished services to the Hunt in carrying on during the difficult years of the war.' As much as anyone who had gone before them in the Club's history, the generosity of these two men had unquestionably averted disaster. The Hunt gradually recommenced fundraising initiatives to help consolidate financial stability, including a successful dance at Moundsmere in aid of the Wire Fund, which had been restarted in December 1945.

Last held in 1939, the point-to-point also resumed on Easter Monday 1946 at a new course on Mr E.C. Holroyd's land at Bentworth, where it remained until a move to Hackwood Park in 1951. In the build-up to the first Hunt race meeting for eight years there had been concerns over the number of horses available to run so soon after the end of war, and that the participation of grass-fed or unfit horses might sully the reputation of the Hunt, however the races over natural hedges and ditches were a great success. The Members' race was won by Mr Andrews's Egyptian Star II, and the meeting turned in a healthy profit of £1,331. Mr Gerald Barnes, a Farmer Member of the Club whose rented land at Bentworth included the start and finish of the figure-of-eight course, assumed the role of point-to-point Secretary in 1947, with an allowance of £50 towards his expenses.

Gerald Barnes had taken the tenancy of Hall Farm, Bentworth in 1936 having moved from Winchester where his family had been involved with horses for over 400 years. He went on to establish a successful hunting livery yard and was widely acknowledged as a wonderful horseman whose perfectly conditioned charges always went well across country and never tired. Along with his close friends and fellow hunting farmers such as Henry Warner, Leslie Aylward, John Highmoor

Above: Captain J.B. Scott's Dacoity (Mr R. Harrap up) wins the last Members' race before the Second World War in 1939.

Below: Mr W. Andrews's Egyptian Star II win the first post-war Members' race in 1946.

and Gilbert Dicker, for many years Gerald donated food and forage for the hunt horses at Ropley. He had four children with his wife Sylvia, three of whom took to riding and hunting like ducks to water. Tom, Mary, and Sheila all showjumped for England on a variety of home-produced mounts, and in 1952 the Hon. Secretary wrote to congratulate Tom Barnes for winning the Leading Pony Showjumper of the Year class at Harringay, along with Brian Butler from Greywell for winning the Daily Mail Cup at White City. Sheila Barnes was junior European champion on Solo in 1961 and two years later came fourth in the Hickstead Derby on Sudden, who became something of a household name throughout Hampshire, winning many competitions and representing England in Nations Cup teams.[6] After his retirement, Sudden was ridden by Gerald Barnes as the starter's hack at Hampshire Hunt point-to-points, and Gerald's equestrian legacy endures through his granddaughter, Floss[7] Heeney, who runs a livery yard at East Worldham.

Herman Andreae agreed to continue hunting the country three days a week from 1947–1948 on a guarantee of £1,500, but with typical generosity offered to return £500 at the end of the season if the Hunt could not afford the full sum. He introduced Brigadier M.W. Selby Lowndes, DSO as his deputy Master and amateur huntsman, with Jack Kealy remaining as kennel huntsman and first whipper-in. Known to his friends as Boy, the Brigadier came from a distinguished hunting family and had been Master and huntsman of several packs before the war including the Handley Cross Harriers in Kent, and military hunts in France, India, Italy, and Palestine. He had also been amateur huntsman to the Tedworth and Wilton, and after the war was Master of the Newmarket and Thurlow for a season before accepting Herman's invitation to move to Hampshire. The Brigadier was said be superb on the horn, and many who heard him blow the long drawn out notes of 'going home' observed that the melancholy call seemed to go on forever.

An immediate improvement in sport followed the Brigadier's appointment, and he was quickly elected to the Hound Committee and invited to wear the Hunt button and collar. Halfway through his first season the Chairman complimented the amateur huntsman on the high standard of sport he was providing and praised Mr Andreae's continued generosity towards the Hunt. Members were so pleased with the improved hunting that an appeal was launched to purchase a second-hand car to

---

[6] The FEI Nations Cup, called Furusiyya FEI Nations Cup since 2013 because of sponsorship reasons, is the most prestigious showjumping series for national teams in the world.

[7] Fiona Heeney, known to all as Floss.

better enable the Brigadier to carry out his duties, a benefit conferred on very few amateur huntsmen before or since. Often short of funds, the Brigadier once took an acting job on a film set as a mounted policeman and was most disappointed when his minor role ended up on the cutting room floor.

On October 8th 1949 Herman Andreae entertained 38 Members and Farmer Members to a bi-centenary dinner at Moundsmere Manor,[8] where he described the HH as the 'Happy Hunt' and the health of both Herman and Mrs Andreae was drunk with musical honours after speeches from General Sir George Jeffreys, Brigadier General Hope and Captain Holmes on behalf of the farmers. The following summer General Jeffreys hosted a party in Herman Andreae's honour at Burkham House to acknowledge the Master's generosity and sportsmanship in continuing in office despite the discomfort and disability he suffered since being severely kicked in the back whilst attending a meet. During the evening Herman was presented with a painting by Lionel Edwards, a silver hunting horn and a book containing the names of everyone who had subscribed to the presentation.

The Hunt had resumed meeting four days a week and was enjoying a purple patch under Mr Andreae's Mastership, but against this backdrop of companionship, good sport, and financial stability ominous storm clouds were gathering. They did not herald an outbreak of further hostilities, but the eventual consequences for hunting were to prove even more catastrophic than either World War. The year before the bi-centenary dinner the Club had received a letter from the British Field Sports Society, which had been founded in 1930 to counter increasing public hostility to all field sports. The missive warned of a Private Member's Bill[9] designed to end hunting and coursing, the latest step in an anti-hunting campaign that was gathering momentum but would not prevail for another 58 years. George Evans proposed that all Members and subscribers join the BFSS,[10] and in 1948 a subcommittee was formed under the chairmanship of Brigadier Selby Lowndes to address the issue. Both the 1949 anti-hunting Private Member's bills failed; one

---

8   It has been stated elsewhere that the 200th anniversary dinner was held in October 1949 as it was not possible to celebrate the Hunt's alleged bi-centenary of 1745 during the war years. The case for the Hampshire Hunt starting in 1749 is set out in the introduction to this book. The Hampshire Hunt Club erroneously celebrated its bicentenary with a dinner at Winchester College in 1995, however a surviving list of Members in 1782 proves that the Club was in existence at least thirteen years prior to 1795.

9   Private Members' Bills are public bills introduced by Members of Parliament and Lords who are not government ministers. The names of Members applying for a bill are drawn in a ballot. These bills have the best chance of becoming law, as they get priority for the limited amount of debating time available.

10 British Field Sports Society.

was withdrawn and the other was defeated on its second reading in the House of Commons.

Not a single day was lost to frost during the 1950–1951 season, when Jack Kealy and Fred Maun whipped-in to the Brigadier and hounds went out 108 times, suffered no blank days, and killed 24½ brace. Herman Andreae resigned his Mastership in 1952 with the keenest regret, since his years at the helm had been 'very happy ones due to the pleasant and friendly atmosphere of the Hampshire Hunt and the unfailing kindness and courtesy received from the followers and farmers.' He offered £1,000 to assist the Hunt the next season despite the fact that he would no longer be Master, and in 1959 presented a silver perpetual Challenge Cup for the Hunt Farmers' Race at the point-to-point. Having provided five seasons of superlative sport as amateur huntsman, Boy Selby Lowndes left Hampshire for Gloucestershire where he joined Lord Bathurst in the Mastership of the VWH.

Sir Arthur Blakiston Bt. MC was appointed Master and huntsman for the 1952–1953 season on a guarantee of £3,500 and accounted for eleven brace before the Opening Meet. Petrol rationing had been suspended in 1950, which led to a significant increase in car followers, but Members ruled out any attempt to cap them for the immediate future. A subcommittee to settle poultry claims had first been appointed in 1886, but in 1953 it was decided to discontinue the practice following advice from the MFHA and a post-war rise in the fox population. The Club was following the example of many other hunts throughout the land in taking this decision, most of which had not paid compensation for loss of poultry to foxes since the outbreak of war.

Members must have decided that Sir Arthur needed the support of a first-class professional in the hunting field, for in January 1953 his offer to continue was accepted on the understanding that he engage a first whipper-in and kennel huntsman 'of reputation' to assist him. He happily consented provided it was the unanimous wish of the Members, but not for the first time, events were soon to be overtaken by fate. Just three weeks after agreeing terms for the 1953–1954 season the Master handed in his resignation due to his wife's illness. The news was received with great regret, for Sir Arthur had worked hard to meet farmers and open up the country. During the ensuing discussion Members considered the benefits of employing a professional huntsman and cutting back to three days a week. A Mastership Committee was appointed and on January 25th 1953 the position of Master of the Hampshire Hunt was advertised in *Horse & Hound* magazine.

A TIME OF GIFTS 1939–1953

Herman Andreae MFH 1944–1952 at Moundsmere in 1950 painted by Lionel Edwards.

Chapter Eleven 1953–1965

The Goschen Era

H.K. Goschen Esq., Major H. Leigh Newton DSO, 1953–1955,
H.K. Goschen Esq., Mrs H.K. Goschen 1955–1965.

Ken Goschen and Major Leigh Newton become Joint Masters in 1953, Bob Jones appointed professional huntsman, point-to-point moves to Hackwood Park, Oney Goschen becomes a Joint Master in 1955, hunting country increasingly difficult to cross, the Hampshire Hunt's standing in the local community, increase of subscriptions and general meetings, foxes and earth stopping, cross country race at Rotherfield Park, car followers, purchase of coverts for the Hunt, death of three long-standing Members, criticism of Bob Jones and his retirement, Dennis Boyles appointed to hunt the doghounds and Ken Goschen to hunt the bitches, the Goschens' retirement and their final day's hunting.

Captain Speid-Soote was appointed Acting Master for the 1953–1954 season with the support of Ken Goschen and Leslie Aylward, however the Captain unexpectedly resigned in June for reasons that were understood by Members, but not recorded. Within a few days Ken Goschen, a wealthy banker and keen hunting man from Froyle, and Major Leigh Newton offered to hunt the country four days a week with a professional huntsman on a guarantee of £3,500, which was formally approved at the AGM in July. At the same meeting Members received an unexpected bonus from Herman Andreae by way of a cheque for £1,000, and Captain Augustus Coryton signalled his intention to stand down as the Hon. Secretary.[1] He was persuaded to share secretarial duties with Mr Venning for the time being and did not formally resign until 1963, when his long service to the Hunt Club was rewarded by the gift of a gold watch. At the following year's AGM in June 1954 it was agreed that the Management and Finance committees should amalgamate into one body, although separate committees would continue to be appointed on an ad hoc basis in addition to the Wire Fund and Hound Committee.

---

1 Augustus Coryton (son of former Master and Chairman, Frederick Coryton) was Hon. Secretary from 1920 to 1934, but resumed this post in 1948 on the death of the incumbent Hon. Secretary, John Highmoor.

The Joint Masters appointed Bob Jones from the Lauderdale as their professional huntsman, who quickly settled to the role and provided consistently good sport with the doghounds on Tuesdays and Saturdays and the bitches on Mondays and Thursdays. The new huntsman took a mixed pack to the Boxing Day meet at the Butts in Alton for the first and last time, since the doghounds had a field day cocking their legs against wheelchairs outside Lord Mayor Treloar Hospital whilst the occupants enjoyed the meet. The bitches scored a four-mile point from Chawton Park Wood to Shell Lane via Rotherfield Park and East Tisted for Bob's second Boxing Day, closely followed by a fast six-mile point from Lower Lanham Copse to Itchen Wood after Wing Commander and Mrs Begg's meet at Armsworth Park on December 30th 1955. In January the Joint Masters expressed their willingness to continue for the following season provided the Club modernise two of the staff cottages at Ropley to include lavatories and baths and make drainage improvements to the kennels and flesh house. The Chairman stated his pleasure that arrangements would remain unchanged and noted that the Hampshire Hunt had once more attained a high standard of sport.

The quality of sport was especially evident during a tremendous afternoon hunt following the meet at Old Alresford House on January 10th 1957, a day that Ken Goschen later recalled as one of the best he ever witnessed. Hounds found in Old Down at 3.30pm and raced away to Ropley Wood and Bramdean Common before circling back into Cheriton Wood and crossing the main road at New Cheriton, by which time hunt staff and two remaining members of the field were already fifteen minutes adrift of the flying pack. The hunt continued at a blistering pace past Hinton Ampner and Bramdean, through the Brockwood coverts and over the Meon Valley road into Hambledon Hunt country before re-entering HH country via Filmore Hill. A farmworker saw the sinking fox here beneath the moonlight only a hundred yards ahead of hounds, who were last seen running hard for Ashen Wood having covered at least twenty miles. The hunt's conclusion was never established, but later that night the entire pack of weary hounds were seen by a motorist padding homewards along the road.

In 1951 the point-to-point had moved from Bentworth, where it had been held since the War, to Hackwood Park by kind permission of Lord Camrose, whose brother, the Hon. Julian Berry, farmed the Hackwood estate and was also a keen hunting Member of the Hampshire Hunt Club. The first fences were built by Ginger Woods, who had been a terrierman for Brigadier Selby Lowndes and was later appointed keeper for Major Berens of Bentworth Hall where he ensured hunting and shooting went together. In the 1950s the requirement that all horses participating in point-to-points must be regularly hunted was rigorously enforced, and grooms were debarred from qualifying. The move to Hackwood precipitated a request from the neighbouring Vine Hunt to run their own Easter Monday meeting at the same course, which lies within the Hampshire Hunt country. This was allowed on the understanding that the profits from both meetings be divided equally, since the Vine had assumed the Easter Monday date for their races after the Hampshire Hunt Club had graciously relinquished the prestigious date back in 1947. By the early 1960s Members were referring to the last Saturday in March as the traditional date for their own races, but there was no doubt which was the more profitable fixture.

Long and protracted negotiations took place between the two Hunts during the years that followed as each jostled for a better position; the Hampshire Hunt controlled the course as it lay within their own country, but the Vine had secured much the best date in the point-to-point calendar. A suggestion that the Vine retain profits from their own meeting and vice versa was given short shrift, and the idea of alternating Easter Monday between both hunts was never adopted. The Vine

Bob Jones (huntsman) arriving with hounds at Treloar Hospital.
Ken Goschen MFH and Tom Smith (whipper-in) to rear.

Bob Jones (huntsman) and Bill Marks (whipper-in) with hounds at Treloar Hospital, Boxing Day 1958.

eventually agreed to pay the Hampshire Hunt a straightforward rent to use the course, but the work and preparation fell mainly to men from the Hampshire Hunt such as George Bennett, John Hewett, Derick Faulkner, Bill Welling and Charlie Corbett. In 2006 the wheel came full circle when the Hunts reverted to the original agreement, whereby income and expenditure from both meetings are pooled and the profits divided equally.

There was further consternation in 1962 when Members first learnt of proposals to build the M3 motorway through the northern end of the Park, which would annexe the London Road entrance. The threat was eventually overcome with some dramatic alterations to the course, resulting in contestants having to race round two and a half circuits in order to complete the obligatory three miles. In 1967 the traditional farmers' point-to-point lunch was replaced by a cocktail party at the RAF Officers' Mess at Odiham, which was deemed to have been a great success. The following year the point-to-point committee applied for Saturday April 8th, only to discover that, not for the first time, the date coincided with the Grand

THE GOSCHEN ERA 1953–1965

National. In order to avoid another clash, the 1968 point-to-point took place on the first Thursday in April, but it was another two years before it moved on a more permanent basis to the first Saturday in April providing the date did not fall ten days either side of Easter.

When Major Leigh Newton left the Mastership at the end of his second season, he was replaced by Ken Goschen's wife, Oney, who had been District Commissioner of the HH branch of the Pony Club since 1938 and was tireless in her efforts to encourage the young to ride and hunt. The Chairman pointed out that the husband and wife team had already worked together successfully on behalf of the Hunt, and that 'the hunt staff were never better mounted, the horses had never looked better and the standard was very good.' Standards were undoubtedly high, but minutes from November 1954 reveal that the Hampshire Hunt country had deteriorated to the extent that it was 'huntable, but hardly rideable for the field.' Landowners were sent a polite letter asking them to keep their estates accessible and free from wire, and since Members disliked narrow hunt jumps, the Wire Fund undertook to build wider fences and erect wings 'practically everywhere.' Such jobs fell to the Wire Fund's employee, Mr Woods, who was instructed not to take his orders from landowners direct as doing so was making it difficult for the Wire Fund Committee to organise his work schedule.

In February 1957 Members, subscribers, landowners, farmers, and supporters returned to the Assembly Rooms in Alton for a general meeting similar to those held during Mr Robinson's Mastership in 1920 and 1921, although the prime reason on this occasion was to justify subscription increases of up to 40 percent.[2] The Wire Fund secretary, Leslie Aylward, explained that keeping the country open and relatively wire free was an expensive undertaking; a full time fence man cost the Hunt Club £425 a year, but when timber, materials and petrol were also taken into account the annual cost was in excess of £700. Leslie believed that the Wire Fund[3] significantly contributed to the Hunt's popularity and ended his address by prevailing on followers to report damage and inform the Wire Fund managers of locations where hunt jumps would improve access.

---

2   The cost of a season's hunting for Members increased from £25 to £35, or from £35 to £45 for more than one horse. Subscribers' costs increased from £15 to £20 for a single horse and from £25 to £35 for two or more. The subscription cost to Farmer Members went up by £5 to £15.

3   The first Wire Committee was established by the Hampshire Hunt Club on October 5th 1896, and sub divided into Monday, Tuesday, Thursday, and Saturday districts. The Wire Fund is first referenced by the Hunt minutes in the 1930s

Ken and Oney Goschen Joint Masters 1955–1965.

Mr Goschen's speech offers an insight into the scale and style of the Hampshire Hunt Club in the late 1950s. In order to hunt four times a week, 55 couple of hounds were kennelled at Ropley under the care of four full-time employees, being Bob Jones, the professional huntsman, first and second whippers-in, and a kennelman. A stud groom and five girls looked after up to twenty horses in the stables; at least five were required for the huntsman, three for the first whipper-in and two for the second whipper-in. Four more horses were needed for the Joint Masters, along with several spares in case of lameness or injury. Staff costs alone absorbed every penny of the £4,000 a year Masters' guarantee, which did not cover the additional expense of feeding hounds and horses, petrol, vehicle, and saddlery repairs. Shoeing bills and rewarding some 135 earthstoppers cost a further £400, on top of which came veterinary expenses, compensation claims, staff clothing and prerequisites. The financial burden would be even greater, Mr Goschen explained, were it not for all those generous people who helped out in so many different ways, especially the puppy walkers and those kind farmers who donated forage,

**HH Cosy '57 Champion bitch at the 1958 Aldershot Hound Show
with Bob Jones (huntsman) and Bill Marks (whipper-in).**

feed, bedding, and flesh. Mr Keep, who described himself as 'a small farmer from the foxiest corner of Hampshire,' paid tribute to the Masters for their efficient management of the Hunt and urged his fellow farmers to allow the Hunt to install jumps and gates on their land. He reminded mounted followers that they were the farmers' guests and asked them to report damage.

No one made reference to the fox population at the general meeting, however the post-war increase was diminishing as game preservation returned. A decade after foxes had been held up in order to reduce numbers, Mr Goschen had to remind Members to encourage foxes on their land, preserve at least one litter of cubs, and use their influence to persuade others to do likewise. He hoped Members would feel 'very sincerely sad' if their coverts were ever drawn blank and made it clear that membership of the Club involved obligations that extended beyond paying an annual subscription. Mr Goschen's pleas must have fallen on deaf ears because he told Members at the AGM fifteen months later that several litters of cubs had already been destroyed. He appealed to them once more to maintain 'the right and proper tradition of killing foxes with a pack of hounds.'

With fewer foxes available to hunt, it was more important than ever that those found above ground did not gain sanctuary below it. In 1958 a letter from Major Bonnor was read out lamenting the lack of earth stopping and complaining that two brace had been run to ground on the first Saturday after Christmas. In fact the Major could not recall a single Saturday when a fox had not gained refuge in an open earth, and he believed it was now time to engage a full time earthstopper. Mr Holman suggested that since most of the keepers were employed by Members, the best approach might be for them 'to get their own men up to scratch.' These and other complaints led to the appointment of a full-time terrierman and earthstopper called Eric Withey, who had suffered from shell shock during the War. Eric was occasionally prone to beating his head against the steering wheel of his Land Rover, much to the consternation of any passengers.

Captain A.F. Coryton, D.L., J.P., reported on a telephone conversation with Sir William Makins in connection with rights of way and bridle paths, and also submitted a letter from the County Surveyor regarding a sub-committee of the County Council which is undertaking a review to ascertain the more important paths and bridle ways in each parish. The committee have also a third category; the long distance routes, many parts of which will be established under the Parks Commission. Apart from consultations with parish councils, the committee are consulting other bodies and authorities, and it is wondered whether the Hunt Club would be interested in suggesting bridle ways which are used as short cuts. It was also stated that one of the County Surveyor's staff would be available to investigate bridle ways if a horse could be provided by the Hunt Club for the purpose. Alternatively, a meeting was suggested by the County Surveyor with Members of the Hunt Club.

After some discussion of the matter it was

AGREED (i) that a sub-committee consisting of Colonel J.B. Scott, D.L., J.P., Captain A.F. Coryton, D.L., J.P., J.W. Simpson, Esq., A.R.L. Aylward, Esq., Lt.-Colonel W.S. Wingate-Gray, M.C., with power to co-opt any Member from a particular area should discuss the matter and then meet the County Surveyor on the lines suggested;

(ii) that a letter of thanks be sent to Sir William Makins and also to H.N. Jenner, Esq., the County Surveyor.

Minutes re bridleways and the Hampshire County Council in 1959.

The Goschens were sometimes frustrated by a shortage of foxes, but their Mastership represented a period of real stability for the Hunt; there were no threats to resign, and although challenging, money to pay the guarantee was always found. Under their leadership the Hunt was a respected institution throughout the local community, working in harmony with public and charitable bodies. Donations were made every year to four different agricultural associations, the Animal Health Trust, and the East Hampshire Stallion Committee, and caps were taken for the Earl Haig Fund and the HSBS. The Hunt Club enjoyed a good relationship with the Selborne Common National Trust Committee and contributed to the cost of cutting out rides, of which the Hampshire Hunt was perhaps the greatest beneficiary. The Forestry Commission willingly unlocked gates and removed wire to provide hunt access, and when the Hampshire County Council conducted a review of the county bridleways in 1959, it was entirely natural that they should offer one of their staff to investigate bridleways on horseback if the Hunt Club could provide a suitable mount. The local vets, Messrs Searles and Darbishire, administered care to hounds and horses free of charge whilst supportive farmers donated hay, straw, and oats as well as fallen stock for the hounds.

On March 2nd 1959 a subcommittee organised the first of several cross county races, which were proving popular with other hunts in different parts of England. The race was run across 4½ miles of natural hunting country on the Scotts' Rotherfield estate, from East Tisted Station to Harkers Crossroads with a loop out to Noar Hill and back again. Although Weatherbys[4] would not allow hunt cross country races to be run for profit, the event was deemed to have been a great success. The 1960 race was run in treacherous conditions following a week of heavy rain and won by Margaret Uloth from the Hursley Hunt riding her mare, Lavender Blue. There were several fallers during the contest including the favourite – a leading national showjumper – who turned a complete somersault at the first fence. Believing that it was hers to keep, Margaret took the winner's Cup to Germany, where her husband had been posted on military service, but later received a letter asking for the Cup to be engraved and returned. Unfortunately the shop she selected to do the work in West Germany was burgled and the Cup stolen, however the jeweller agreed to create a replica from a sketch supplied by Margaret. The result was a much bigger and better solid silver Cup, which was duly returned to the Hampshire Hunt without anyone noticing the difference. There was another

---

[4] Weatherbys administer racing and point-to-pointing on behalf of the Jockey Club.

successful cross country race in 1961, but no further references to the contest in Hunt correspondence until 1968 when it resumed at Rotherfield Park in October.

Meanwhile Bob Jones continued to provide good sport, hitting an especially purple patch during March 1961 when hounds ran non-stop from 11.15am to 6.30pm following the meet at Dora's Green and produced two four-mile points before the end of the month. Points of even four miles were beginning to be regarded as a triumph over the odds, the odds being ever increasing numbers of car followers who frequently ruined a good hunt by heading the fox. The subject had been given an airing during the 1957 general meeting, and in January 1961 a subcommittee, formed to address the problem of those who 'unwittingly ruin sport,' recommended the appointment of car Field Masters to direct traffic out hunting. Colonel Wingate Gray suggested that the car Master should acquaint his charges with plans for the day at the meet and identify himself by flying 'a flag or suchlike' from his vehicle. However car followers were not soldiers, and although well intentioned, efforts to marshal them on public roads were doomed to failure. The practice was quietly allowed to drop, but the problem did not go away. The continual heading of foxes prompted local hunting correspondent and immaculately attired foot follower, Peter Warren, who used the pen name Ramle Vale, to appeal to car followers to show greater consideration. In November 1964 he repeated farmers' complaints about hunt followers driving their vehicles across private land without permission and asserted that the best car is the one parked up where it can cause no obstruction or annoyance.

Car followers were not the only threat to sport. Public opposition to hunting was gathering momentum, and in 1960 Members and subscribers were urged to join the RSPCA in order to vote on the charity's forthcoming policy regarding foxhunting. Against this backdrop Ken Goschen had the foresight to urge landowners to reserve sporting rights to the Hunt when selling off land, and thanked Mr John Trimmer for doing exactly that when parting with Butlers covert in 1961. When the good hunting coverts of Old Down, Sutton Wood and Bower's Grove were put on the market by Winchester College early the following year he asked Members to assist with their purchase, which was successfully accomplished by a small syndicate before the end of the year. Such important acquisitions would have met with the approval of three of the Hunt Club's most distinguished Members who reached the end of long and successful lives around this time. George Evans died in 1956, and three years later Members again stood in silence to remember the life of Major F.H.T. Jervoise, from Herriard Park. In January 1961 it was the turn of General the Lord Jeffreys, who had been a Member since 1902, and apart from a short absence on military duties in India, served as Chairman of the Hampshire Hunt Club from 1922 until his death. A stickler for the highest standards of etiquette on and off the hunting field, this titan of the Hampshire Hunt was succeeded as Chairman by Colonel Jervoise Scott[5] of Rotherfield Park.

At a second general meeting in December 1961, Ken Goschen warned that the proposed M3 motorway would cut the country in half and act as a barrier to the run of foxes. When the Chairman invited questions from the floor the huntsman, Bob Jones, was criticised by some of the ladies present for being too slow and lacking in urgency. Sam Scott disclosed that a cavalry officer of his acquaintance had intended to hunt this season, but finding sport totally inadequate compared to pre-war days, had given up on the idea. The old adage that a huntsman is only as good as his last day rang true at the meeting, for Bob's detractors must have forgotten the run of excellent sport he had provided at the end of the previous season. Leslie Aylward spoke up on his behalf, saying that all huntsmen were criticised, even George Evans and Brigadier Selby Lowndes, and that there was a great deal more to consider than a huntsman's performance in the field. Several present were keen for a vote to be taken on Bob Jones's future, but they were reminded that a general meeting had no authority to make such decisions. Sam Scott was worried that an influx of visitors from London would be fed in at the bottom of the subscribers list, until eventually the Hampshire Hunt would be known as a 'Hospital' country.

Bob Jones remained in office for another year but stood down at the end of the 1962–1963 season, which was compromised by one of the worst winters in living memory. There was no hunting or racing during the big freeze of 1963 as plummeting temperatures froze lakes and several rivers solid from late December until early March. After Members accepted Ken Goschen's offer to share hunting the hounds with a professional for the 1963–1964 season, Dennis Boyles was appointed to hunt the doghounds on Tuesdays and Saturdays. The new team made a good start, catching nearly thirty brace during their first season and providing consistently good sport to large fields. The electrocution of a valued doghound on the railway line near Alice Holt during the course of a fine hunt in January 1965 was a low point in an otherwise excellent season, but the hunt was successfully

---

5 Captain Jervoise Bolitho Scott, known to his friends as Jarvie, was MFH 1926–1929 with George Evans. In 1962 Colonel J.B. Scott DL, JP was created a Baronet in New Year's Honours list and became Colonel Sir Jervoise Scott Bt., DL, JP He was also Chairman of the Hunt Club from 1960 until June 1965, the year of his death.

THE HAMPSHIRE HUNT 1749–2022

HAMPSHIRE HUNT

Rates of Subscriptions Season 1964/65

Minimum Subscriptions

1. **Members.**
   Non-hunting Members elected after 1st November, 1909, minimum subscription—£25.
   Members hunting one horse—£40.
   Members hunting more than one horse—£55.
   This subscription of £55 will enable the Member and his family, if resident with him, to hunt.
   In addition a compulsory Wire Fund subscription of £5 for all hunting members (except for owners or occupiers of land exceeding 50 acres in the Hampshire Hunt Country) shall be payable with the annual subscription.

2. **Farmer Members.**
   Non-hunting Farmer Members—£10.
   Hunting Farmer Members—£15.
   A Farmer is one whose principal means of livelihood are derived from farming, and who farms in, or closely adjacent to, the H.H. Country.

3. **Subscribers.**
   Subscribers hunting one horse minimum subscription—£30.
   Subscribers hunting more than one horse—£45.
   This subscription of £45 will enable the Subscriber and his family, if resident with him, to hunt.
   In addition a compulsory Wire Fund subscription of £5 for all hunting subscribers shall be payable with the annual subscription (except owners or occupiers of land in the Hampshire Hunt Country exceeding 50 acres).

4. **Serving Officers of H.M. Forces.**
   Serving Officers of H. M. Forces, who are not Members of the Hunt Club, to pay half the Subscribers' subscription and £5 subscription to the Wire Fund payable with the annual subscription.

5. **Riding Establishments.**
   Proprietors of Riding Establishments to pay the subscription applicable to Subscribers.

6. **Caps.**
   Hunt Club Caps £3 per day to include 10/- in respect of Wire Fund.
   Serving Officers of H.M. Forces to pay half the Cap, namely £1/10/- to include Wire Fund.

7. **Children (i.e., those under the age of 18).**
   Children of Hunting Members, Hunting Subscribers and Farmers will be allowed to hunt without payment but will only become entitled to a Button upon payment of £3/3/-.
   All other children will have the option of paying either 10/- per day inclusive of Wire Fund or £3/3/- for the Season (inclusive of Wire Fund) for which they will receive a Button.

P.T.O.

Rates of subscription for season 1964–1965.

8. **Damage.**
   Damage to fences and gates, crops, etc., must be reported immediately to the Wire Fund Area Managers, as follows:—
   Monday Country: Mr. John Gray, North End Farm, Cheriton, Alresford. Tel. Bramdean 307.
   Tuesday Country: Mr. A. R. L. Aylward, Hall House, Farringdon. Tel. Tisted 275.
   Thursday Country: Mr. J. Rowsell, West Stoke Farm, Stoke Charity. Tel. Sutton Scotney 220.
   Saturday Country: Mr. N. Patrick, Bunces Farm, Runwick, Farnham. Tel. Farnham 6561.

9. **Point to Points.**
   Members and Subscribers are reminded that in order to be qualified to run in Point to Points, Hunters require a Certificate from the Masters stating that the horse has been "regularly and fairly hunted during the present Season with the H.H. by a Member, Subscriber or Farmer (or their children) or the Huntsmen or Whippers-in of the Hunt) and is, in the Master's opinion, a genuine hunter. A Subscriber is defined in the rules as "a person who has paid by February 1st of the current hunting season the minimum annual hunting subscription."
   The Masters require that horses shall be fairly hunted not less than eight times. Horses being qualified should be shown to the Masters at the Meet and cards (which can be obtained from the Hon. Secretaries) brought up for signature after 2 p.m. on the same day.

10. It would assist the Secretaries if Members and Subscribers would pay their Subscriptions by Bankers' Order, for which purpose a form is enclosed.
    Cheques should be made payable to the "Hampshire Hunt Club," and sent to A. R. L. Aylward, Esq. Members and Subscribers will assist the Hunt by paying their Subscriptions as soon as possible after the commencement of the Season, i.e., 1st May, 1964, and in any case not later than October 1st.

11. **The British Field Sports Society.**
    It is hoped that all followers of the H.H. and all well wishers of other Sports of the countryside will become members of the above Society.
    The minimum Subscription is 5/- a year, and further particulars can be obtained from the B.F.S.S. Hon. Local Secretary, N. H. Patrick, Esq., Bunces Farm, Runwick, Farnham, Surrey.

12. **Hunting Appointment Cards** may be obtained from Messrs. C. Mills & Co., Normandy Street, Alton, at 10/6d. for the season.

13. **Dates.**
    Autumn Dance, Aldershot, 30th October, 1964.
    Hampshire Hunt Ball, Winchester, 29th January, 1965.

Joint Honorary Secretaries:

A. R. L. Aylward, Esq., O.B.E.,
Hall House,
Farringdon, Alton.
Tisted 275.

R. R. Edgar, Esq.,
Newton Valance Place,
Nr. Alton.
Tisted 256.

concluded by the rest of the pack.

By 1964 it was costing the Goschens £1,150 of their own money[6] to run the Hunt, but the senior Master told the attendees of a third general meeting in 1964 that he was more concerned by a shortage of foxes than the size of his guarantee. In January 1965 the Goschens tendered their resignation at the end of the season, citing escalating costs and insufficient foxes. When Members met to discuss the best way forward, they calculated that it would cost at least £8,000 to run the hunt four days a week, but only £6,000 if they cut back to three. It was decided to keep an open mind as to future arrangements and to advertise the Mastership in *Horse & Hound* magazine. It took the selection committee less than a month to appoint an Acting Mastership of Colonel Archer Shee, Major General R.H. Barry, CB, CBE, Geoffrey Gregson and John Gray to hunt the country on Tuesdays, Thursdays, and Saturdays with a professional carrying the horn.

With the exception of the Acting Masters' own horses, the Hunt Club undertook to pay all expenses in connection with running the Hunt and authorised expenditure of up to £6,500 for the coming season. When these arrangements were announced in early February the Goschens asked if they could hunt a fourth day in the eastern part of the HH country at their own expense. Some Members favoured this proposal, but others felt that it would divide the country. After a lengthy discussion on the subject, a proposal to allow the Goschens' request was narrowly defeated by twenty-two votes to eighteen. Ken Goschen stated that he and his wife would loyally abide by the decision and do their best to ensure that the new arrangements were successful, but that is not quite how events unfolded over the following years.

The season closed earlier than usual on April 3rd at the Goschens' Silvesters Farm in Froyle, where a large, mounted field came to wish the retiring Masters well, and the couple rode away from the meet down a road lined with cheering foot followers. A busy day followed beneath glorious spring sunshine that included a fast afternoon hunt from Lee Wood to Slade Heath, Locks Grove, Perryland, and on to Clare Farm near Wimble Hill. The highest standards had been maintained throughout the Goschens' twelve-year Mastership during which George Evans's post-war stamp of light framed, active hounds had been maintained at Ropley. The Goschens' departure marked the end of hunting four days a week, that with the

---

6 The Goschens' guarantee was £5,100 but in 1964 Ken Goschen revealed it was costing £6,250 a year to run the Hunt.

exception of the war years and immediate aftermath, had endured for more than two hundred years. As one episode of the Hunt's story drew to a close, so another began, and the appointment of a brand new Mastership in 1965 heralded the dawn of what was to become another golden era in the Hunt's long history.

Chapter Twelve 1965–1975

The Quartermasters and Beyond

Major General R.H. Barry, CB, CBE., Colonel J. Archer Shee, G. Gregson Esq., MC, and J. Gray Esq., 1965–1967, G. Gregson Esq., MC, J. Gray Esq., and A. Edgar Esq., 1967–1970, G. Gregson Esq., MC, J. Gray Esq., and E. A. Thomas Esq., MC, 1970–1971, J. Gray Esq., E.A. Thomas Esq., MC, and the Hon. Mrs Cowen 1971–1972, J. Gray Esq., E.A. Thomas Esq., MC, the Hon. Mrs Cowen and G. Gregson Esq., MC, 1972–1974, J. Gray Esq., the Hon. Mrs Cowen and G. Gregson Esq., MC, 1974–1975.

Major General R.H. Barry, CB, CBE, Colonel J. Archer Shee, Geoffrey Gregson MC., and John Gray become Acting Joint Masters in 1965, Frank Hazeltine first season as huntsman, the Hampshire Hunt Supporters Club, Anthony Edgar joins the Mastership in 1967, terriermen Eric Withey and Kruger North, Ken Goschen's private pack and MFHA resolution in 1968, foot and mouth disease in 1967 and 1968, Brian Walters becomes huntsman, cross country race at Rotherfield, improvements to accommodation at kennels and Miss Atherton legacy, Edward Thomas joins the Mastership in 1970, The Hon. Shelagh Cowen joins the Mastership in 1971, Brian Walters accident and is replaced as huntsman by Geoffrey Gregson, saboteurs appear for the first time, Michael Bowman-Manifold, Masters' guarantee.

Apart from the First World War, when Frederick Coryton's committee had run the Hunt, Joint Masterships of the Hampshire Hunt had never exceeded three individuals, but the appointment of several Masters to share the burden of organising increasingly challenging hunting was to become the new normal throughout hunting England. In appointing a quartet of respected local men, the selection committee had chosen carefully and well. Major General R.H. Barry, CB, CBE,[1] who would later succeed Sir John Floyd as Chairman of the Hunt Club,

---

1   Major General R.H. Barry, CB, CBE was known as Dick by all his many friends.

had enjoyed a distinguished war career with the Special Operations Executive, and became an enthusiastic follower in his Land Rover after he gave up riding. Colonel Jack Archer Shee was another long-standing Member of the Hunt Club, whose home at Inadown near Newton Valence was a popular meet in the old Tuesday country. Geoffrey Gregson MC won his Military Cross during the Second World War and was the second son of the renowned Molly Gregson, who had been a Master of the Crawley and Horsham from 1939 until 1961. Geoffrey lived on a farm in the Chiddingfold country near Alford with his second wife but thought nothing of driving an hour or more several times a week to reach meets of the Hampshire Hunt. Of the four Quartermasters – as they quickly became known throughout the Hampshire Hunt country – John Gray, a farmer from Cheriton near Alresford, was destined to remain at the helm of the Hampshire Hunt for by far the longest time.

Born into a farming family in 1921, at just nineteen years of age John found himself owner of 30 heavy shire horses and tenant of some 1700 acres around Martyr Worthy and Itchen Abbas after his father died prematurely from cancer. Some of these tenancies were relinquished in the late 1940s, but he had been unable to afford the asking price of £10 an acre for Bridget's when given the opportunity to buy that farm as a sitting tenant. In the early 1950s John took on the tenancy of North End Farm near Cheriton, which was being farmed half-heartedly by the Tichborne estate since the departure of the previous occupant, and in 1959 he succeeded in purchasing the farm that would be home for the rest of his life. Come rain or shine, John Gray rose early every morning to ride his horse around the farm wearing leather boots and gaiters before returning to breakfast, which was often followed by a long day riding to hounds. A gifted stockman blessed with a sense of humour, sound common sense and a quiet, understated charm, John Gray was to blossom as a Master of Hounds in the mould of his popular predecessor from another century, Henry Deacon.

The widely respected hunting farmer was equally relaxed sharing a drink with a peer of the realm or a gamekeeper, but he was also a pragmatist with the unerring ability to call the right shot on complex conundrums, year in year out. A family man to the core, John had taken his two younger brothers and sister under his wing following the death of their father, and together with his wife Pat raised three fine daughters. He found time to encourage others too, notably young Hopper[2] Corbett, who was also destined for high office within the Hunt. Hopper refers to her hunting

---

2   Since a very young age, Lucinda Corbett has been known as Hopper.

mentor as Uncle John and remembers how he commanded instant authority from all. 'John Gray didn't rule with an iron hand' she says, 'he ruled with a velvet glove. But no one ever questioned his authority.' Such attributes stood John in good stead during his 28 years as a JP, and for an even longer term on Cheriton Parish Council.

The new Mastership appointed Frank Hazeltine in place of Dennis Boyles, who left to hunt the Atherstone and went on to crown a distinguished career in hunt service as huntsman to the Devon & Somerset Staghounds. Frank went well across country and was good on the horn but was something of a dour character. When asked by John Gray how a whipper-in was getting on a fortnight into his new job, Frank replied, 'I don't know Guv'nor, I haven't spoken to him yet.' The new huntsman provided the best Opening Meet sport for some years, which was written up in *Horse & Hound* by Ramle Vale, who filed regular hunting reports for the *Hampshire Chronicle* but reserved red letter days for a magazine read by hunting enthusiasts throughout the UK and beyond. His observations are a reminder of how many farmers grew kale in the sixties and seventies, including Leslie Aylward, whose field above Farringdon provided the first fox of the new season in 1965. After an excursion downhill into the Hartley Vale, hounds found again in Mr Bowtell's kale and pursued a third fox into the Hambledon country at White Horse Gorse during a brilliant day when they hunted through five different parishes. Hounds returned to Newton Valence in February and marked their fox to ground in Bush Down after another exceptionally busy day. Ramle Vale noted that the pack were all on at the earth, and that Leslie Aylward was the only surviving member of the field, despite feeling sore after a disagreement with an iron gate the previous week.

The 1966 Opening Meet at Newton Valence.

In June 1965 former Master, Hunt Trustee, landowner and longstanding Member, Colonel Sir Jervoise Scott Bt., DL, JP resigned as Hunt Chairman, the position being filled by Lieutenant Colonel John Floyd from Lovington near Alresford. The Hampshire Hunt Supporters Club was also started this year under the chairmanship of Dick Smith, and immediately set to work organising fundraising events that included terrier shows, clay pigeon shoots, barbeques, and a dance at Herriard Park. Within a year the Supporters Club had enrolled over 300 paid up members and went on to provide stewards for the hunter trials, sponsor the Members' race at the point-to-point, sell race cards, and run a Grand National draw. The HHSC[3] contributed £500 to the cost of a walk-in freezer at the kennels, but when its new Chairman, Geoffrey Newberry, gave a résumé at the 1968 Hunt AGM he lamented a depressing lack of enthusiasm from certain areas of the Hunt, saying, 'members of the Supporters Club felt rather left out in the cold by Hunt Club Members.' Matters were not helped by a suggestion from the floor that HHSC members should wear badges and post car stickers to aid identification when both methods of recognition were already in place.

The Acting Masters assumed greater financial responsibility for the 1966–1967 season and became bona fide Joint Masters on a guarantee of £6,500 in an agreement whereby the horses, saddlery, vehicles and hounds remained the property of the Hunt Club. There was a run of good sport during November 1966 that included three four-mile points, but hunting was suspended for three weeks in January 1967 due to an outbreak of foot and mouth disease in the south of the county; despite the disruption, hounds ended the season in March having killed 32½ brace in 90 days hunting. The Quartermasters resigned after two years in office,[4] but Messrs Gregson and Gray agreed to continue with Anthony Edgar replacing General Barry and Colonel Archer Shee. Anthony was the son of Robin and Esme Edgar, who lived at Newton Valence Place where they hosted a succession of Opening Meets during the sixties and seventies. Anthony and his first wife, Roberta, lived at Lower Green, Hawkley where they also laid on generous meets after which the enthusiastic host took great pleasure in leading the field over his park railing en route to the first draw.

By now well into his seventies, Eric Withey also retired at the end of the season after many years' service to the Hunt. The popular terrierman was presented

---

3   The Hampshire Hunt Supporters Club.

4   Some records incorrectly state that Major General Barry and Colonel Archer Shee left after their first season. They retired on May 1st 1967 having completed two seasons in office.

THE QUARTERMASTERS AND BEYOND 1965–1975

H.H.
Two outstanding hunts with points of four miles

More excellent sport has been enjoyed of late. From Brockwood Dean there was a painstaking hunt from Bramdean Common to the main road. Then a fox found near the West Meon Hut led hounds to the garden at Pursers, on to West Tisted Manor and over Mr. Samuel's land to the lime quarries at Ropley.

Hounds ran on to Little Down and then into the thick row at Lyeway. There were excursions to Mr. Morgan's farm buildings and then the edge of Old Down before they were stopped at a late hour when the fox finally "bedded down" somewhere in Mr. Morgan's buildings. This hunt included a four-mile point.

Another capital hunt followed the Hedge Corner fixture on November 21. A fox believed disturbed by our neighbours was seen by Mr. Leslie Aylward entering the H.H. country, and hounds were laid on his line. He was a bold traveller, and they ran from near the White Horse, over the farms of Mr. Dick Hughes, Mr. Kinney and Mr. Collard, through Goleigh Wood and Lyewood and raced on to Noar Hill.

Running round the hill, the line was taken to Blackmoor and then the Lythe at Selborne. Crossing over the top to Long Copse hounds marked to ground, having recorded another four-mile point and left most of the 90 followers spreadeagled across country. RAMLE VALE.

Above: Two four-mile points in November 1966.

Top left: John Gray MFH 1965–1996.

Left: Presentation to Eric Withey at the 1967 Opening Meet following his retirement as terrierman.

Mr. Eric Withey (73) receives a cheque in recognition of his 12 years' service in charge of the H.H. Ropley Terrier Kennels. The presentation was made at the Hunt's opening meet at Newton Valence on Monday by Mr. G. G. A. Gregson (Joint Master). Mr. Withey's retirement comes after a lifelong interest in hunting.

– 163 –

with a cheque for £200 at the 1967 Opening Meet at Newton Valence and his photograph, flanked by three Joint Masters, was published in the local press. Eric returned to the fold three years later to help marshal traffic on hunting days but was replaced as terrierman by Kruger North whose long wheelbase Land Rover was loaded with fencing materials and sandwich boards. The signs were positioned on busy roads when hounds were in the vicinity and had the words 'Hounds Please' depicted in large capital letters on one side and 'Thank You' on the other. Kruger unwittingly featured in a typical John Gray anecdote when he was sent by the Joint Master to warn his eight year old daughter that he had temporarily deserted the hunting field. 'Miss Jane' said Kruger when he eventually caught up with the bewildered girl 'your father said to tell you his horse has dropped dead, and he has gone home to fetch another.'

Former Master and Hunt Trustee, Ken Goschen, caused something of a ripple at the AGM in July 1968 when announcing that he had made an application to the MFHA for part of the Hampshire Hunt country lying east of an imaginary line from Froyle to Odiham to be allocated to his own private pack of hounds, which he founded with drafts from the Hampshire Hunt and Duke of Beaufort's after resigning the HH Mastership in 1965. He reminded Members that his previous request for this country had been narrowly defeated and believed there was still considerable support for his project. He felt there was plenty of room for both the Hampshire Hunt and his own hounds and asked that there should be no ill feeling. The Chairman, Lt. Colonel Sir John Floyd, thanked Mr Goschen, but explained that the Trustees of the country were not in a position to give away any part of it, after which Mr Goschen departed the meeting.

After the completion of any other business, Members resumed discussing Ken Goschen's request. Colonel Archer Shee reported that the Chiddingfold and Leconfield Hunt had already allocated Mr Goschen a small piece of country that the Hampshire Hunt considered to be their own, and that he, together with Messrs Gregson, Gray and Aylward, would shortly be attending an MFHA meeting to resolve the issue. After others expressed concern that Mr Goschen's application to hunt the Froyle country might be considered at the same meeting, it was decided to advise the Association in writing that the Hampshire Hunt would not discuss or agree to this additional proposal. However there was also some sympathy for Mr Goschen who lived and owned land in the Froyle area, and suggestions that a 'local arrangement' might be amicably attained.

Later that month the MFHA defined the country under dispute and confirmed that it belonged to the Hampshire Hunt. The Association stated that they had no power to reallocate any country registered to the Hampshire Hunt and stressed the necessity of maintaining hunt boundaries 'in these days of development,' but also ruled that consideration for Mr Goschen's hounds should be given so long as he is Master. The MFHA Committee hoped that the Masters of the Hampshire Hunt would grant Mr Goschen as many invitation days as possible provided that he keep to the specified draw. The Masters allowed him five days hunting in the Hampshire Hunt country the following season but granted further concessions as time went on. Ken's private pack continued operating until the early nineties by which time the landscape in his eastern corner of the country was becoming too urbanised to hunt across. Mr Goschen's hounds left their kennels at Isnage Farm, Bentley on March 30th 1991 for their final day after 25 years during which their followers had never been asked to pay a subscription. Several, including Mrs Anne Inskip who walked puppies for both Hunts and was secretary to Mr Goschen's hounds for a decade from 1965, resumed hunting with the Hampshire Hunt.

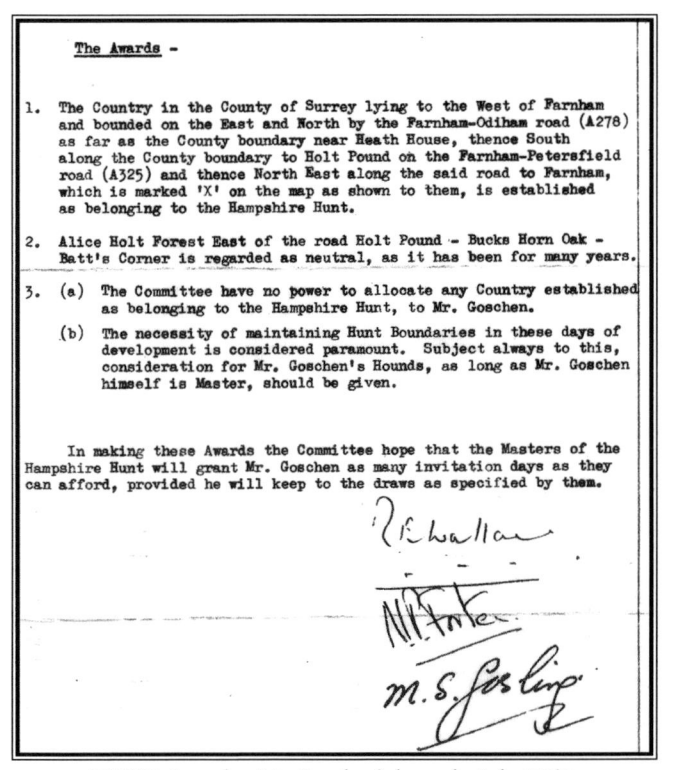

The Awards –

1. The Country in the County of Surrey lying to the West of Farnham and bounded on the East and North by the Farnham-Odiham road (A278) as far as the County boundary near Heath House, thence South along the County boundary to Holt Pound on the Farnham-Petersfield road (A325) and thence North East along the said road to Farnham, which is marked 'X' on the map as shown to them, is established as belonging to the Hampshire Hunt.

2. Alice Holt Forest East of the road Holt Pound – Bucks Horn Oak – Batt's Corner is regarded as neutral, as it has been for many years.

3. (a) The Committee have no power to allocate any Country established as belonging to the Hampshire Hunt, to Mr. Goschen.

   (b) The necessity of maintaining Hunt Boundaries in these days of development is considered paramount. Subject always to this, consideration for Mr. Goschen's Hounds, as long as Mr. Goschen himself is Master, should be given.

In making these Awards the Committee hope that the Masters of the Hampshire Hunt will grant Mr. Goschen as many invitation days as they can afford, provided he will keep to the draws as specified by them.

MFHA Award re Mr Goschen's hounds, July 1965.

The dreaded foot and mouth disease returned shortly after the Opening Meet in 1967, and there was no hunting at all from November 16th until February 1st 1968 when the Minister of Agriculture allowed sport to resume under strict conditions that included a ban on any visitors. Hunting restarted the day restrictions were lifted with a lawn meet at John and Pat Gray's North End Farm, after which the field were entertained by foxes from Cheriton Wood and Bramdean Common. Frank Hazeltine left at the end of this difficult season and was replaced as professional huntsman by Brian Walters, who commenced cubhunting in September 1968 amongst the commons in the south east corner of the country. He made an excellent start by catching his first fox after twenty minutes' hard pursuit, and in early October provided a four-mile point from The Straights via Kingsley to Bordon Station where hounds again caught their quarry. The cross country race – now described as a ride so as not to fall foul of Weatherbys – reappeared at Rotherfield Park in mid-October, where Geoffrey Gregson won the lightweight division and 27 competitors galloped over four miles and 23 fences. Afterwards 180 guests sat down to lunch inside the house, and since the ride was now able to operate as a fundraiser, the Hunt Club benefited by £181.

Without the likes of Herman Andreae and Ken Goschen to generously prop up finances in times of difficulty, the Hunt Club appreciated every pound raised from activities such as the cross country ride together with donations from the thriving HHSC. In addition to the usual running expenses, modernisation of hunt staff accommodation at Ropley was still something of an ongoing project. The conversion of a loft into living space for girl grooms and the renovation of the Hunt Lodge for the benefit of Masters and Members were both financed by a generous bequest from Miss Atherton, who in 1967 left the residue of her estate to the Hunt Club, 'in memory of the good days spent with the Hampshire Hunt and the friendship and courtesy shown to her by its Members.' In 1969 a thatched cottage to the east of the kennels was sold after it had become uninhabitable, and the difficulties of attracting hunt staff to live in such conditions had become apparent. The sale raised enough money to finance the construction of two three bedroom prefabricated bungalows at a cost of £3,000 each.

During the 1969–1970 season seven days were lost to snow, but hounds went out 63 times after the Opening Meet and killed 36½ brace, their best tally since reducing to three days a week. A successful winter was complemented by a brilliant summer on the flags that got underway when Brian Walters garnered an armful of rosettes at the South of England Show at Ardingly in June. The following month hounds were shown at Peterborough where Lurcher won the best single doghound from the restricted unentered couples class and Drummer, who had been walked as a puppy by Lady Scott at Rotherfield Park, was awarded the reserve doghound championship having triumphed in the open unentered class. Both unentered dogs were by Heythrop sires, and their achievements in the showring were a fitting tribute to the sound breeding polices of Geoffrey Gregson, who had assumed control of hounds and kennels when joining the Mastership five years earlier.

Anthony Edgar left the Mastership in 1970 and ten years later joined Captain Wallace as a Joint Master of the Exmoor Hunt. Anthony was replaced by Edward Thomas, who joined Messrs Gregson and Gray on a guarantee of £7,500. Edward and Ruth Thomas lived at South Warnborough Manor, which was the setting for generous meets and a succession of Pony Club hunter trials. Edward was invariably mounted on a roan hunter; his wife never rode but was a terrific supporter of the hunt and a provider of superb hunting teas. Their son, Hugh, whipped in around the time his father was a Joint Master, and after a successful eventing career went on to become Director of Badminton Horse Trials. In February 1971 heads were bowed at Harkers Crossroads in memory of Leslie Aylward described by Ramle Vale as a farmer and foxhunter extraordinaire, which was followed by the best day of the season to date.

Geoffrey Gregson retired at the end of an especially open season, leaving John Gray and Edward Thomas to continue with The Hon. Mrs Shelagh Cowen, who lived at Pipers Hill near Sutton Scotney and was known to all as Toddy. Lord Rank's daughter was a popular and much loved part of the Hunt, and together with her sister Urkie,[5] had been brought up in the Old Surrey and Burstow country. The foot followers presented Geoffrey Gregson with a book of G.D. Armour's hunting paintings at his final meet at Bentworth Lodge on April 3rd 1971, to mark their appreciation of an MFH who had, 'always been kind and helpful to the dismounted brigade and never lost his temper.' Ramle Vale observed that the retiring Master, who had been responsible for managing both kennels and stables at Ropley, 'leaves a first rate pack of hounds, and a well foxed country that has been fairly hunted during his six seasons as a Joint Master.' David Randall also left as first whipper-in to go the Albrighton Woodland and was replaced by Ron Quarmby, who would soon be taking on more duties than he anticipated.

---

5   Ursula, always known as Urkie, became Urkie Newton after marriage and went on to found the Melton Hunt Club in Leicestershire.

Hounds leaving Newton Valence Place after the 1970 Opening Meet, painted by John King. From left to right; in the foreground Brian Walters (huntsman), Anthony Edgar, Geoffrey Gregson MFH, John Gray MFH, Sir Arundel Neave, John Rowsell, Colonel Archer Shee, Lt Colonel Sir James Scott, Greenie Fuller, Violet Coryton, Sue Maxse, Shelagh Cowen, Will Ings, Leslie Aylward, Simon Harrap, Peter Andreae, Pam Sharples, General Barry, Lyn Holmes, Undine Gregson, Nicholas Embiricos (on pony) and Edward Thomas; standing Colonel Coryton, Mr and Mrs Robin Edgar.

THE QUARTERMASTERS AND BEYOND 1965–1975

Geoffrey Gregson was absent from the sharp end of hunt business for no more than a few months, for in 1971 Brian Walters broke both his legs in an horrific car crash a week before the start of cubhunting. Left without a huntsman, and with a new whipper-in who did not know the country, Members appealed to Geoffrey to help out as amateur huntsman for the rest of the season with Ron Quarmby turning hounds. The new team provided an excellent day from the Opening Meet at the Edgars' Newton Valence Place in November, but later that month hunt saboteurs appeared for the first time during a meet at The Star Inn, Bentworth, where they sprayed hounds and horses with Anti Mate. The press reported that the hunt was abandoned after a few hours, however thanks to the meticulously compiled hunting diaries of Michael Bowman-Manifold, we know that a busy hunting day followed.

Michael Bowman-Manifold could have represented any number of people throughout England for whom life during winter revolved around foxhunting. A research radio engineer and physicist by training and vocation, the bachelor's detailed hunting diaries and press cuttings from 1951–1981 have provided valuable information, without which there would have been many gaps in the narrative of the Hunt he so cherished. Born in 1902, he was taught to ride by Gerald Barnes's father at Winchester and came to the Hampshire Hunt after switching allegiance from the Chiddingfold in 1951. Michael kept his somewhat steady but much loved hunters at livery with Gerald Barnes at Hall Farm, and like the character from a famous Surtees sketch,[6] did not hunt to astonish others, but for his own pleasure. This had little to do with hounds, but everything to do with personal triumphs and disasters on the back of his own horses. His diary entries are accompanied by his weight (between thirteen and fourteen stone), and the number of fences jumped (rarely more than a dozen) for every day hunted, the text liberally peppered with abbreviations and annotations. Half a jump equalled a refusal, three points signalled his horse had hit the top rail and the word 'exit' written in the appropriate place besides one of Ramle Vale's hunting reports indicates the point when Michael turned for home. He is still remembered for his exclamation, 'loose pony with a child on top' as a young and out of control John Maxse careered past him on a 12.2hh pony in the 1970s.

Geoffrey Gregson re-joined the Mastership on May 1st 1972 to hunt hounds on a guarantee of £8,500. A good season followed during which the predominantly Heythrop-bred hounds accounted for 35½ brace in 36 mornings' cubhunting and 65

---

[6] 'Happy are those who hunt for their own pleasure, and not to astonish others' is taken from one of the humorous sporting sketches of the writer and satirist, Robert Smith Surtees (1805–1864).

Simon Harrap qualifying Major E. T. O'Reilly's Morning Air at Rotherfield Park in 1967.
Geoffrey Gregson MFH riding his own Comforting Wave, winner of the HH Members' race in 1972 and 1973.

days proper, the season only marred by the death of two hounds in a road accident. Edward Thomas left the Mastership at the end of the following season and was written up in glowing terms by Ramle Vale. 'Always pleasant and cheerful he has been a popular member of the HH field for many years and during recent years has been an active Master and played an invaluable role in the Saturday country in which he lives.' The early seventies were also notable for the success of fundraisers such as dances, a hunt ball, hunter trials, hunt ride and the point-to-point which contributed nearly half the cost of the Masters' £8,500 guarantee. As this sum only covered two thirds of their expenditure, the Masters' allowance was raised to £10,000 for the 1973–1974 season, together with an undertaking from the Hunt Club to pay the new VAT tax should it become due on the guarantee.

In 1974 the long running and contentious issue of Lady Members was resolved when they were finally invited to join the Hampshire Hunt Club. The topic had last been considered in 1966 following a letter from Lady Charlotte Bonham Carter, who thought the time had come to consider the point in greater detail, however 'there was (sic) by no means unanimous feelings' on the divisive subject and the Chairman decided the matter should be postponed for discussion until the next meeting. Although Oney Goschen had been elected an Honorary Member in 1966, the privilege of being the first fully fledged Lady Member of the Hunt Club fell to Sue Maxse, who recalls feeling very honoured, but that the only tangible change was replacing the plain HH buttons on her coat with ones bearing the Prince of Wales's crest.

Both Shelagh Cowen and Geoffrey Gregson left the Mastership in 1975. Geoffrey went straight to Northumberland to take up his new appointment as Joint Master and huntsman to the Tynedale, a county that later attracted Shelagh Cowen to join the Duke of Northumberland in the Mastership of the Percy Hunt in 1988. Geoffrey Gregson went out on a high note after the bitch pack scored a four-mile point following the closing meet at Newton Valence Place and finished his last season, during which gate shutters were trialled for the first time, with a record tally of 37 brace. Ron Quarmby, who was moving to the Puckeridge and Thurlow, showed the young hounds at an April puppy show at which the retiring Joint Master and amateur huntsman was presented with a painting by John King of hounds being collected at Horsedown Common. Geoffrey Gregson thanked everyone warmly for their help during his Mastership and paid tribute to his hound breeding predecessors George Evans and Ken Goschen. The onlookers included a slim, immaculately turned out figure who had made quite a name for himself as the North Cotswold's professional huntsman. In just a few weeks' time Steve Andrews would move from Gloucestershire down to Ropley to take up the same position with the Hampshire Hunt.

Michael Bowman-Manifold (on left) and Will Ings.

Chapter Thirteen 1975–1981

A New Broom Sweeps Clean

J. Gray Esq., M.R. Porter Esq., A.J. Maxse Esq., 1975–1981,
J. Gray Esq., M.R. Porter Esq., A.J. Maxse Esq.,
F. Momber Esq., 1981–1983.

Anthony Maxse and Michael Porter join the Mastership in 1975, Steve Andrews appointed huntsman and his first season, rampant inflation and financial challenges for the Hunt Club, sale of snuff box and property, Peter Andreae and Hunt equity portfolio, cross country ride at Rotherfield, HHSC and Tally Ho! magazine, sponsored ride, 1979–80 season and visit of HRH the Prince of Wales, financial recovery and Hunt philanthropy, Frank Momber joins the Mastership in 1981.

On May 1st 1975, John Gray, who was the only remaining Master from the original 1965 Quartermasters, was joined by Anthony Maxse and Michael Porter in an Acting Mastership to hunt the country twice a week up until February 1st, and three days thereafter. Tony Maxse hunted as a child with his great uncle's[1] Leconfield pack in West Sussex, and after Eton and Sandhurst joined the Coldstream Guards. During his army career he was Aide-de-Camp to the Governor of Cyprus but also found time to enjoy hunting in Leicestershire from Melton Mowbray. Tony, Sue and their three children lived at Pelham Place, which was the venue for meets in winter, the junior Pony Club camp in summer and fundraising evenings on behalf of the Hunt throughout the year. Amongst the most popular of these events were a private viewing of the film, *The Belstone Fox*, and a dinner with the Speaker of the House of Commons, Bernard Weatherill. Tony was a popular Saturday Field Master and later, as Treasurer, ran a tight ship when in charge of administering accounts and invoices for the collection of fallen stock. Tony was to remain as the Hunt's Treasurer right up until 2017, when he was succeeded by the equally efficient and hardworking Kate

---

[1] Charles Henry Wyndham, 3rd Baron Leconfield, GVCO, MFH.

Andrews. After retiring from the saddle he followed hounds enthusiastically on foot with his border terrier, and his passion for walking led to the Maxse Walk each spring. This hundred-mile trek was often accompanied by hounds and hunt staff during the early stages and raised such huge sums for cancer research that Tony was awarded the MBE for his services to charity.

Michael Porter hunted with the Aldenham Harriers in Hertfordshire as a boy, where he helped out in kennels and on the hunting field, before his family moved to Sussex after the war where Geoffrey Gregson's mother was firmly in charge of the Crawley and Horsham. He later took a farming position in Leicestershire and enjoyed riding his cob with the Fernie Hunt before moving south in 1962 to manage Headley Wood Farm in the eastern part of the Hampshire Hunt country. On becoming a Joint Master, Michael assumed responsibility for running the kennels, overseeing the hound breeding, and organising the puppy show, which was an opportunity to showcase the quality and active stamp of hound he was determined to maintain at Ropley. In common with his close friend, Joint Master and fellow farmer, John Gray, Michael harboured old fashioned values and stood for no nonsense. He ran the unfashionable Tuesday country surrounding his own farm, an often trappy landscape of commons and heathland that became increasingly important as shooting interests put pressure on other areas of the Hunt country. The Blackmoor estate, Longmoor Ranges, Ludshott Common and Downlands were generally well foxed, and the setting for many a fine hound hunt.

The appointment of Steve Andrews to hunt hounds sent ripples of excitement across Hampshire, for the Masters could hardly have chosen anyone better qualified, or more dedicated to the pursuit of excellence. The huntsman's impeccably timed arrival at a prominent and historically important Hunt would consolidate a glowing reputation, and over the next sixteen years Steve would endear himself to all with his dedication, style, and bravery across country. He started in hunt service with the Cowdray before moving to the Atherstone in 1950 to turn hounds to Captain Brian Parry and the professional Sidney Littleworth. When Sidney left in 1953 Steve was promoted to hunt the doghounds in his place, and six years later moved with his new wife Joann as huntsman of the South Staffordshire. Getting wind of that Hunt's pending amalgamation with the Meynell, he accepted an offer from his old mentor, Captain Parry, to hunt the North Cotswold hounds in 1962. After twelve happy seasons in Gloucestershire, the professional huntsman was obliged to make way for the arrival of Captain Brian Fanshawe in 1975, who was to hunt hounds as an amateur.

A NEW BROOM SWEEPS CLEAN 1975–1981

As Hopper Cavendish explains, the North Cotswold's loss was to be the Hampshire Hunt's gain. 'I can still recall the enormous effect on the Hunt when Steve Andrews first arrived,' she remembers, 'suddenly we had this dynamic, immaculate huntsman who rode beautiful horses and whose absolute number one priority was to make it fun for the ladies and gentlemen. He quickly found his way around the country, built countless new hunt jumps, and almost immediately the Hampshire Hunt were flying in some style. When hounds found, his excitement in cheering them on would almost stop your heart. He encouraged farmers and young people to hunt, and if someone showed the slightest interest, he would lend them a horse and get them out.' Hounds were in top form for his first Opening Meet at Newton Valence on November 4th 1975, where entertainment was provided by foxes from Bush Down and Mr Derick Faulkner's kale at Norton Farm. The huntsman took a heavy fall negotiating an awkward fence in the morning but despite being badly shaken kept going until blowing for home at dusk.

This was the shape of things to come, for Steve Andrews was fanatical about recovering as quickly as possible from any accident or mishap that might prevent him from going hunting. Further red letter days followed, including several four-mile points, and by December, Ramle Vale was informing readers of the *Hampshire Chronicle*, 'that hounds have never looked sharper,' and predicting 'that given fair scenting conditions Steve Andrews will handle many foxes.' Steve had no enthusiasm for showing during summer except at the puppy show, which may have been a disappointment to those accustomed to seeing Hampshire Hunt hounds in the ribbons at Ardingly and Peterborough. Existing lines at Ropley were further enhanced by the introduction of North Cotswold blood, which blended well with the pedigrees of hounds nurtured by Michael Porter's predecessors, George Evans, Ken Goschen and Geoffrey Gregson.

Sport could hardly have been more exciting in the hunting field, but in 1975 the Hunt Club was facing a loss of £2,700[2] and the Masters a shortfall of £1,500 in their guarantee against a backdrop of rampant inflation. By 1976 the economic outlook was so bleak under Harold Wilson's Labour government that the Chancellor of the Exchequer, Denis Healey, warned of 'possible wholesale domestic liquidation…the magnitude of this threat is quite incalculable.' No organisation was immune from the dire financial situation, and the Hunt Club Chairman, Major General Dick Barry, appealed to all Members and subscribers to donate an extra

---

2   £2,700 was the size of George Evans's entire guarantee sixty two years earlier in 1913.

£20 to help the Hunt through a very difficult period. Finances would have been even worse were it not for the generosity of farmers such as John Gray, his brother David, cousin George Gray, Michael Porter, Simon McCowen and others who provided all the hay, straw, oats, and sugar beet pulp required for the horses at Ropley.

In addition to the routine costs of running the Hunt, there were ongoing problems with the sewerage and drainage systems at the Ropley kennels, which were a constant source of trouble and expense. In order to rectify this problem and put the Hunt on a sound financial footing, Members considered selling off the family silver, which included property, coverts, and artefacts. Recently retired Master, Shelagh Cowen, organised a fundraising auction in July 1975 where the lots included a silver snuff box featuring a galloping fox and embossed with 'Tally Ho!' on the lid, which had been presented to the Hunt Club by George Lowther in 1812. The box had previously been produced for Members to admire in 1900 and 1948 and was collected from the bank for its third recorded appearance on March 9th 1975, where there was unanimous agreement that the treasure be sold. Mrs Cowen's auction made £3,200 but there is no record of who purchased the silver snuff box.

Members also discussed dispensing with the farmers' cocktail party, which had replaced their point-to-point lunch of old, and even considered asking farmers to contribute towards the cost of running the event. When it was suggested that The Gullet be sold to raise funds, Peter Andreae said he would like to discuss this proposal with his family, since the covert had originally been bought by his grandfather, and former Master, Herman Andreae, and later donated to the Hunt Club. The Andreaes had no objection to the sale, which Members decided to postpone for the time being. However it was agreed to sell the Hunt Lodge, a substantial Victorian house that had been home to George Evans, for not less than £15,000. The proceeds would clear the Hunt's anticipated debt and leave a residue of £9,000 to carry forward; the property duly realised £15,859 when it was sold in 1975. Later the same year the sale of two cottages at Ropley raised a further £16,000 and put the Hunt in a sound financial position.

Members could rest assured that the proceeds of sale would be invested wisely in bonds and equities by Peter Andreae, who managed the Hunt Club's equity portfolio and had been a loyal Member of the Hunt Club since 1964. As his grandfather lived at Moundsmere, Peter and his four siblings were brought up by their parents, Sonny, and Clodagh, at Bentworth Lodge. Sonny hunted with the New

A NEW BROOM SWEEPS CLEAN 1975–1981

Forest and the Hampshire Hunts and gave his name to a covert at Bentworth called Sonny's Bank, which enjoyed the reputation of a sure find on hunting days. In 1976 Peter purchased Thedden estate next to Bentworth much to the benefit of hunting, and in the fullness of time also inherited Bentworth Lodge and the surrounding land from his father. Hounds continue to receive a warm welcome across both estates throughout the season, which always closes with a hunt breakfast and final meet at Shalden Farm.

The cross country ride, which had been run on and off since the inaugural race in 1959, enjoyed a purple patch between 1975 and 1981, when the Rotherfield event was hugely popular with competitors and spectators alike. The race was now run in January and usually followed by a midday meet of the hounds, but in 1979 it had to be postponed until the end of February due to prolonged severe weather. The rescheduled race was won by Charlie Petre on Paper Round, who just beat Simon Harrap[3] riding Don Aire, and Hopper Cavendish was the first lady home. Charlie's father had won the 1946 Grand National on Lovely Cottage, a 25-1 shot trained by Tommy Rayson on the gallops at Worthy Down, where the race for the Hampshire Hunt Cup had been run in the late 1700s. Other winners of the cross country ride included Janie Swinburn, wife of General Richard Swinburn who commanded the Aldershot Garrison, and Duncan Munro-Kerr who represented Britain as a showjumper. In 1981 the cross country ride moved to a different part of the Rotherfield estate at Colemore, as permanent grassland surrounding the house was needed for a British Horse Society event, however the new course was beset by flints and the race was not repeated. After two successful years the BHS[4] event at Rotherfield became a Three Day Event which ran for eleven years and hosted two Junior and Young Rider European Championships. Although run by the BHS, the Hunt Club benefitted financially since they were able to charge for the provision of several ancillary services.

Meanwhile the Hampshire Hunt Supporters Club went from strength to strength and consolidated its position as a key benefactor to the Hunt, providing amongst other items, half the cost of a new Land Rover in 1977 and a new flesh trailer two years later. In 1979 Angela Cooper, who lived on the Rotherfield estate with her husband Harry and the ubiquitous terrier, became Secretary of the

---

3 Simon Harrap went one better six weeks later when winning the 1979 Members' race at the HH point-to-point from Sir James Scott's Albergian, ridden by his son Alex in the fastest contest of the day.

4 British Horse Society.

HORSE AND HOUND, November 28, 1975
The H.H. meet at Bentley

Huntsman Steve Andrews leads the H. H. hounds from their recent meet at Marsh House, Bentley. Andrews joined the H. H. this season after having previously been huntsman to the North Cotswold, and with him as first whipper-in went his son Stephen (*bottom right*). The H. H. is now a committee-controlled pack and Mr. A. J. Maxse (*top right*) is one of the three Acting-Masters. *Left*: Among those at the meet was Sir Humphrey Prideaux.

Horse & Hound report from the meet at Marsh House, Bentley in November 1975.

HRH Princess Anne with Steve Andrews (mounted) and John Gray MFH at the European Junior Three Day Event Championship Horse Trials at Rotherfield Park in 1982.

Supporters Club, and remained the driving force behind all its activities for nearly thirty years. Angela is still remembered for her old HHSC jumper, whose logo of a running fox had become so stretched over the years that it resembled a sausage dog instead of a fox. One of her many achievements was to replace the newsletter with a more comprehensive and stylish booklet named *Tally Ho!* which featured reports on hunting, social and fundraising events and a smattering of fascinating anecdotes relating to the Hunt's past history and characters. It is thanks to the inaugural edition of this excellent publication that we know over 400 guests attended the farmers' cocktail party at The Officers' Mess at RAF Odiham on April 6th 1979.

In addition to publishing *Tally Ho!* there were numerous fundraising events such as the summer horse show at Rotherfield to organise, and the provision of volunteers to help with the point-to-point at Hackwood and other equestrian events run by the Hunt Club. These included the HH hunter trials, which took place over an all grass course at Drury Farm, Bentworth where Gerald Barnes's son, Tom, had set up a successful livery yard of his own. Dave Marsh, who was Chairman of HHSC from 1983–1988 and later President, was another key player within the organisation. He lived conveniently close to the kennels and together with his wife, Lou, was a prolific walker of hound puppies. Dave became a good friend to Steve Andrews and spent countless hours helping prepare for the puppy show in summer and driving the hunt lorry carrying second horses in winter.

Other fundraisers included a sponsored ride organised by Giles Rowsell and George Gray, the Joint Master's cousin, which ran for twenty years from the mid-seventies onwards. The ride took place in late October on the Sunday immediately before the Tuesday Opening Meet, along a seven mile route offering a selection of optional fences across the organisers' land at Stoke Charity and Wonston. The jumps were built by Henry Mustill from Stockbridge, who was also responsible for the point-to-point fences at Hackwood and knew how to construct an obstacle that would stand the test of time. Thanks to generous sponsorship from forty or so local businesses, the considerable profits from this event were shared by the Hunt Club, the BFSS and three other charities selected on a yearly basis. The event was so popular, and sufficiently close to the conurbations of Basingstoke and Winchester, that it attracted up to 500 participants each year.

By 1979 Steve Andrews knew the country inside out and had endeared himself to all with his determination to provide first-class sport. The 1979–1980 season started brilliantly with a 4½-mile point from Park Copse following the

Angela Cooper long-standing Secretary of the HHSC.

The inaugural issue of *Tally Ho!* published by the HHSC in the summer of 1979.

A NEW BROOM SWEEPS CLEAN 1975–1981

Opening Meet at Moundsmere, which was now home to Herman Andreae's grandson, Mark, and keepered with foxes very much in mind by Ben Knight. There was great excitement surrounding the visit of HRH the Prince of Wales less than a fortnight later on November 10th, 65 years after the Hunt Club had invited a previous Prince of Wales to join them in the hunting field. Prince Charles, who was hunting regularly at the time, stabled his horses for three nights with Tony and Sue Maxse at Pelham and wore his customary dark blue hunting coat with scarlet collar and cuffs. As was his custom, the Prince did not attend the meet at Manor Farm, Farringdon but hacked on to the first draw with his hosts and the Crown Equerry,[5] Sir John Miller.

To the immense disappointment of all, a poor day followed due to an acute shortage of foxes, succinctly summed up by the entry in Hopper Cavendish's hunting dairy; 'Poor Steve Andrews, P.O.W. and no fox.' Despite the lack of sport and the fact that his mare stopped twice at a fence off the Rotherfield drive, HRH wrote a gracious letter of thanks to Tony Maxse; 'it was great fun adding another pack to my growing collection and, despite the problem of finding foxes (obviously you are doing your job properly!), it was a lovely day to be out and to see the country. It also made me feel much better after a fairly busy week in London.' He was a little less enthusiastic about the day when meeting a gentleman wearing the HH button out hunting with the Quorn in High Leicestershire a few years later. Sir John Miller also wrote from the Royal Mews to thank Tony Maxse for stabling the Royal hunters. 'It was most interesting to see your lovely pack of hounds, and I hope the expenses were settled satisfactorily although it sounded rather inadequate to me.'

Members must have wished HRH was there to see hounds at their absolute best on February 21st 1980, when they achieved an exceptional hunt following the meet at Wyards Farm on a fox found in the Will Hall coverts between Hungry Copse and Great Wood. During the early stages of the twenty-mile run the fox sought refuge under a shed in the Misses Tristrams' garden at Bentworth. Molly and Ruth Tristram were terrific supporters whose overgrown garden often provided a fox, but on this occasion the hunted one was quickly evicted to continue past Gaston to Trinity Firs. He got to ground under another shed near Medstead cemetery before leading hounds past The Gullet and on to Alresford Pond where

---

5   The Crown Equerry is the operational head of the Royal Mews of the Royal Household of the Sovereign of the United Kingdom.

HRH The Prince of Wales with the Crown Equerry, Colonel Sir John Miller,
far right and the Maxse family at Pelham Place, November 1979.

Thank you letter from HRH The Prince of Wales to Tony Maxse MFH
following his day with the HH in November 1979.

the hunt ended on Peter Mills's farm. Hounds had scored a brilliant 8½-mile point during which they had been accompanied for much of the way by a cur dog after Mrs Mitchell's terrier slipped its lead to join in the fun.

Hunt finances were in much better shape by the early eighties, when the Hunt Club began contributing to a pension fund set up on behalf of their huntsman. The initial contribution was £400 a year, but the sum had increased to £700 by the end of the decade. In December 1982 Members authorised a £300 budget for the important spring task of covert laying, and the following year agreed a donation of £40 by covenant to the National Trust to help defray the cost of keeping rides accessible on their property at Selborne Common. The Hunt Club was sufficiently flush to send the Aldershot Beagles £50 to assist with a court case against hunt saboteurs in 1980 and a further £250 towards the Devon & Somerset Staghounds' legal costs in 1985. By the start of the 1987 season Members' subscriptions had increased from £255 in 1982 to £400, and from £220 to £320 for regular subscribers.

The 1981 Members' race at Hackwood was full of incident. Hopper Cavendish, having her first ever ride in a point-to-point went at the third fence, soon followed by Stephen Andrews,[6] whose mount, Scottish Monarch fell at the open ditch despite having carried his father all season out hunting. Michael Opperman and Choral Lodge parted company at the same fence, leaving Albergian and Alex Scott to battle it out with Simon Harrap, who unwittingly handed the race to the Chairman's Albergian, after his horse was carried wide of a red marker and disqualified. Undeterred by his fall in the first race, Michael Opperman declared Choral Lodge for the Adjacent Hunts race, which he duly won.

A few weeks later the Quartermasters were resurrected in a different format when dairy farmer and incumbent Chairman of the HHSC, Frank Momber, joined Messrs Gray, Maxse and Porter in the Mastership for the 1981–1982 season. Frank, his wife Phil and their two children hunted at every opportunity, often riding homebred horses, from their base in the Tuesday country at Hatchmoor Farm near Greatham. Frank learnt all about farming and hunting as a mud student on Exmoor before going on to marry Phil and manage a dairy farm near Swindon. The young family and a single shared hunter moved to Hampshire in 1968 after Phil's father, Commander Pumphrey, asked them to run the dairy farm he had bought some years earlier, having retired from a distinguished career in the Royal Navy. Rather

---

6 The professional huntsman was Steve Andrews; his son is referred to throughout the text as Stephen Andrews.

like his good friend John Gray, who once emerged from a fall with his cigarette still clenched between his teeth, Frank also enjoyed tobacco, but preferred his inside the bowl of a pipe. He liked to ride on a long, easy rein and was one of the few who invariably had a second horse.

Above: Sir James Scott's Albergian with Alex Scott up wins the first of his three Members' races at the 1978 point-to-point.

Top left: Mark Andreae winning the 1977 Members' race on his own Henry Morgan.

Left: Anne Moore leads in Sir James Scott's Lilting Spirit (Mr R. Downes up) following his victory in the 1976 Members' race.

Chapter Fourteen 1981–1991

The Best of Times

J. Gray Esq., M.R. Porter Esq., A.J. Maxse Esq., F. Momber Esq., 1981–1983, J. Gray Esq., M.R. Porter Esq., F. Momber Esq., Mrs A.J. Maxse 1983–1985, J. Gray Esq., F. Momber Esq., Mrs A.J. Maxse 1985–1986, J. Gray Esq., F. Momber Esq., Mrs A.J. Maxse, The Hon. Mrs J. Cavendish, 1986–1990, J. Gray Esq., Mrs A.J. Maxse, The Hon. Mrs J. Cavendish, 1990–1991.

Steve Andrews breaks leg in 1981, John Gray's résumé of contemporary hunting, Sue Maxse joins the Mastership 1983, Kruger North and the Butler Boys, David Herring deputises for Steve Andrews, hunt saboteurs and the law, 21st anniversary dinner for John Gray, Hopper Cavendish joins the Mastership 1986, Hunt Scurry, résumé of seasons 1986–1991, Steve Andrews's final day as huntsman in March 1991.

In November 1981, Steve Andrews broke a leg in a fall near Lasham airfield after which hounds were hunted by the whipper-in, Andrew Phillis, with Richard Broadley and Stephen Andrews helping to turn hounds. Steve was back in the saddle for the meet at Bighton Manor in early January and presided over a superb second half of the season, which included a 5-mile point in February following the meet at Armsworth Park. That spring John Gray wrote an illuminating résumé on the current state of the Hampshire Hunt country for *Tally Ho!*, in which he reflected on the Hunt's good fortune to have access to so many large shooting estates whose owners not only welcomed hounds but also joined them in the field. He paid tribute to the old established farming families in the country which are so closely involved with the Hunt and explained that although hedges have been grubbed up and there is more winter corn than ever, young cereal crops carry a far better scent than bare arable. He pointed out that the busy motorways are generally out of harm's way on the Hunt boundaries, and that housing and industrial developments have been mostly confined to a strip of country running from Basingstoke to Andover and down to the coast at Southampton. All in all, he concluded in 1982, the country was no more difficult to hunt than when Ken Goschen was Master in the late fifties and early sixties.

Tony Maxse left the Mastership at the end of the 1982–1983 season and was replaced by his wife, Sue, who was also District Commissioner of the Pony Club. Sue was brought up in the Puckeridge country where she played junior tennis for Cambridgeshire, hunted, and rode in point-to-points. Her impeccably turned out quality hunters were often homebred, and she was a popular Master held in high esteem by all, especially the Hunt staff who appreciated her lighter feminine touch whenever she called in to check that all was going well at Ropley. After her husband had been presented with a retirement painting of his favourite hunter at the 1983 puppy show, it was Kruger North's turn to receive a cheque from the Hunt Club in grateful recognition of his sixteen years' service as terrierman.

Kruger was officially replaced by Jim, Pete, and Michael Butler, but the three hunting mad brothers from Slys Farm at Bramdean had been lending a hand with terriers and spades ever since Steve Andrew called in to solicit their help soon after his arrival in Hampshire. The dairy farming brothers, referred to by all as 'The Butler Boys,' were flattered to have been asked by a man for whom they had considerable respect. Their unkempt but delectable farm at Slys was an oasis of grassland, hedges and foxes across which hounds were always welcome. The Butler Boys were said to spend all day and half the night putting-to earths before hunting, so that foxes were above ground and available to hunt. Somehow these most traditional and genuine of countrymen always found time to milk their cows, and in the case of Michael and Pete find a bride as well. Michael married Diana Martin, who had been the stud groom at Ropley, while Pete married Julie Civil, who is a successful accountant and owner of point-to-pointers. Over the years Julie and Pete walked many hound puppies for the Hunt, and in 2001 Julie became a Joint Master of the Hursley Hambledon and remained in office for fourteen years. Pete died in 2019, however the bungalow left to Julie by Ormond Theyer is now home to the Butlers' son, Fred and his wife, Rose. Fred works for his mother's accountancy firm and helps to maintain the old tin-roofed church close to Bramdean Common that Ormond also took care of for most of his adult life.

In 1984 Steve Andrews missed the entire cubhunting season having been stood down by the doctors after suffering a mild heart attack. David Herring, a former MFH and amateur huntsman accepted the Joint Masters' invitation to hunt hounds until Steve was able to resume duties. There is no doubt the dedicated professional found it particularly hard to hand over his beloved pack to another man, but he was firmly back in the saddle in time for the Opening Meet, attended by a handful of unwelcome hunt saboteurs, who had become increasingly disruptive

THE BEST OF TIMES 1981–1991

Sue Maxse MFH 1983–1991 with huntsman Steve Andrews in 1984.

From left to right, Joint Hon. Secretary John Newcomb, huntsman Steve Andrews and terriermen Michael, Pete (holding his daughter Lucy) and Jim Butler, and Ken Civil.

Dinner in 1985 to celebrate John Gray's 21st year in office. From left to right, Sir James Scott, Sue Maxse MFH, John Gray MFH, Pat Gray, Captain Ronnie Wallace MFH (Exmoor), Frank Momber MFH.

over the last few seasons. Foxhunting was a legitimate pursuit conducted by permission on privately owned land, and it would be another decade before the Criminal Justice and Public Order Act of 1994 created an offence of trespassing with the intention of disrupting a lawful activity. Until then trespass was a civil offence, and the police were often reluctant to intervene. In December 1984 the Hunt Club Chairman met with the Chief Constable of Hampshire to thank his police force for their assistance, but also pointed out their lack of consistency when dealing with saboteurs. Despite the intermittent attention of unwelcome visitors another good season ensued, which included an outstanding day from Becksteddle, where Angela and Harry Cooper entertained a large field and hounds caught their fox deep inside the Hambledon country after a very fine hunt.

    Michael Porter left the Mastership at the end of the season to become a Joint Master with Ken Goschen but continued to manage Headley Wood Farm where the Hampshire Hunt were always afforded a warm welcome, and in the fullness of time he would return to the fold. The Hunt Club gave a dinner at the Guildhall in Winchester on November 1st 1985 to celebrate John Gray's 21 successful seasons as a Master to date, during which he had gained the respect of all connected to the

Hunt. According to his daughter, Gillian, 'hunting was the answer to everything' for her father, who even rode to hounds the day her sister, Joanna, was born. The health and prosperity of a man who appeared impervious to the cold and never carried a hip flask or went home before hounds was proposed by Major Robin Cowen. After John Gray had responded, Captain Ronnie Wallace MFH proposed the health of the Hampshire Hunt Club, to which Lt. Colonel Sir James Scott responded in his capacity as Chairman.

Six months after John Gray's celebratory dinner he, Frank Momber and Sue Maxse were joined in the Mastership by Lucinda Cavendish, who John Gray had taken under his wing when she was a teenager growing up at nearby Beauworth with her brother, Charlie Corbett. Their paternal grandfather, the Reverend Lionel Corbett, moved to Hockley House, Cheriton in 1903 and was a member of Frederick Coryton's small committee who had acted as Masters during and immediately after the First World War between 1915 and 1919. Horses and hunting ran thick in the Corbett siblings' blood, and Lucinda – who from an early age insisted on being addressed as Hopper – won her first gymkhana rosette at a tender age in 1958. She was blooded at Rye Common eleven years later, and during the seventies her horsemanship was refined to advanced level eventing standard by Jennie Loriston-Clarke at Brockenhurst. In 1976 Hopper married the Hon. John Cavendish, who does not hunt himself but has been a rock of support to his wife ever since, and over many years an enthusiastic supporter of so many different Hunt functions and activities.

The Cavendishes came to live at Leslie Aylward's old home, Hall Farm, Farringdon, in 1978, from which base they have hosted many meets and walked generations of hound puppies. Hopper had also spent several seasons assisting the huntsman, Steve Andrews, in the field and bringing on his young horses. As to be expected with such a background, she took to Mastership like a duck to water and thoroughly enjoyed her first season in office, which included a five-mile point on Boxing Day after hounds had been introduced to the elderly patients at Treloar Hospital. The season ended on a high note following the farmers' meet at Moundsmere. 'After a dismal start hacked to Herriard Park where we found a fox that gave us a wonderful hunt,' reads the entry in Hopper's hunting diary for March 26th 1987. 'A brilliant hunt much enjoyed by the field consisting of hunting farmers, some who hardly ride – a superb end to my first season in the coat with brass buttons. I have enjoyed it very much and hope I shall be lucky enough to do many more.'

The 1986–1987 season also included the inaugural running of the Hunt Scurry, which was organised by Hopper's brother, Charlie Corbett, at his Holden Farm, which straddles both HH and Hursley Hambledon countries. The Hunt Scurry was named after a Ferneley painting hanging in the Maxses' dining room but was really the continuation of a cross country race that had been run for the first time at Rotherfield in 1959 before morphing into the cross country ride, which had not taken place since 1981. Under its latest guise competitors wore hunting dress and raced in separate divisions of children, ladies, and gentlemen over a three-mile course built by Charlie and his farm staff. Afterwards around 200 guests including competitors, spectators, and sponsors, sat down to lunch during which prizes were presented and speeches made. On one memorable occasion, the principal sponsor and driving force behind the event, Irishman, land agent and auctioneer, Hume Jones, led a rousing rendition of the Hampshire Hunt Song, which had been composed by the Reverend C. Powlett in the late eighteenth century.

Under its new guise, the first Hunt Scurry was held on January 10th 1987 when the Hon. Geordie Herbert won the men's division, whilst the ladies' race was won by the Joint Master's daughter, Sarah Maxse, riding a horse called Snap that had been hunting four days earlier. A day later there would have been no race at all because it was freezing hard by nightfall and hunting was not able to resume until January 27th. In 1990 Charlie Corbett became a Joint Master of the Hursley Hambledon, after which the Scurry became a joint fundraiser and a tremendous social occasion usually held between Christmas and the New Year. Members of the Maxse family were frequently in the shake up, and on more than one occasion Charlie captured the first hunting farmer prize, and his great friend and sponsor, Hume Jones, the best heavyweight. The event, which was covered by the inimitable *Hampshire Chronicle* and occasionally the *Horse & Hound* magazine, was run for the last time in 1999.

The 1987–1988 season was an especially open one, with just one day lost due to the great October storm that flattened acres of mature woodland and in some areas provided superb cover for foxes where there had been only thin lying before the storm. In November 1987 John Gray presented the Hunt's oldest subscriber, Ruth Tristram, with a cake to celebrate her 90th birthday at the meet at Bentworth; she had enjoyed her first day with the HH back in 1923. Around this time John Gray was arrested for striking a saboteur on the arm after the thug had grabbed hold of his horse's rein, and as a consequence had to stand down as a much respected local Justice of the Peace. 'He was a JP back in the days when they were appointed for being good men and true,' his daughter Gillian remembers, 'my father respected

THE BEST OF TIMES 1981–1991

Above: Peggy Close's Great Crack with Mr J. MacKay up, winner of the 1982 Members' race and second in the 1980 Foxhunters' Chase at Aintree.

Above: Hume Jones; sponsor, competitor and devotee of The Hunt Scurry.

Right: Lady Scott presenting Charlie Corbett with the Members' race trophy after his victory on Hardy Turk in 1983.

1983 – Lady Scott presents the cup to Mr. R. A. C. Corbett, owner and rider of HARDY TURK

The Hon. Mrs John (Hopper) Cavendish MFH 1986–2004.

Frank Momber MFH 1981–1990.

Steve Andrews with Hounds at Bentworth Lodge on his final day March 23rd 1991.

different views to his own, but drew the line at harm done to people, horses, or hounds.'

There was some doubt as to whether Steve Andrews would be fit to hunt hounds for the 1989–1990 season following an operation to his back in July, but although he missed hound exercise, he was back in the saddle with customary determination in time to start cubhunting on September 19th. Hounds went out on sixteen mornings prior to the Opening Meet, after which saboteurs continued to make a nuisance of themselves, much to the huntsman's disgust and frustration. Frank Momber left the Mastership at the end of this season after nine years in office and is remembered by his many friends as a larger than life character, full of enthusiasm and energy, who departed this world far too young in 2009. The following season HH hounds, hunt staff and seventeen mounted followers hunted in Dorset on January 31st 1991 by invitation of the Cattistock Hunt, whose own hounds were coughing, and marked two brace to ground during a busy day. Back in Hampshire the saboteurs were again out in force from the meet at Tunworth a few days later, but hounds were undeterred and hunted beautifully throughout the day.

By then Steve Andrews had only a few precious days left as huntsman, for he had given notice to draw stumps on a long and illustrious career at the end of the season. Sue Maxse was also stepping down as a Joint Master, bringing to a close sixteen successful and consecutive seasons of Maxse service to the Hunt. At the end of his last day on March 23rd 1991 Steve Andrews blew the long drawn out notes of 'going home' for the final time before leading his hunter down the Shalden Farm drive surrounded by adoring hounds as Joann walked alongside him. Later that year the Hunt Supporters Club and General and Mrs Swinburn on behalf of the Hunt Club hosted retirement parties for the couple who had endeared themselves to so many throughout Hampshire and beyond, and Steve took up a new position as gamekeeper to the Elwes family at Aylesfield.

Chapter Fifteen 1991–1996

The End of an Era

J. Gray Esq., The Hon. Mrs J. Cavendish, M. Andreae Esq.,
M.R. Porter Esq., 1991–1994, J. Gray Esq., The Hon.
Mrs J. Cavendish, M. Andreae Esq., F. Faulkner Esq., 1994–1996.

Michael Porter rejoins the Mastership in 1991, Mark Andreae joins the Mastership in 1991, Bob Collins appointed huntsman, Bob and Carol Collins and new team at Ropley, Ormond Theyer and Bramdean Common, Bob Collins's early seasons, last Boxing Day meet at The Butts at Alton, death of Sir James Scott, Derick Faulkner joins the Mastership in 1994, farmers' days at Moundsmere, retirement of John Gray after 31 years as a Master.

Michael Porter returned to the Mastership on May 1st 1991 following the disbandment of Mr Goschen's Hunt, where he had been a Joint Master since 1985. John Gray and Hopper Cavendish also invited Mark Andreae, whose grandfather had done so much to help the Hunt recover when Master after the Second World War, to join their team. Mark derived enormous pleasure from welcoming hounds and followers onto his Moundsmere estate, where hunting took precedence over shooting. Well foxed and accessible via numerous beautifully maintained hunt jumps and inviting thorn hedges, Moundsmere was a perfect venue for the Opening Meet. Mark also kept horses at livery in the Duke of Beaufort's country where his friend Captain Ian Farquhar was hunting hounds, but would unfailingly telephone Hopper every Sunday morning when back in Hampshire to ask if there was anything he could do to help. Sometimes he was dispatched in his Range Rover, yellow labrador on the seat beside him, to smooth over troubled waters with a bottle of whisky and a famously winning smile.

John Gray and Hopper had set about finding a professional huntsman to replace Steve Andrews as soon his retirement from hunt service was announced more than a year in advance. The search led them to Itton Court[1] in Wales after

---

[1] The Curre Hunt was started in 1896 by Sir Edward Curre of Itton Court in Monmouthshire.

Richard Barlow MFH had urged Hopper to consider the Curre huntsman when he met her at the Ardingly hound show in June 1990. Within a month the Masters had appointed Bob Collins to replace Steve Andrews the following season and accomplished a daunting mission with impressive alacrity. Back in Hampshire the arrival of a new huntsman was anticipated with great excitement, but although Bob was destined to forge an equally successful career as his predecessor, the two men could hardly have been more different. Both were sticklers for etiquette, but Bob loved the summer game and took great pleasure in showing hounds at Ardingly, Peterborough and even Lowther hound shows. His cheery, west country demeanour injected fun and enthusiasm into endless puppy show practices, visits to Pony Club camps, and just about every other social occasion.

Friendly and outgoing, Bob encouraged all comers to join him on mounted hound exercise before the start of cubhunting, during which his wife, Carol, provided coffee breaks and picnic breakfasts. Carol quickly became a mainstay of the Hunt and a rock of support to her husband both on and off the hunting field, where she was frequently dispatched to watch a busy road from the back of her grey horse. Carol played an active and prominent role within the local community, where her interests included the Ropley Horticultural Society, the Women's Institute, and arranging flower displays for the village church. She was also an enthusiastic

Mark Andreae MFH at Moundsmere in 1995 painted by John King.

photographer and film maker, always on hand to record memorable and interesting events, which would later be screened to an appreciative audience whilst raising funds for the Hunt.

The Collinses' arrival, along with Darren Beeney as whipper-in, his wife Alison as stud groom and Richard Markham as kennelman and second whipper-in, represented a complete clean sweep at the kennels and stables, which on May 1st 1991 did not include a single member of hunt staff from the previous regime. Thankfully Hopper was on hand to provide continuity, identify hounds, and show the new huntsman where he could enjoy hound exercise in safety during the summer months. Bramdean Common, which was within easy hacking distance of the kennels, was a favourite early morning destination that could be reached without having to ride down a tarmac road. The Common was home to long-standing puppy walkers, Rose and Ormond Theyer, who lived at Plantation Bungalow where hounds were always welcome to unbox or load up at the end of a day's hunting, and the innocuous brown teapot on their kitchen table contained whisky, not tea.

Ormond's arrival as a very small boy into the area he would call home for the rest of his life is a tale of mystery and intrigue. In 1926, his unmarried mother discovered that she was pregnant and was sent to Australia to have the baby. Having given birth she resolved to bring her son up in England and returned home on a ship called the Ormond, after which her son was named. The two settled in Bramdean, and when Ormond left the Coldstream Guards after the Second World War his mother bought him Plantation Bungalow together with some woodland that he cleared for pasture. After his marriage to Rose he was able to buy more land from Oxford's Magdalen College and increased his holding to around 200 acres, which the Hunt was always encouraged to cross. Bramdean Common was a sure find, and for many years Ormond donated all the timber required to build and maintain hunt jumps. After Ormond lost his wife, Carol Collins lightened the burden of old age by regularly calling into Plantation Bungalow with food and good cheer. The Hampshire Hunt lost a dear friend when Ormond died in 2006 and joined Rose in the graveyard beside the tiny tin-roofed church he had personally maintained for so many years.

Following an outbreak of kennel cough, Bob was not able to start his first season's cubhunting until September 16th, after which he made up for lost time by going out four mornings a week up until the Opening Meet. So great was the new huntsman's enthusiasm that when the lady Master arrived 40 minutes early for

THE HAMPSHIRE HUNT 1749–2022

Huntsman Bob Collins with his wife Carol.

Michael Porter MFH 1975–1985 and 1991–1994.

Carol Collins (wife of huntsman, Bob) and Ormond Theyer.

the first morning, she found hounds and hunt staff ready and waiting with horses wearing headcollars and ropes under their bridles.[2] By Christmas it was clear that Bob was a much quieter huntsman than his predecessor, but was every bit as consummate a horseman, who rode light despite being a heavy man, and frequently popped a big fence without breaking out of a trot. As a nod to his time in Wales, he liked to include at least one broken coated hound in the pack, which coincidentally retained Itton Court blood originally introduced after the Second World War by George Evans. The huntsman's other idiosyncrasies included a ban on hunt staff wearing poppies at any time except during remembrance week – he once tore the poppy off a whipper-in's lapel after it had not been removed in time – and an insistence that the girls bringing out second horses wore a gleaming stirrup leather across their shoulders as has been the long-standing custom at Milton.[3] These included the glamourous Dominique Davies and Chantelle Rowlands, who were not only superb grooms for several seasons during Bob's era, but so beautiful that in 1999 they featured as one of the prestigious frontispieces in *Country Life* magazine.

On Boxing Day 1992 hounds met at the Butts in Alton for the last[4] time after Hampshire County Council refused permission for hounds to meet or hunt on their land going forward. The decision did not overly affect the Masters who the following year moved the meet to Will Hall Farm[5] less than a mile away, but it must have been a huge disappointment to the patients at Treloar Hospital, for whom the festive occasion was a highlight of the year. The Council's ban prompted Jack Jervoise from Herriard Park to write to Mark Andreae with his own interpretation of the ban as 'a very serious infringement of speech and action and shows an intolerant attitude to minorities that we might expect in a communist country, but not in a democracy.' Many thousands agreed with these sentiments, and the BFSS sought a judicial review on behalf of the Hunt Club, claiming that Hampshire County Council was acting ultra vires when they banned hunting and coursing on their land. The judicial review was granted by Mr Justice Latham to Hampshire farmers Mark Andreae and Miles Hudson, but not everyone thought this was such

---

2   Headcollars and ropes allowed the hunt horses to be secured safely whenever the hunt staff had to hold up hounds at an earth or take to their feet for any other reason. The appendages did not appear after the Opening Meet.

3   The Fitzwilliam (Milton) Hunt kennels are at Milton Park near Peterborough. Their hunt staff wear a stirrup leather across the shoulders out hunting (but not during autumn hunting) and when showing hounds in summer.

4   The Hampshire Hunt resumed meeting at The Butts at Alton on Boxing Day 2010.

5   Will Hall Farm belonged to Winchester College and was farmed by John Gray's godson, Chris Martin.

THE HAMPSHIRE HUNT 1749–2022

The HH at Herriard Park

1. The mounted field move off.
2. The Hon. Mrs. J. G. G. Cavendish MFH and Bob Collins the huntsman.
3. Bob Collins.
4. Mr. Michael Porter MFH with Bob Collins.
5. Hounds moving off.
6. The HH Joint-Masters, Mr. J. Gray, the Hon. Mrs. J. Cavendish, Mr. Michael Porter and Mr. Mark Andreae.

The HH in 1992. (The meet was actually at Pingasson, Weston Patrick).

a good idea. The leader of Hampshire County Council wrote to the Joint Master, Michael Porter, counselling against taking any further action against the mighty HCC. He suggested the BFSS should bring a test case against a county 'that has no large urban population, which does not have a politically skilful and anti-field sports leadership, and which does not have the large resources and skilled legal department enjoyed by Hampshire.'[6]

The last meet at Alton was also the first Boxing Day for some years without any saboteurs, which was possibly a consequence of Bob's laissez-faire attitude to his tormentors, there being little fun in provoking someone whose only reaction is cheery words and a smile. Occasionally the smile took some mustering, as was the case when the huntsman rode up to the lady Master, removed his hat, mopped his brow, and asked somewhat wearily, 'and where now Madam?' after a long blank draw. 'We'll go to Stoney Brow,' came the quick response, 'and we *will* keep smiling.' Perhaps that conversation took place in March 1992 when Hopper's diary records a day best forgotten; 'Antis not foxes, no jumps or anything to make me smile except my horse bucking at the meet. Spent all day embarrassed with a large Saturday field.' There was nothing to smile about on November 2nd 1993 either, when the Hunt Club lost its Chairman and most stalwart supporter with the death of Sir James Scott after a busy day's hunting on his own land at Rotherfield Park. Sir James had been there to view a fox away from Plash Wood in the morning, holding his top hat aloft against a clear, cold blue sky, but later felt unwell and dismounted. Hamish Rowsell, who was out qualifying a point-to-pointer, led Sir James's hunter back to the stables, and within hours its owner had passed peacefully away.

Michael Porter stepped down in 1994 having been a Joint Master of either the HH or Mr Goschen's for nineteen consecutive years and following Sir James's death became Chairman of the Hunt Club. Michael was replaced in the Mastership by Mr Derick Faulkner,[7] who farmed at Selborne in the Farringdon Vale, where the HH point-to-point races had been run in the 1930s. Derick was able to purchase Norton Farm from the Hartley estate after a spark from the fireplace inside the principal residence at Hinton Ampner House landed on a sofa and burnt the stately home to the ground in April 1960. In order to finance the extensive repair costs, the owner

---

6 It has not been possible to establish the outcome of the judicial review. There is a strong possibility that the Council leader's advice may have been followed.

7 Frederick Ralph Faulkner always known as Derick.

HH Supporters Club meet at Kennels 1993. Presentation of the horse Odd Job ridden by whipper-in Richard Markham to Hunt Club Chairman Sir James Scott by Supporters Club Chairman Colin Potts.

Ralph Dutton[8] sold off several rented farms that the tenants clubbed together to buy. Derick was at the heart of the local farming community and well placed to keep a tricky part of the country open for hunting. He also assumed responsibility for the hunt staff and worked assiduously on the point-to-point course at Hackwood, where he became the assistant Clerk of the Course. Wendy Faulkner, who was born at the same nursing home in Blackberry Lane as her future husband, was an accomplished Master's wife organising fundraisers for the Hunt and producing lavish hunting teas whenever hounds met at Norton Farm. This was usually around the time of her father-in-law's birthday in November, after which the first draw was Frenchmere Copse, a sure find possibly named after French prisoners of war who had once laboured nearby.

That Derick became a Master at all was largely thanks to Steve Andrews encouraging the farmer and his neighbour, Chris Butler from West End Farm at

---

8   Ralph Dutton became the 8th Baron Sherborne on the death of his cousin Charles Dutton, 7th Baron Sherborne, in 1982. He died without heirs in 1985 and left Hinton Ampner to the National Trust. If the Hartley estate had not been sold to finance the rebuilding of Hinton Ampner House, hunting across the estate would have been prohibited in November 2021 when the National Trust banned legitimate trail hunting on all their properties.

Froyle, to take up riding and join him in the hunting field. Throughout the 1980s Steve and John Gray encouraged as many farmers as possible to go hunting to such good effect that there were often a dozen or more amongst the mounted field on a Tuesday. For a number of years the Masters arranged a special farmers' day immediately after the season had officially ended, which Mark Andreae was delighted to host at Moundsmere. Despite being held towards the latter end of March, these days frequently turned out to be amongst the best of the season, and in 1985 hounds ran like smoke during the farmers' day to catch their fox after a nine-mile hunt. By 1995 Mark Andreae's private meet had become so popular that it was attended by farmers from seven different hunts, who enjoyed a full English breakfast at the Yew Tree pub and a convivial hunting tea in Mark's farm office at the end of the day. Bob Collins embraced the initiative from the outset and continued to encourage farmers such as Andrew Shirvell, the Shalden farm manager, to ride a horse and come hunting. There was widespread hilarity amongst Andrew's colleagues when they learnt he was planning to attend the farmers' meet, but he had been visiting Tom Barnes's stables on a daily basis for clandestine early morning rides. He was a competent horseman by the time he appeared at Moundsmere on Odd Job, the most reliable of all the horses stabled at Ropley, but history does not relate if there was a winner to the sweepstake on how long it would take before they parted company.

On February 22nd 1994 John Gray presented Mrs Pam Begg with flowers at her 47th and final lawn meet in the snow at Armsworth Park, where Squire Evelyn had kennelled his private but short-lived pack in the mid eighteenth century, long before the H had been dropped from the Park's name. Despite shooting pressures, and thanks to the enthusiasm of their huntsman and commitment of the Masters, hounds were able to cubhunt at least four days a week throughout the nineties, usually managing more than 30 mornings prior to the Opening Meet on the last Tuesday in October. However as the organisation of hunting became increasingly challenging, the concept of traditional Tuesday and Saturday country gradually lapsed as hounds met wherever they could be accommodated.

On December 2nd 1995 Bob provided a busy day on the house side of Sir James Scott's[9] Rotherfield estate, whilst the head keeper, Michael Gray, organised an equally successful day's shooting on the other side of the A32 at Colemore. During

---

9   Sir James Scott succeeded to the baronetcy after his father, also Sir James Scott, but known to his friends as Jim, died soon after viewing a fox away from Plash Wood in 1993 as recounted earlier in the chapter.

Hunting Farmers

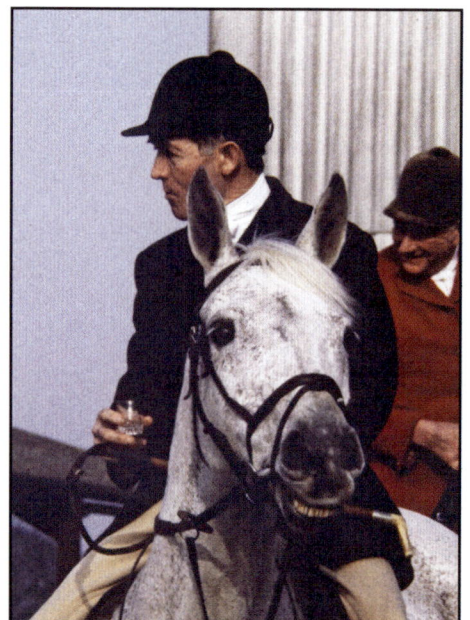

George Gray.

Bill Welling.

Charlie Corbett.

Chris Butler.

THE END OF AN ERA 1991–1996

Above: Michael Butler with his son Michael.

Above left: Mark Cheyney.

Above right: David Gray.

Right: Russell Martin (left) and Andrew Shirvell.

January 1996 nine days were lost due to heavy snow, and in March that year Richard Markham, who was moving as first whipper-in to the Belvoir on May 1st, had the opportunity to hunt hounds after Bob was concussed in a fall. The huntsman was back three days later, jumping a gate off the road in his customary inimitable style. Hounds were in absolute top form for the last month of the season, impressing all with their drive and accuracy until the first harrows and rollers appeared in the pastures, which had always been Bob Collins's cue to bring the season to a close.

On March 23rd 1996 John Gray hosted the meet for his final day's hunting as a Master, having guided the fortunes of the Hunt he loved for a remarkable 31 years. More than a hundred riders and many more on foot came to North End Farm to wish John well and see him receive a magnificent painting by Susie Whitcomb featuring himself, Bob Collins, and hounds against a backdrop of rolling Hampshire countryside and the infallible Rookery Copse. The wonderful day that followed included two scintillating runs across John's own farm and ended with a huge hunting tea in the barn, where Uncle John was heard to say many times, 'we've had a very fair day, a *very* fair day.'

Presentation to John Gray MFH during his final meet as a Master on 23rd March 1996. From left to right: Derick Faulkner MFH, Mark Andreae MFH, Hopper Cavendish MFH, Tony Maxse, Sue Maxse, John Gray MFH, Shelagh Cowen, Michael Porter, Geoffrey Gregson, Frank Momber and Dick Barry.

Chapter Sixteen 1996–2005

Listen to Us!

The Hon. Mrs J. Cavendish, M. Andreae Esq., F. Faulkner Esq.,1996–2001, The Hon. Mrs J. Cavendish, M. Andreae Esq., S. Harrap Esq., 2001–2003, The Hon. Mrs J. Cavendish, M. Andreae Esq., S. Harrap Esq., T. Floyd Esq., 2003–2004.

National Trust ban on staghunting, Labour gain power in 1997, Hyde Park Rally in July 1997, Countryside March in 1998, Campaign for Hunting levies, hunting from 1999–2001, foot and mouth disease in 2001, Simon Harrap joins the Mastership in 2001, The Newcombs retire as Hon. Secretaries and are replaced by the Webbs, Liberty and Livelihood March in September 2002, Tom Floyd joins the Mastership in 2003, the point-to-point at Hackwood, passage of the Hunting Act through Parliament, vigil and protest in Parliament Square, Hunt Club decision to continue hunting within the law, Bob Collins final season and last day's hunting before the ban.

In April 1997 the National Trust banned staghunting on all of its properties following the Bateson report,[1] which did not directly affect the Hampshire Hunt Club, but did mark the beginning of a gradual and irreversible decline in the Trust's support for hunting with hounds that eventually led to a suspension of even legally exempt hunting in 2021. The HH continued to visit the Trust's land at Selborne Common until the early 2000s, by which time the volume of walkers was making hunting there impractical. A month later, and exactly a year to the day since John Gray gave up his 31 year reign as a Joint Master, Tony Blair's Labour government won a landslide victory that threatened a fieldsport that had endured throughout Hampshire for the previous three centuries and contributed so much to the history and fabric of the county. The Labour victory also marked a turning point in the strategy for the ongoing defence of hunting; instead of stalking the corridors of power in Westminster, it was now time for hunting to shout its case loudly from

---

1 On March 11th 1997 Bateson and Bradshaw published a report, entitled *Behavioural and Physiological Effects of Culling Red Deer*. The National Trust responded by banning stag hunting on their properties the next day.

the rooftops and fearlessly publicise the many important roles it played within rural communities.

This new approach was soon evident when the Countryside Alliance[2] organised a huge rally in Hyde Park on July 10th 1997 as a response to the threat to traditional hunting with hounds in particular, and a whole rural way of life in general. The event was promoted by a series of marches from different corners of the UK, including Coldstream in the Scottish borders, Caldbeck in the Lake District, Plas Machynlleth in Wales, and Madron in Cornwall with the intention of converging at Hyde Park on July 10th. The Scottish marchers were approaching Morpeth on June 16th when it was announced that the Labour MP for Worcester, Michael Foster, who had won the ballot to introduce a Private Members Bill, would bring his anti-hunting bill before Parliament the following day. Whilst this was a worrying development, the threatened legislation generated favourable publicity for core walkers wearing T-shirts emblazoned with the legend, *Listen to Us*, trudging through towns, villages and cities on their way to Hyde Park.

Hopper Cavendish spearheaded the organisation of transport to Hyde Park, filling five coaches and a double decker bus with HH supporters who joined a mighty crowd listening to a succession of motivational speakers that included Yorkshire cricket captain David Byas, champion jockey Willie Carson, Lembit Opik MP and the actor, Jeremy Irons. Baroness Ann Mallalieu rose the hair on the back of a hundred thousand necks during a spellbinding address to the crowd that spoke of freedom, a love of animals and the countryside and the sacrifices made by those who had marched hundreds of miles to be there. She ended by quoting Shakespeare's famous passage from Henry V to thunderous applause and set the seal on the most memorable of all protests between 1997 and 2005. These included a second gathering in the capital on March 1st the following year when a quarter of a million individuals marched peacefully to the Houses of Parliament in protest against Michael Foster's invidious bill and the government's general disregard for rural issues. This time Sio Axel-Berg[3] and Penny Aikenhead filled nineteen buses from the HH country. Meanwhile Bob Collins, for whom the 1997 rally had been his first ever visit to London, ended the season with a respectable 29½ brace. In addition to devoting much time, energy and expense to supporting numerous public

---

2   The Countryside Alliance was formed on July 10th 1997 from three organisations: the British Field Sports Society, the Countryside Business Group, and the Countryside Movement. The Alliance was formed to help promote and defend the British countryside and rural life, both in the media and in Parliament.

3   Fiona Axel-Berg, always known as Sio.

Hounds and hunt staff parading at the Royal Show in 1997. Huntsman Bob Collins, Derick Faulkner MFH, Hopper Cavendish MFH, Mark Andreae MFH and whipper-in Adrian Smith.

relations initiatives, the Hunt Club was also asked to make significant contributions to the Countryside Alliance and MFHA Campaign for Hunting. The defence of hunting did not come cheap, but individuals and Hunts throughout the country rose to the challenge and raised many thousands of pounds for the cause. In April 1996 the Hunt Club donated £5,000 to the Campaign, but three years later the sum had quadrupled to £20,000, partially to help finance the MFHA's contribution to the Burns Report.[4]

A visit to the Duke of Beaufort's country was a highlight of the 1999–2000 season. Those who travelled up to Gloucestershire cherish memories of hacking out from Badminton Park in the morning and washing off hounds and horses in the famous lake at the end of a busy day during which hounds were rock steady to red deer, a species rarely encountered back home. In February the Hampshire Hunt met at The Grange near Northington for the first time in 40 years, and the following November recently retired National Hunt jockey, Luke Harvey, was the guest speaker at a Millennium dinner at the Langrish House Hotel. On February

---

4   The Burns Report famously concluded that hunting seriously compromises the welfare of the quarry species but did not find the practice to be cruel or draw any conclusion on whether hunting should be banned or should continue.

2nd 2001 John Gray's 80th birthday was celebrated with a meet at North End Farm, which was followed by an exhilarating day and the obligatory convivial hunting tea inside his kitchen. As if fighting for the survival of hunting was not enough, the dreaded foot and mouth disease that had shut down sport in the late sixties returned to force a premature close to the 2000–2001 season in early February. The Masters sent their kennelman, Michael Murphy, to Cumbria to help other volunteers from the hunting community with the grisly task of slaughtering infected farm stock. The rest of the season was lost, together with the first half of the following one, before hunting was allowed to resume in December 2001, but there was much rejoicing when Bob Collins won the horn blowing competition at the *Horse & Hound* Ball. In July 2001 Members of the Management and Finance Committee were warned that new regulations forbidding the collection of bovine fallen stock over the age of 30 months would result in a shortage of flesh for the hounds. This news was another headache for beleaguered Masters to address and overcome, and they were authorised to spend £3,000 on a boiler to facilitate mixed feeding.

Derick Faulkner left the Mastership in 2001 and was replaced by Simon Harrap, who was encouraged to join the fray by Mark Andreae's confidential assurance that he need not worry too much, for Hopper does most of the work. The Harrap family enjoy a long connection with the Hampshire Hunt, having owned and occupied Marsh House since 1908. Simon's grandfather was formally congratulated by Members for a good show of foxes back in 1925, and his aunts, Aileen and Jean Harrap, were amongst the first ladies to be invited to wear the Hunt collar three years later. Simon had been a successful point-to-point jockey, winning the Members' race at Hackwood on a number of occasions, whilst his wife, Diana, was hugely supportive of her husband's new role, overseeing the stables at Ropley and sourcing horses for the hunt staff to ride. Their three children were all brought up to ride and hunt, and their eldest daughter, Louise Daly, has been a Joint Master of the Ledbury since 2011. Although Simon runs a small shoot on his farm at Bentley, hunting has always come first, and the Harrap family welcome hounds to Marsh House on the first Saturday after the Opening Meet.

Also in 2001, John and Margaret Newcomb stepped down from being joint Hon. Secretaries having worked tirelessly behind the scenes on behalf of the Hunt Club for 26 years. They both hunted regularly from their home at Newton Valence, John on a chestnut with flowing flaxen mane, and Margaret on a dun which she shared with their daughter Jackie. The couple seldom missed a meet after they had given up riding, easily identifiable by their West Highland White terriers and old

Huntsman Bob Collins with hounds in Badminton Park in 1999.

Lou Marsh, Sidney Bailey (VWH huntsman), Ian Langrish (Garth & South Berks huntsman), Dave Marsh, Douglas Hunt (Hursley Hambledon huntsman), and Carol Bailey at the 1998 HH puppy show.

Above: John and Margaret Newcomb joint Hon. Secretaries from 1975–2001.

Left: Derick Faulkner MFH 1994–2001.

Below: Simon Harrap MFH 2001–2011 with his wife, Diana.

green Land Rover. The vehicle was a magnet for their many friends at the annual point-to-point, where the Newcombs dispensed generous hospitality throughout the day. John ran a respected independent land agency practice from an office in Alton and his forestry expertise was invaluable in the management of Hunt coverts such as The Gullet, Bowers Grove, Sutton Wood and Old Down. One of his last acts as joint Secretary was to oversee the sale of Old Down Wood, which was no longer effective as a fox covert due to the proximity of Four Marks and the busy A31. The covert, which realised £140,000,[5] had been the start of many a fine hunt in the past including an exceptional twenty-mile run that ended beneath moonlight in 1957.

In Nigel and Tessa Webb, the Newcombs handed over to another dedicated husband and wife team who were to remain in office for a decade. The Webbs and their three children all loved hunting and had moved to Kilmeston in the HH country from the Vine and Craven in 1995. Always immaculately turned out, the Webbs were popular and diligent Hunt secretaries and the driving force behind numerous fundraising events, where the food was often provided by their daughter's catering company. Before retiring from a successful career in the city, in 1999 Nigel set up the National Association of Air Ambulances with support from the AA whom he persuaded to put in fifteen million pounds worth of sponsorship. The national network of air ambulances flourishes to this day and is a regular attendee at various hunting and equestrian accidents throughout the year, whilst the business acumen that created it has been an invaluable asset to the Hunt.

The 2002–2003 season got off to an inauspicious start when it became apparent that neither the lady Master nor the huntsman's wife would be available for most of the season. Hopper was recovering from a nasty fall sustained judging the hunters at Dublin Show in August and Carol Collins was injured whilst hunting at Perryland in October. Autumn hunting[6] was the driest for many years and was interrupted by a call to arms for every countryman and woman to set aside September 22nd and join what turned out to be the largest demonstration of any kind to have taken place in Britain. Staged against the backdrop of an imminent ban on hunting with hounds, the Liberty and Livelihood March from Hyde Park to the Houses of Parliament drew an estimated 407,000 participants from every sphere of rural life. Thousands arrived in the capital under their own steam, but others

---

5   The Hunt Club's share of the proceeds of sale from Old Down Wood amounted to £50,400.

6   Always a misnomer, around this time the term *cubhunting* was replaced with the more accurate description, *autumn hunting* by direction of the MFHA.

came into London on thirty one specially chartered trains and two thousand five hundred coaches. The event grabbed front page headlines around the world and was generally well received by an incredulous press; one reporter invited his readers to imagine an FA Cup final crowd walking down Whitehall every hour, for hours on end. There were many gamekeepers amongst a large contingent from Hampshire, including Dougie Maynard who was in charge of the perennially accommodating Herriard Common shoot and Zac[7] Kench from the equally obliging Horsedown Common shoot. As the escalator carried Zac underground to catch the tube he was heard to remark, 'I cannot imagine what would ever induce a fox to go to ground.'

After the success of this event the mood was buoyant back in Hampshire, where Bob and his whipper-in, Will Hudson, provided several good days, including a memorable run following the meet at Holden Farm on New Year's Eve. It was the Quartermasters once more in May 2003, when Tom Floyd joined the Mastership and remained in office for eleven years until standing down after his appointment as High Sheriff of Hampshire in 2014.[8] As a child Tom hunted with the Avon Vale and became Master of the Eton College Hunt before going up to Oxford in 1969, where he spent four years either whipping-in or hunting the Oxford University Drag Hounds. Tom's job with Unilever had necessitated living in disparate countries around the world, but in 1987 he and Sarah moved to Shalden with their sons, Harry and John. From then on they hunted regularly with the Hampshire Hunt, where Tom's uncle, Lieutenant Colonel J.D. Floyd, had been Chairman from 1965–1969. Tom was an excellent Field Master, popular with the farmers and conscientious in organising his part of the country.

Following a run of unfortunate accidents, which resulted in her being advised against continuing to ride, Hopper Cavendish stood down from the Mastership at the end of Tom's first season after eighteen years in office and became Chairman of the Hunt Club on the resignation of Michael Porter. The following November grateful Members, subscribers and supporters presented her with a stone statue of a lurcher at the Opening Meet at Moundsmere, which now occupies pride of place inside the Cavendishes' home at Hall Farm. Two months after Hopper's resignation Members learnt that Nigel Webb and Charlie Corbett had successfully negotiated a five-year lease of the point-to-point course at Hackwood Park, for an annual rent

---

[7] Bob Collins nicknamed George and Carol Kench, Zac and Mandy, after characters in the television soap opera, Emmerdale, and the names stuck.

[8] When Tom Floyd was sworn in as High Sheriff of Hampshire he became the fifth Member of the Hampshire Hunt Club to be granted this honour since 2000.

LISTEN TO US 1996–2005

Huntsman Bob Collins with hounds and children at the Pony Club Camp.

Hunting gamekeepers George (Zac) Kench, Horsedown Common shoot (left),
and Dougie Maynard, Herriard Common shoot, (right).

of £2,262. This was a bold commitment against the prevailing mood of uncertainty and sent out a clear signal that it would be business as usual for the Hampshire Hunt Club going forward.

The signing of this lease in 2003 is an opportune moment to consider some of the many individuals who over the years gave freely of their time to sustain and support a great HH institution. John and Fay Hewett were involved at the sharp end as Clerk of the Course and Secretary respectively for many years with the assistance of keen hunting farmer and Hackwood Park manager, George Bennett, to undertake practical course work when required. Kenny Freeman, known to all as Acker, was also employed by the Hackwood estate and assumed fence building duties after Henry Mustill retired. Wynne Tufnell took over from Peter Lewis as the official course inspector at Hackwood in 1973 and continued with that job for the next 45 years, combining the last twelve of them with the role of starter. Wynne's connections with the HH point-to-point go back further still, for he rode his first winner there in the maiden race in 1962 and later trained several winners from the family home at Binsted. These included Mick and Peggy Close's Great Crack, who was second in the Foxhunters' Chase at Aintree in 1980, and Hotel, a prolific winner of ladies' point-to-point races with their daughter Carol in the plate.

There were several changes in 1987 when John Gray MFH became Chairman and Charlie Corbett, who had already won two Members' races on Catherston Thunderstorm and Hardy Turk, succeeded John Hewett as Clerk of the Course. William Hamer, who had enjoyed a successful career between the flags on his own HH qualified horses, became Treasurer and Anne Moore, whose husband had hunted the Chiddingfold Farmers Hunt before moving to Rotherfield as Sir James Scott's stud groom, took charge of the number cloths. Both were embedded in the fabric of the point-to-point for the next thirty odd years, as was Annie-Lou Gibbs who assumed responsibility for PR and sponsorship. Generous sponsors who were delighted to align themselves with the Hampshire Hunt Club included Christies, Hill Morrison, the NFU and Rathbones. When Charlie stood down as Clerk of the Course in 2004, this important position was filled by Bill Welling, a keen hunting farmer and expert on grassland management.

Within weeks of the Liberty and Livelihood March it became clear that the Labour government had little intention of listening to more than 400,000 people who had travelled to London in September. In December the DEFRA Minister introduced legislation that would have allowed some licensed hunting, but the bill was amended by the left wing MP, Tony Banks, to ban hunting in its entirety. After the bill was eventually rejected in October 2003 by a 212 majority in the House of Lords an identical one was reintroduced into the lower house on September 9th 2004, which triggered a protest vigil outside the House of Commons. Volunteers from the Hampshire Hunt provided cover for 24 hours, the overnight slot falling to Sio and Luke Axel-Berg, who recruited the Earl of Portsmouth, Adrian de Ferranti and Rupert Harvie to join them. Sio remembers London nightlife unfolding over their nocturnal shift, firstly workers and MPs wending their way home, then raucous diners and finally inebriated stragglers in the small hours. Passing cars and taxis hooted their support against a backdrop of Winston Churchill's boarded up statue, but Adrian's attempts to persuade a disbelieving pizza company to deliver hot food were unsuccessful.

The vigil ended on September 15th with a protest in Parliament Square as the Hunting Act was being given its third and final reading inside the House of Commons. The crowd was swelled by supporters from Hampshire, including the Joint Master, Simon Harrap, who was hit over the head by a policeman attempting to restrain an angry, jostling crowd. The bleeding was so profuse that Simon got some very strange looks from customers inside the café where he later sought refuge and a cup of tea. During the commotion eight young men led by Otis Ferry were able to dupe security and gain access into the chamber of the House of Commons where their intervention briefly halted proceedings. The 'invasion' achieved widespread and largely sympathetic publicity but following a short adjournment the House went on to approve the Hunting Bill by a majority of 356 votes to 166. Members and supporters also attended the Labour Party Conference at Brighton on September 28th where Sio Axel-Berg provided naked bathers staging their own protest in the sea with Countryside Alliance stickers to protect their modesty. The triumphant atmosphere that accompanied the Liberty and Livelihood March only two years earlier seemed but a distant memory on November 16th 2004 when the Parliament Act, a rare legislative device that had only been deployed on six occasions since its inception 93 years earlier, was invoked to allow the House of Commons to overrule the Lords and put in place a ban on hunting with dogs that was to come into force on February 18th 2005.

Huge uncertainty surrounded the future of hunting, but at a General Meeting of the Hampshire Hunt Club on December 4th 2004 it was decided that hounds would continue to meet and hunt within the law until every legal challenge had been explored. The determination to keep going was further reinforced at an

Tom Floyd MFH 2003–2014 leading the field.

Below: Simon Harrap (inset top right) injured during the protest in Parliament Square on September 15th 2004.

Above: Adrian de Ferranti, Luke Axel-Berg and Rupert Harvie supporting the all-night vigil at Westminster in September 2004.

Extraordinary General Meeting at the Alton House Hotel on February 6th 2005 when the rules and constitution of the Hampshire Hunt Club were given their most comprehensive overhaul since 1795. Most significantly, Rule 1 was amended as follows: 'The Club shall consist of landowners, farmers, and others interested in lawful hunting and in preserving the tradition of hunting in Hampshire so far as is consistent with the law. The Club shall be called the Hampshire Hunt Club.' At the same meeting Simon Harrap gave an assurance that hounds would continue to go out twice a week until the end of the season and explained the Masters' plans for the future. He emphasised the importance of maintaining the Hunt's infrastructure and ensuring that valuable bloodlines are never lost from the kennels at Ropley.

The many protests and demonstrations during the 2004–2005 season somewhat overshadowed sport, but hounds went out three mornings a week during September and October and accounted for a larger tally than normal. Bob had already announced his decision to retire in 2005 and was invited to hunt the HH hounds in the Duke of Beaufort's country at Tormarton, the Crawley and Horsham at Angmering Park, and the Curre at Itton Court in Monmouthshire. As the February 18th deadline drew near, ever more people turned out on foot and mounted to offer support and solidarity to foxhunting, but many also came to pay their respects to Bob during his final and fourteenth season with the Hampshire Hunt. During his time at Ropley Bob had nurtured several young men who went on to hunt hounds themselves, including Gareth Bow and William Hudson, whilst Daniel Cherriman learnt his hunting ropes helping out at the kennels during his school holidays.

The final meet before the Hunting Act became law was at Tom and Sarah Floyd's Clover Farm at Shalden on Thursday 17th February 2005. Over 200 supporters enjoyed breakfast in the barn, which was followed by rousing speeches from the Hunt's Liaison Officer, Luke Axel-Berg, and Mark Andreae, who paid tribute to the retiring huntsman. A huge cheer rang out when Bob Collins left the meet, and soon afterwards hounds were running in full cry on a fox well found in Shalden Plantation. The best hunt of the day took place later in the afternoon all around Bentworth Lodge before a thick, late afternoon mist came down to lacquer the fields a sombre grey, and Bob Collins reluctantly blew for home. The long, drawn-out notes signalled not only his last proper day as a huntsman, but the end of hunting as he, and everyone else, had ever known it.

After the dust had settled the HH Supporters Club organised an evening in Bob and Carol's honour in April, which was followed by a formal retirement dinner inside a marquee on the lawn at David and Gail Sinclair's house in Isington. Willie Poole was invited to be the guest speaker, but when Hopper met him off the train at Alton, he was clearly the worse for wear. 'I fell amongst thieves at Boodles, my dear' he slurred, 'what I need is toast and marmalade.' Thankfully he recovered in time to deliver a moving speech and pay tribute to Bob's long and illustrious career in hunt service. During the evening guests sat at tables named after coverts in the

Hampshire Hunt country, and as Hopper explained in her own tribute to the retiring huntsman, the event was sold out months in advance. The Masters also expressed their gratitude to Bob and Carol in their end of season report in the HH Blue Book[9] and complimented him on the exceptionally high standards he maintained throughout his fourteen years' service to the Hunt.

---

9 The Blue Book is published annually in late spring by the Hampshire Hunt Club and contains a list of Members and subscribers as well as the Masters' report on the previous season.

Chapter Seventeen 2005–2016

Stormy Waters

M. Andreae Esq., S. Harrap Esq., T. Floyd Esq., 2004–2006,
M. Andreae Esq., S. Harrap Esq., T. Floyd Esq., Mrs L. Axel-Berg
2006–2007, S. Harrap Esq., T. Floyd Esq., Mrs L. Axel-Berg,
2007–2008, S. Harrap Esq., T. Floyd Esq., Mrs L. Axel-Berg,
P. Rowse Esq., 2008–2010, S. Harrap Esq., T. Floyd Esq.,
Mrs L. Axel-Berg, P. Rowse Esq., R. Harvie Esq., 2010–2011,
T. Floyd Esq., Mrs L. Axel-Berg, P. Rowse Esq., R. Harvie Esq.,
2011–2014, Mrs L. Axel-Berg, P. Rowse Esq., R. Harvie Esq.,
Mrs N. Rowsell, 2014–2015, Mrs L. Axel-Berg, R. Harvie Esq.,
A. de Ferranti Esq., Mrs N. Rowsell, 2015–2016

Hunting under the new Act, Sio Axel-Berg joins the Mastership in 2006, her first season, John Gray's memorial service, Peregrine Rowse joins the Mastership in 2008, hunt staff and Members convert to wearing blue coats in the hunting field, Rupert Harvie joins the Mastership in 2010, Hounds return to The Butts at Alton on Boxing Day 2010, Will and Nicki Hudson's wedding, different fundraising initiatives, dinners and hunt balls, sponsored ride and the Hunt's history of supporting charitable causes, Nicola Rowsell joins the Mastership in 2014, Adrian de Ferranti joins the Mastership in 2015, retirement of three long-standing and experienced Masters between 2014 and 2016.

In the fullness of time it was to become clear prosecutions for contravening the Hunting Act would be few and far between, but considerable uncertainty surrounded what was left of the 2004–2005 season. The day after the Hunting Act became law on Saturday February 19th the meet at Moundsmere was attended by a mounted field of 117 riders and a remarkable 2500 people on foot who came to demonstrate that come what may, hunting will never be banished from the British countryside. Giles Harrap, Simon's youngest brother and a barrister who did not approve of bad legislation, gave a stirring speech before Bob Collins laid his beloved hounds onto an artificial scent in Bradley Firs, allegedly concocted from a mix that included fox urine and sardines. Hounds ran like smoke to the far corner of

Moundsmere estate, leaving almost everyone behind and ended up marking at an earth close to where the trail had finished. The fox was duly and legally accounted for by the terriermen and Bob, clearly bemused by the whole sorry proceedings, turned to his whipper-in with a tear in his eye and simply said, 'I cannot do this anymore' before hacking home. Will Hudson, who had whipped in to Bob since 2001 and already been appointed to replace him on May 1st, took over hunting hounds for what was left of the season and rose to the challenge of hunting within the new law.

A year later the first complete season under the new Act was judged to have been a resounding success, thanks in no small part to the overwhelming support of farmers and landowners, who gave written permission for the hunt to conduct legal activities across their land. Traditional meets such as the Opening Meet at Moundsmere, the November fixture at Marsh House, the Christmas meet at Rotherfield Park, and the Old Rectory at Tunworth in February all retained their place in the hunting calendar as generous hosts continued to welcome the Hunt just as they had always done. Hounds bred for centuries to perform one job, and one job alone, also had to adapt to a new and confusing style of hunting. The modern English stamp of foxhound was maintained at Ropley by using stallion hounds from the Exmoor, Hursley Hambledon and VWH Hunts, and during Will's time a smattering of Dumfriesshire blood was also introduced into the kennels.

On May 1st 2006 Sio Axel-Berg joined Mark Andreae, Simon Harrap and Tom Floyd in the Mastership and stayed for ten years. In many ways this was a long overdue appointment since Sio had already spent three decades raising money for the Hunt. She was brought up at Alresford in the heart of the HH country and joined the Hunt's Autumn Dance committee when just seventeen years old. Sio and her brother, Andrew Lyndon-Skeggs, later took over running the Hunt ball in Winchester which routinely attracted up to 500 guests. She kept a horse at livery in order to hunt regularly whilst a student at Sparsholt Agricultural College and has never looked back. Her husband, Luke, acted as the Hunt Liaison Officer during the years leading up to the ban and has also served on the Hunt Club's Management and Finance committee.

Harvest was so far advanced during the summer of Sio's first season that Will Hudson was able to commence hunting on August 21st. Hounds went out three mornings a week throughout autumn, then twice weekly after the Opening Meet until reverting to three days after the shooting season had ended. In February the whole Hunt mourned the loss of Uncle John, who had always hoped to die in the hunting field – 'four strong men and a gate to carry me out on.' That wish had not been granted, but Charlie Corbett paid eloquent tribute inside a packed Cheriton church at John's memorial service, invoking memories of a countryman who was more at home on a horse than behind the wheel of a car, and one who stood out by maintaining the values of rural England of the 1930s. Three months later Mark Andreae stood down as a Joint Master, leaving a triumvirate of Joint Masters to continue from May 1st 2007. Their new season started well in early September but was halted within ten days by an outbreak of foot and mouth disease near Guildford. The Opening Meet at Moundsmere was consequently delayed until November 20th when hounds ran hard all day, and the HH was given a glowing write up by the *Horse & Hound*'s hunting correspondent.

Peregrine Rowse, who lives with his wife Peppy just inside the old Garth & South Berks country, joined the Mastership on May 1st 2008. Peregrine's mother was brought up hunting with the Hampshire Hunt, where her family owned land between Bentley and Headley, but her son became captivated with hounds and venery when following the Pimperne Beagles as a schoolboy at Milton Abbey. Having since enjoyed many happy seasons with the Hampshire Hunt in the

Above: Sio Axel-Berg MFH 2006–2016 with Treasurer since 2017, Kate Andrews.
Left: Tony Maxse MFH from 1975–1983, later Treasurer and keen foot follower.

company of his three hunting daughters, Peregrine was delighted to be given the opportunity to join the Mastership and put something back into the sport he loved. His first season in office was disrupted by a month's stoppage due to kennel cough from mid-October and then by an outbreak of strangles, which resulted in the Opening Meet being postponed for the second year running.

The season proper eventually got underway on November 25th at Moundsmere, where the hunt staff wore blue coats for the first time since the end of the eighteenth century. Members had agreed to the change during a heated debate the previous December after Charlie Corbett's proposal that dispensing with red coats should be a temporary measure for the duration of the ban won the doubters over and is still firmly in place fourteen years on. Three years later the wearing of blue coats was extended to Members, overturning a resolution that red coats must be worn in the hunting field more than two centuries[1] after it was first introduced. These changes were not universally popular, and Peregrine recalls a Member asking him how the field could be expected to follow a blue coat at the head of affairs. 'In much the same way you have followed Mrs Cavendish in a blue coat for the last sixteen years,' came his swift response. Sport was further compromised by the sudden and unanticipated departure of the first whipper-in halfway through the season. His place was admirably filled by Rupert Harvie, a farmer from outside the country near Godalming, with additional support from Nicola Dimond and Kate Andrews. After kennel cough, strangles and staff shortages, hard weather curtailed sport during February, but a frustrating and difficult season ended on a high note with a brilliant day from Shalden Farm.

On May 1st Rupert Harvie cemented his long-standing relationship with the Hampshire Hunt by joining the Mastership. Rupert and his wife Becca live at Heath Farm near Godalming in Surrey, a former dairy enterprise that is now home to a flourishing livery yard and Munstead Horse Trials. Although the farm lies a good forty minutes' drive from the kennels at Ropley and many of the meets are more than an hour away, the distances have never dampened his enthusiasm. Rupert helped out at the kennels several times a week throughout Bob Collins's era and describes the former huntsman as the hunting mentor who taught him everything he knows about the sport. Rupert whipped-in as an amateur for many years before field mastering full time after joining the Mastership, and his knowledge of hounds'

---

1 On January 18th, 1799 Mr Graeme's proposal that red coats should be worn in the hunting field instead of blue was carried unanimously.

STORMY WATERS 2005–2016

Will and Nicki Hudson at The Grange on the occasion of their marriage April 2nd 2011.

Tom Floyd MFH 2003–2014, flanked by his wife, Sarah, and Adrian de Ferranti MFH 2015–2017.

Nigel (on foot) and Tessa Webb (mounted with arm band), Joint Hon. Secretaries from 2001–2011 with their daughter, Georgie.

Emmy and Roddy Watt, Joint Hon. Secretaries from 2011–2018.

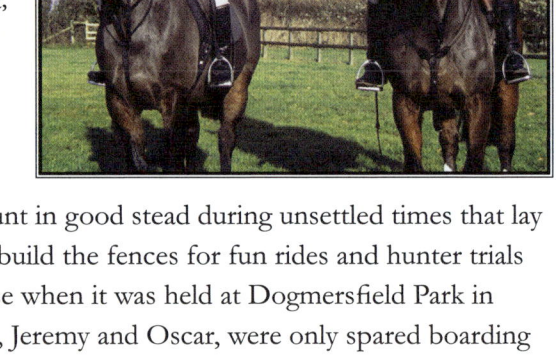

names and traits would stand the Hunt in good stead during unsettled times that lay around the corner. He also helps to build the fences for fun rides and hunter trials and worked on the team chase course when it was held at Dogmersfield Park in the early nineties. The Harvies' boys, Jeremy and Oscar, were only spared boarding school because their father did not want them to miss out on Saturday hunting, which in a roundabout way has led to Jeremy going into hunt service with the Wheatland.

Rupert's first season as an MFH saw hounds return to the traditional Boxing Day venue of The Butts at Alton after the senior Joint Master, Simon Harrap, had successfully presented the Hunt's case to Alton Town Council the previous March. As it turned out the first meet there since 1992 had to be held on foot due to very severe weather, but snow was a distant memory by April when Will

Hudson married Nicki Dimond at Northington Church. There were shades of George Evans's wedding on another spring day 82 years earlier when the couple rode away from the ceremony in full hunting dress for a reception overlooking the lake, which was followed by a private afternoon hunt around the park. Simon Harrap left the Mastership at the end of the season, which was also an appropriate time for Nigel and Tessa Webb to relinquish secretarial duties since all three had started out as Hunt officials ten years earlier. It was retirement in name only for Nigel who succeeded Peter Andreae as a Hunt Trustee in 2016 and has continued to work assiduously on behalf on the Hunt. The secretaries were replaced by another husband and wife team, Roddy and Emmy Watt, who were made Honorary Members of the Hunt Club[2] when they stood down after seven years' service in 2018.

The battle to save hunting had run down the Hunt's financial resources, and in the years that followed the Hunting Act it became increasingly important to supplement subscription income with imaginative fundraising. Ambitious targets such as £40,000 the Management and Finance committee budgeted to receive from fundraisers for the 2009–2010 season were only achievable because so many individuals gave freely of their time and energy to organise new events and revitalise old ones. These included private days' hunting sold off at Hunt breakfasts and a lucrative Auction of Promises at Bonhams in May 2011, where the lots included stays at Tim and Beverley Guinness's villa on Lake Como and Ralph and Patricia Kanter's apartment in Venice. Ironing services courtesy of Annie Fisher, horse clipping and transport, valeting of coats and boots, and flyfishing on the River Itchen were amongst the more affordable lots. The evening was a huge success, but it was agreed that generous donors should not be asked to contribute more than once every two or three years.

Guests at fundraising dinners wore Hunt evening dress or white tie and were entertained by speakers such as General Barney White-Spunner, Giles Rowsell and an opera singer who encouraged everyone present to join in the singing. Several dinners were held at Charlie and Sarah Bullen's Avington Park, and on one memorable occasion at the Gurkha Museum in Winchester, where the tables were adorned by regimental silver and guests dined beneath a portrait of HM The Queen. Hunt balls have been an intermittent feature of the Hampshire Hunt's social calendar ever since the Duchess of Bolton hosted a dance at Hackwood Park in

---

[2] All Hon. Secretaries are made Honorary Members of the Hampshire Hunt Club on retirement.

honour of the Prince of Wales after hunting on January 26th 1791. History doesn't relate which band provided the music on that occasion, but some two centuries later Anthony Ward-Thomas's band, The Swamp Donkeys, entertained revellers at the Harraps' Marsh House on more than one occasion. Since Anthony was an intrepid amateur jockey whose removal firm sponsored the Members' race at Hackwood, this was an entirely appropriate choice. The 2013 Hunt ball was held inside the Reids' Olympic sized indoor arena at Swaines Hill Manor, where young ladies disguised as foxes dispensed shots of vodka and the entertainments included an indoor human steeplechase involving mini tiger traps, straw bales and copious amounts of port.

In the early 2000s the lapsed sponsored ride at Stoke Charity arose phoenix-like from the ashes, in the shape of a new sponsored ride at the Matthews's Swarraton Farm in the Candover Valley. The October event later moved to The Grange at Northington, where a ten-mile route across glorious Hampshire countryside attracted hundreds of participants and raised large sums for the Hunt Club and charities such as the Injured Jockeys Fund and the Countryside Alliance. These organisations were the latest in a long list of charitable causes the Hunt Club

Anthony Ward-Thomas with his daughters Lizzie and Catherine after winning the Members' race in 2000.

has supported throughout its long history. Previous beneficiaries include Ropley village school, the RABI and HSBS, the National Trust, a field hospital in the Boer War, and the Hampshire farmers for whose benefit Frederick Coryton set up the Shire Horse Society before the Great War. In March 2017 the inimitable Sio Axel-Berg and four hunting friends collected more than a thousand confectionaries for a gigantic cake sale at St Maurice's Covert in the centre of Winchester. In one exhausting day the five ladies raised £10,000 for the Hampshire and Isle of Wight Air Ambulance, part of the national network rescue service that has collected many casualties from the hunting field since being founded by Nigel Webb in 1999.

Left: Peregrine Rowse MFH 2008–2015, Chairman of the HH Club since 2018, and walker of Drama '12, best working hound at the 2013 puppy show.

Below: Nicola Rowsell MFH 2014–2016, with her daughters Florence and Cassia.

Tom Floyd left the Mastership in 2014 after eleven years of diligent service and was replaced by Nicola Rowsell, whose parents, Lieutenant Colonel Bill and Margaret Stanford were also staunch supporters. The Rowsells live at West Stoke Farm near Sutton Scotney with their three children, where Nick has run the family farm since the early nineties. As a teenager Nicola represented the HH Pony Club in equestrian events that included the Weston Park open horse trials and a Pony Club tour to Zimbabwe in 1988, and by 2014 was point-to-point Secretary, hunting liaison officer for the HH branch of the Pony Club, and an enthusiastic puppy walker. When combined with a flair for communication, Nicola's marriage to a progressive farmer who enjoys shooting opened doors to the Hunt that had been closed for years. These included the lovely Blackmoor estate near Selborne and the countryside around the Rowsells' home patch that now provides three mornings' autumn hunting and a precious Saturday in the middle of the shooting season. The new Mastership was given a boost in June when Pepsi, whose breeding is pure Hampshire Hunt blood for four generations on her sire's side, won the prize for the best local hound at Ardingly as an unentered bitch. Peregrine left the Mastership at the end of the following season but remained at the centre of Hunt affairs by succeeding Hopper Cavendish as Chairman of the Hampshire Hunt Club. He was replaced as a Joint Master by Adrian de Ferranti on May 1st 2015, who has lived at College Farm, Ellisfield since 1980, which is strategically located between the important hunting estates of Moundsmere and Farleigh. Adrian grew up hunting with the Cheshire and Wynnstay packs, but after moving south Adrian, his wife Christian and their four children all became keen followers of the Hampshire Hunt. Ludo de Ferranti enjoyed himself so much that he went on to spend three seasons whipping-in as an amateur to the Haydon, Heythrop and Warwickshire Hunts.

Much to everyone's regret, within two years of becoming a Joint Master Nicola was compelled to stand down on doctor's orders after donating a kidney that ultimately saved her husband's life. The disappointment caused by her unavoidable departure was compounded by Sio Axel-Berg's retirement after completing a decade as Joint Master. In the space of just three years the Hunt had parted company with a young Master of great promise and in Tom Floyd, Sio Axel-Berg and Peregrine Rowse, three others with a combined total of nearly thirty years' experience at the sharp end of hunting. Through a combination of circumstance and sheer bad luck their leaving was to mark the beginning of a particularly unsettled and challenging period in the Hunt Club's history of long and secure Masterships.

Chapter Eighteen 2016–2022

The Music of the Hounds Will Never Die

R. Harvie Esq., A. de Ferranti Esq., The Earl of Portsmouth DL,
2016–2018, R. Harvie Esq., The Earl of Portsmouth DL,
B. Dyer Esq., 2018–2019, R. Harvie Esq., B. Dyer Esq., 2019–2020,
R. Harvie Esq., Miss S. Evans, 2020–

The Earl of Portsmouth joins the Mastership in 2016, HHSC and its fundraising initiatives, Ben Dyer joins the Mastership in 2018, Will and Nicki Hudson leave in 2018, two unsuccessful huntsmen in three years, Rob Dix hunts hounds for remainder of 2019 season, Hackwood Park lost as the venue for point-to-point, Sally Evans joins the Mastership in 2020, sale of remaining four hunt coverts in 2020, Simon Dunn returns to hunt hounds in 2020, appointment of Country Captains to help organise hunting, hospitality for farmers and gamekeepers, fun rides and the HH branch of the Pony Club, traditions that endure.

Many believed that the Hunting Act would be overturned if and when a Conservative government regained power, but prospects of repeal faded following the May 2010 general election, which resulted in a Conservative and Liberal Democrat coalition. There was a glimmer of hope that a Statutory Instrument[1] might be deployed to introduce a beneficial amendment the following year, but after that fell by the wayside it became increasingly clear that further opportunities to amend or repel the divisive Act would be few and far between. There were few silver linings to the Hunting Act, however the forcing through of bad law undoubtedly persuaded many who were previously ambivalent about hunting to embrace the sport as a protest against an outrageous curtailment of liberty.

---

1 Statutory Instruments are a form of legislation which allow the provisions of an Act of Parliament to be subsequently brought into force or altered without Parliament having to pass a new Act.

There are examples all over Britain of hitherto unsympathetic farmers welcoming the hunt back onto their land, and in Hampshire at least one individual was inspired to take up the sport as his own protest against bad law. The Earl of Portsmouth enjoyed hunting on Dartmoor as a child but moved to the family estate at Farleigh Wallop in Hampshire in 1976 and into the principle residence, Farleigh House, thirteen years later. Quentin Portsmouth was a keen shot who understood the threat posed to his own sport by a Labour government opposed to foxhunting, which led to him joining many of the pro-hunting demonstrations that took place between 1997 and 2005.

After the Parliament Act had been deployed to force the Hunting Act onto the statute books in November 2004, Quentin borrowed clothes for a lawn meet at Farleigh House and joined the field for a day's hunting over his own land. He has been a regular presence in the hunting field ever since, and in 2016 replaced Sio Axel-Berg and Nicola Rowsell as a Joint Master. His deeply held conviction that hunting is the noblest of all field sports echoes sentiments expressed by others connected to the Hampshire Hunt through the ages. These include Alfred Eggar, who spoke on behalf of the farmers at a general meeting in 1919 and noted to warm applause, 'that hunting beat shooting hollow as a sport.' Looking back on hours of excitement, fun and camaraderie since he returned to the saddle, Quentin pays tribute to the friends he has made, the horses he has owned and the glorious countryside he has ridden across behind hounds. He also points out the supreme irony that, to paraphrase Whyte-Melville's[2] famous quote, 'I freely admit that the best of my fun, I owe it to Tony Blair.' Quentin and Annabel Portsmouth, who moved to Home Farmhouse, Farleigh Wallop in 2015, have generously hosted champagne hunt breakfasts inside the magnificent dining room at Farleigh House and the Elizabethan barn at Home Farm. Hounds visit the Farleigh estate regularly during the hunting season, which is also the venue for some of the re-branded fun rides.

In October 2020 Quentin donated the sale proceeds from his lorry to the Hunt Club so they could purchase a new one to transport hounds and horses. Other desirable items such as a quad bike, flesh trailer, horse walker and a new blue coat for the huntsman have been provided by the Hampshire Hunt Supporters Club, whose members prefer to donate specific items to the Hunt rather than allow their

---

2   'I freely admit the best of my fun, I owe it to horse and hound' is a line taken from George Whyte-Melville's (1821–1878) poem, *The Good Grey Mare*. The quote has adorned the front cover of every issue of *Horse & Hound* magazine since it was first published in 1884.

THE MUSIC OF THE HOUNDS WILL NEVER DIE 2016–2022

The Earl of Portsmouth (MFH 2016–2019) leads the field from the meet at Farleigh House in January 2012. From left to right: Rupert Harvie MFH, Lord Portsmouth, Peregrine Rowse MFH, Sio Axel-Berg MFH.

Floss Heeney and friends celebrate adopting Dragon with Sally Evans MFH and the hunt staff in April 2022.

hard-earned cash to be swallowed up by general expenses. There was something of a hiatus within the Supporters Club when the Chairman, Jane Evans, and the majority of her committee retired after years of hard work in 2016, but Lee Thurgood, who consolidated the roles of Secretary and Treasurer, was instrumental in forming a new committee. Jo Young now produces a thrice yearly newsletter, which is a natural successor to the former *Tally Ho!* magazine that began life back in the seventies.

The committee currently raises around £15,000 annually at events ranging from coffee mornings at the kennels in May – which are also heaven-sent opportunities to recruit new puppy walkers – to a horse show at the same venue in late summer. During lockdown most of their fundraising moved online, where innovations included a Grand National sweepstake, a virtual Christmas Market and an auction to choose hound puppies' names, which has raised over £2,500 to date. Hound sponsorship is also popular, especially when it concerns a broken coated young doghound named Dragon, which Simon Dunn acquired from the Llanwrthwl Hunt in Wales after deciding to reinstate Bob Collins's tradition of running a woolly hound with the pack. The demand to sponsor the distinctive Welsh hound was so high that he was also auctioned online, and 'sold' to a syndicate of five friends for £250. The successful bidders were rewarded by a morning at the kennels where they joined Simon on hound exercise before sitting down to a sumptuous breakfast cooked by the lady Master, followed by a photo shoot with Dragon centre stage.

New fundraising ideas became more important than ever following Simon Berry's decision not to renew the point-to-point lease at Hackwood Park from April 1st 2018, although the writing for the Hunt races had been on the wall for some time. The March 2013 meeting was postponed due to bad weather, and despite the stupendous efforts of all involved, only managed to break even as a result. At the subsequent Management and Finance Committee meeting Members recognised the landlord's goodwill but were frustrated by his insistence on lease negotiations being conducted through his agents. At the same meeting it was also suggested that the combined resources of the point-to-point committee could be better deployed organising an alternative and less precarious event elsewhere. The Jervoise family kindly offered their land at Herriard for a new course after Hackwood was lost, but the costs of starting again from scratch were prohibitive, nor was there a realistic prospect of securing a more appealing date from the British Horseracing Authority. The point-to-point has not been run since, but the Members' race scrapbook started by Simon Harrap in 1986 survives as a record of contestants' triumphs and disasters in their quest to win the Challenge Cup presented by Captain J.B. Scott in 1939.

THE MUSIC OF THE HOUNDS WILL NEVER DIE 2016–2022

On May 1st 2018 Rupert Harvie and Lord Portsmouth were joined in the Mastership by Ben Dyer, whose father had bought Hackwood Park Farm on the east side of the A339 following the breakup of the Hackwood estate. Ben's arrival coincided with Will and Nicki Hudson's departure to the Wilton after fourteen years' service with the Hampshire Hunt, during which the popular couple had made many close friends as Will pioneered hunting within the new law. If the loss of three experienced Masters between 2014 and 2016 had shaken the Hunt's stability, the resignation of its longstanding huntsman two years later had further dire consequences, for his replacement turned out to be wholly unsuitable and was dismissed within weeks of arrival. In late June Oliver Harding was recruited at short notice to take over the reins at Ropley. Although a gifted huntsman who provided fine sport during his first season, Oliver's second year was blighted by discord, and in November 2019 he closed the kennel doors behind him for the final time and walked away from the job.

Rupert Harvie had anticipated this unfortunate turn of events and made plans to ensure that hunting would continue for the rest of the season. The hero of the hour came in the unlikely form of Rob Dix, who lived on a council estate near Godalming and worked on the Joint Master's farm. Rupert had encouraged Rob to ride, hunt, and then whip-in as an amateur whenever duties permitted and had no hesitation in asking him to step into the breech. 'Okay, I'll give it a go,' was the 28 year old's response before going on to hunt hounds successfully for the remainder of the most challenging season in the Hunt's peacetime history. Hounds were looked after at Ropley by the young kennelman Josh Slade, with help from Paul Glover who came up from the west country to lend a hand. Rupert Harvie and Rob Dix also took it in turns to attend kennels every day until the return of former whipper-in, Simon Dunn, to hunt hounds on May 1st 2020.

When Quentin Portsmouth left the Mastership in 2019 he was replaced by Sally Evans, who had recently retired from her job travelling the world as a Global Brand Director. Sally had been introduced to hunting on foot with the Vine Hunt by her grandmother when she was just a year old, and from then on dreamt of being given a pony for Christmas. She had to wait many years before buying her own horse out of a field in 2005, but by the early nineties was hunting on Exmoor and hiring the occasional horse from Tom Barnes for a day with the Hampshire Hunt where her mother, Jane, was a keen foot follower and later Chairman of the HHSC. Former Master, Peregrine Rowse, who had replaced Hopper Cavendish as Chairman in 2018, and addressed the turbulence following Will Hudson's departure

THE HAMPSHIRE HUNT 1749–2022

Rob Dix who hunted hounds during 2019–2020 season.

Huntsman since 2020, Simon Dunn, with hounds during an autumn hunting morning.

with resolute good cheer, tact and diplomacy, saw a potential Master in Sally and persuaded her to come on board over lunch. Although Sally's first season was testing in the extreme, the challenges thrown up by three changes of huntsman within a single year did little to dampen her enthusiasm. Two seasons on, she is enamoured by all aspects of a job that she says is a fascinating combination of people, animals and the Hampshire countryside.

During Sally's first winter in office the Hunt Trustees were asked to consider the sale of The Gullet, together with Bowers Grove, Sutton and Northfield Woods. The Andreae family had generously donated The Gullet to the Hunt Club, but the other coverts were owned in partnership with different investors. Many were past or present Members or their heirs, but the Trustees were granted unanimous approval to market the Club's woodland assets at a General Meeting of the Hunt Club in July 2020, and subsequently accepted offers in excess of the asking prices. The sale proceeds from these historic woodlands has been invested to secure financial stability for years to come, but their disposal drew a line under the farsighted policy of purchasing and managing woodland for the benefit of foxes, which had stood the Hunt in such good stead prior to the 2004 Hunting Act. Hunt coverts represented sanctuaries where access to hounds could never be denied, and being undisturbed by shooting, they were also reliable finds.

Their names crop up with unerring frequency in hunt reports published by the *Hampshire Chronicle*, throughout the archived diaries of past Masters, and in books describing hunting down the ages in Hampshire. Sutton Wood is particularly favoured, the covert being named as a stout fox's refuge at the end of an eight-mile point when Henry Deacon was huntsman in 1876, and the start of a brilliant evening hunt to Rotherfield Park following the Opening Meet in November 1902. In 1923 the covert committee had recommended the Hunt Club purchase Sutton Wood for £400, but their advice was not acted upon until Ken Goschen oversaw the purchase of Old Down, Sutton Wood and Bower's Grove from Winchester College nearly forty years later. There is no record of how much it cost Mr Goschen's syndicate to buy these coverts in 1962, but Old Down realised £140,000 when sold in 2001 and the 52 acre Sutton Wood made £320,000 nineteen years later.

When Ben Dyer sold up in Hampshire and moved to Yorkshire in 2019 his departure left just two Joint Masters in charge for the first time since the Goschens' husband and wife team in the sixties. Since their retirement in 1965, subsequent Masters had divided up the country between themselves so that each assumed responsibility for organising hunting and field mastering within their own area. To spread the workload after Ben's resignation, Country Captains were appointed to liaise with the farmers, landowners and shoots in their areas, although Rupert continues to manage the country between Farnham and Alton, and Sally arranges hunting around the kennels at Ropley. The remainder of the country is shared between Jonathan Moseley, Floss Heeney, Alex Gregory and Ben Robinson, stalwarts all who give generously of their time to perform a crucial and demanding role.

The appointment of Simon Dunn to return and hunt hounds in 2020 drew a line under two years of turmoil, although his first season was curtailed by Covid-19 virus restrictions that shut down hunting from December onwards. Since his return to Ropley with his wife Ellie, who runs the Hunt social media accounts, and their young son Ralph, Simon has worked hard to build relationships with farmers, gamekeepers and shoot organisers. He has emulated George Evans's policy of befriending keepers and involves himself in their sport by picking up with his labradors at local shoots such as Shalden and Moundsmere. In their report for the Blue Book after the season had ended, the relieved Joint Masters commented on the new huntsman's positivity and enduring cheerfulness. He has been, they wrote, 'a breath of fresh air.' Simon currently has around 40 couple of hounds under his care at Ropley, which continue to be bred on modern English lines first introduced between the Wars, and acknowledges the Hunt's good fortune to be blessed with so many wonderful puppy walkers that there will be eleven couple of promising young hounds to enter in 2022. He also pays tribute to the assistance he receives in the hunting field from the Hunt's long serving countryman, Peter Bogrish, a renowned breeder of working terriers who sells logs, does some deer stalking for local landowners and is never far from the action when out hunting on his quad bike.

The current Masters are determined to maintain the sense of community within the Hunt and have devised new ways – and resurrected old ones – of entertaining those who welcome hounds onto their land and shoots. In George Evans's day farmers were treated to a lavish lunch at the point-to-point races, which later evolved into a cocktail party at RAF Odiham. That was superseded by drinks parties at Moundsmere and inside a marquee at the point-to-point, but a valuable opportunity to thank and entertain farmers fell by the wayside when the Hackwood Park venue was lost.

In 2021 the cocktail party of old returned in the form of a September drinks party for farmers and landowners at the kennels, which also provided compensation

THE MUSIC OF THE HOUNDS WILL NEVER DIE 2016–2022

Rupert Harvie MFH since 2010, Simon Dunn (huntsman) and Sally Evans MFH since 2019 with hounds at the HH kennels at Ropley.

Sir James Scott Bt. of Rotherfield Park, senior Trustee of the HH Club.

Rotherfield Park, sketched by Phil Momber.

Current Hon. Secretary Sarah Daniels.

THE HAMPSHIRE HUNT 1749–2022

Above and opposite: The HH kennels and stables at Ropley.   The HH Club ballot box.

for the cancellation of Alresford Show due to Covid. In July the Masters organised a clay pigeon shoot and buffet lunch for gamekeepers and shoot organisers at Chris Sole's shooting ground in Alton. In 1910 the first prize was a hammerless double barrelled gun valued at £15; more than a century later Chris Brown, the Tisted keeper, won a bronze trophy of a spaniel, whilst the senior Joint Master was awarded the clay conservation prize for the most misses.

Sponsored rides have been replaced by fun rides that raise large sums for the Hunt Club and charitable causes and are also enjoyed by non-hunting members of the local equestrian community. Spring and autumn rides attract up to 300 participants to Cheriton, Chilton Candover, Farleigh and Herriard, where the Jervoise family have hosted numerous Pony Club camps, summer shows and horse trials since the 1950s.

Herriard Park was also the setting for a special competition to celebrate the HH Branch of the Pony Club's 90th anniversary in 2021. The organisation's strong links with hunting are maintained by the current Joint District Commissioners, former Master, Nicola Rowsell, and Lucy Hunter and the special Pony Club meet during the February half term at Norsebury House is often followed by some of the best hunting of the season.

The Hampshire Hunt has a momentous anniversary of its own to look forward to in 27 years' time, but the manner in which Members are elected to this ancient Club has altered little since the rules were first written down at Winchester on April 25th 1795. Many of the sixteen resolutions listed in copperplate ink inside a faded leather-bound minute book have since been modified or abandoned; membership is no longer limited to 25 gentlemen, the current subscription is rather more than 25 guineas, and hunt dinners are not served at *precisely 5pm*. However rule number twelve, *One black ball to exclude*, for the balloting of anyone proposed and seconded in writing for membership of the Hampshire Hunt Club has survived[3] for 227 years. The incumbent Hon. Secretary, Sarah Daniels, still presents Members with the wooden box that her predecessors offered to tailcoated Members by candlelight inside the Swan Inn at Alresford in the late eighteenth century. The rectangular box has a circular aperture resembling a porthole at the front, which is just large enough to accommodate a clenched fist clasping a single black bean. Inside there is a draw divided into two compartments marked *Yes* or *No* in raised wooden lettering on the exterior. After each Member has deposited their bean, the box is unlocked with a tiny key and the draw pulled open for all to see. If the No compartment is empty the candidate is admitted to one of the oldest Hunt clubs in the world.

The Hampshire Hunt continues on an unstoppable, roller coaster journey that began with the arrival of Thomas Ridge and his hounds to hunt the undulating wooded countryside surrounding Kilmeston Manor close to the Itchen's source in 1749. Members and staff ceased wearing blue coats out hunting in the last year of the eighteenth century, but reversion to the original livery after more than two centuries in scarlet is one of many ways in which the Hunt has evolved and adapted in response to changing times, attitudes and legislation. Since its earliest beginnings the Hampshire Hunt has confronted and surmounted inconceivable challenges, from an acute shortage of foxes first experienced in the early 1800s, to the menace of barbed wire, the deprivations of two World Wars, saboteurs and the most formidable challenge of them all, the Hunting Act of 2004. The Hampshire Hunt Club has overcome each and every one through a unique combination of decency, decorum and diplomacy and never relinquished its philanthropic sense of duty to the local community and beyond.

For nearly three centuries hounds and huntsmen, both professional and amateur, have shown consistently good sport against a merry canvas of camaraderie

---

3   In 1795 a single black ball dashed any hope of election, but in 2005, this rule was amended from a single black ball (or bean) to exclude membership to one black ball per seven votes. The proposer or seconder of a prospective Member may also be invited to speak on behalf of his or her nominee before votes are placed. These minor changes became necessary after an unknown Member black balled all new candidates as a matter of course.

and fun. It is no coincidence that Herman Andreae's reference to the 'Happy Hunt' during the bicentenary dinner at Moundsmere in 1949[4] is as appropriate today as it was then. The Hampshire Hunt continues to be afforded a generous welcome by farmers whose own ancestors followed hounds across the very same fields, and by a new, younger generation of landowners at the helm of sporting estates whose history is intertwined with the Hunt.

The greatest constant of all, the unbroken golden thread running through the fabric of the Hampshire Hunt's long and illustrious history has been, and will always be, the hounds themselves. Their music will reverberate across Hampshire's rolling hills, broad valleys and ancient woodlands when the Hampshire Hunt celebrates its tercentenary in 2049. Then, and for evermore.

---

[4] The 200th anniversary dinner was held in October 1949, which is the bicentenary of Thomas Ridge's Mastership. It has been claimed this celebration took place four years late due to the Second World War, however there is no evidence to link Squire Evelyn's private pack, which existed between 1745 and 1749, with the Hampshire Hunt.

Members and staff of The Hampshire Hunt Club at The Grange, Northington on Saturday 27th November 2021.

Mounted Members

1. Lord Portsmouth (former Joint Master)
2. Mrs Floss Heeney
3. Mrs Sarah Daniels (Hon. Secretary)
4. Mrs Annie Lou Gibbs
5. Mrs Kate Andrews (Hon. Treasurer)
6. Mr Dougie Lowe
7. Mrs Liz Cowper Coles
8. Mr Peregrine Rowse (Chairman & former Joint Master)
9. Mrs Sio Axel-Berg (former Joint Master)
10. Mr Rob Dix (first whipper-in)
11. Mr Simon Dunn (huntsman)
12. Mr Red Orr (second whipper-in)
13. Mr Rupert Harvie MFH
14. Miss Sally Evans MFH
15. Mr Charlie Corbett (Trustee & Vice Chairman)
16. Mr Jonathan Moseley
17. Mrs Sarah Barnes
18. Mrs Julie Butler
19. Mr Johnny Cowper-Coles
20. Mrs Ali Bedford
21. Mr Ian McNeil

Members Standing

22. Mrs Nicola Rowsell (former Joint Master)
23. Mrs Susannah Hardman
24. Mrs Tessa Webb (former Joint Hon. Secretary)
25. Mr William Swan
26. Mrs Gail Sinclair
27. Mr Simon Harrap (former Joint Master)
28. Mr Tim Walters
29. Mrs Annie Fisher
30. Mr Andrew Shirvell
31. Mrs Antonia Camilleri
32. The Hon. Mrs Hopper Cavendish (former Joint Master & Chairman)
33. Mr Andrew Hazel
34. Mr Christopher Reed
35. Mrs Susie Corbett
36. Mrs Annie Stevenson
37. Mrs Sona Harrap
38. Mr Nigel Webb (Trustee & former Joint Hon. Secretary)
39. Mrs Cherida Cannon
40. Mr Phillip Sykes
41. Sir James Scott Bt. (Chairman of the Trustees)
42. Mrs Ginny Freer-Smith
43. Mr Ralph Kanter
44. Mrs Susannah Dennis
45. Mr Martin Moore QC
46. Mr David Cowley CBE
47. Mrs Effie Andreae
48. Mr Anthony Cooke
49. Mr Anthony Boswood QC
50. Mr Peter Andreae
51. Mrs Penny Ackroyd
52. Mrs Rebecca Caplan
53. Mrs Mel Petre
54. Mrs Sue Maxse (former Joint Master &Vice Chairman)
55. Mrs Phil Momber
56. The Hon Mrs Alex Macpherson
57. Mrs Emmy Watt (former Joint Hon. Secretary)
58. Mrs Jill Rowsell
59. Mr John Jervoise
60. Mr Derick Faulkner (former Joint Master)
61. Mrs Sarah Floyd
62. Mr John MacMahon
63. Mr Tom Floyd (former Joint Master)
64. Mrs Sue Marriott
65. Mr Tim Guinness
66. Mr Charlie McCowen
67. Mr Bill Welling (former point-to-point Clerk of the Course)

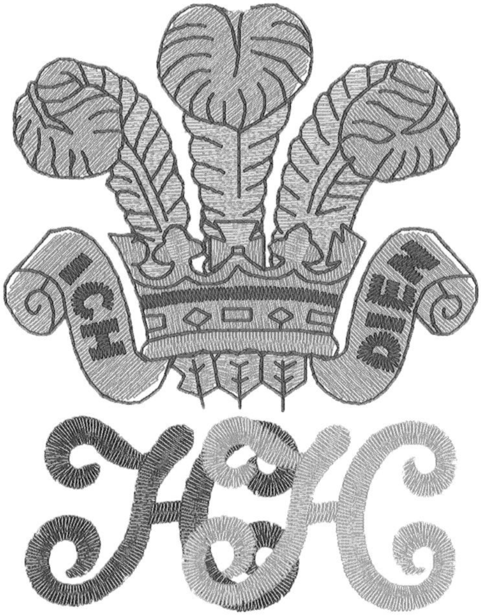
ICH DIEN
HH

Bibliography

Books and sources consulted include the following:

Sporting Reminiscences of Hampshire from 1745 to 1862, by Aesop.
The Hampshire Hunt, a privately printed book by C.F.G.R. Schwerdt published in 1929.
Hampshire Hunt Club minute book 1795–1809.
Hampshire Hunt Club minute book 1856–1888.
Hampshire Hunt Club minute book 1888–1912.
Frederick Coryton's hunting diaries 1889–1909.
Frederick Coryton's book of press cuttings from 1884 to 1920.
The Sportsman Second Series, Volume XIX July to December 1848.
Hampshire Hunt Club Letter Book 1894.
The Foxhound of the Twentieth Century, by Cuthbert Bradley, published 1914.
Evelyn Baring's scrapbook begun in 1914.
A History of Hunting in Hampshire, by Brigadier General J.F.R. Hope published in 1950.
Hampshire Hunt Shire Horse minute book 1891–1914.
Hampshire Hunt Shire Horse minute book 1914–1916.
Correspondence between the MFHA and the Ministry of Food during the First World War.
George Evans's Game Registers dated 1896 and 1905.
Hampshire Hunt Club Letter Book 1912.
George Evans's leather bound hunting diaries 1891–1892, 1894–1914 and 1926–1939 inclusive.
Hampshire Hunt Club minute book 1912–1936.
Hampshire Hunt Club minute book 1936–1954.
Joyce Kemp's handwritten notes on the HH branch of the Pony Club in the 1930s and 1940s.
Hampshire Hunt Club Finance Committee minute book 1952–1970.
Hampshire Hunt Club minute book 1954–1970.

The Hampshire Hunt branch of the Pony Club, a booklet produced in 1954.

Michael Bowman-Manifold's hunting diaries Volumes 1 to 7 covering the 1950s, 1960s, 1970s and early 1980s, and press cuttings contained therein.

Geoffrey Gregson's hunting diaries from the 1960s and 1970s.

Copies of *Tally Ho!*, produced by the Hampshire Hunt Supporters Club in the 1970s and 1980s.

Hampshire Hunt Management and Finance Committee minute book 1970–1989.

Members' race point-to-point scrapbook covering 1936–2017.

Hunt Scurry scrapbook 1987–1999.

Hopper Cavendish's hunting diaries from 1980s–2004.

Masters' reports from H.H. Blue Book 1980s onwards.

Hampshire Hunt Club minute books from 2000–2016.

Miscellaneous articles from *Country Life*, *The Field*, *Horse & Hound* and *Shooting Times & Country Magazine*.

Baily's Hunting Directory.

Miscellaneous press cuttings, newsletters, correspondence, maps, agreements and other documentation from the Hampshire Record Office in Winchester.

Index

A
Abbotstone Down 24, 29, 40, 77, 110
Actaeon 36
Aesop 36
Agriculture Hall, Islington 63
Aikenhead, Penny 208
Aintree 216
Albert Gate, Knightsbridge 74
Aldershot 107, 109, 112, 122, 123, 133, 177, 183
Alford 160
Alice Holt 46, 59, 89, 155
Alresford Pond 100, 181, 222, 241
Alresford Town Band 64
Alresford xii, 16, 18, 21, 36, 41, 43, 54, 59, 68
Alresford, Town Hall 51
Alton 20, 25, 37, 49, 54, 67, 68, 93, 98, 131, 146, 195, 199, 201, 213, 219, 221, 238, 241
Alton House Hotel 218
Amery Wood 25
Andover 185
Andreae, Herman 131, 135, 136, 138, 140, 141, 142, 145, 166, 176, 181, 243
Andreae, Mark 195, 199, 203, 207, 210, 219, 221, 222, 223, 227
Andreae, Mrs 141
Andreae, Peter 173, 176–177
Andreae, Sonny and Clodagh 176–177
Andrews, Joann 174, 193
Andrews, Kate 173–174, 224
Andrews, Mr 138
Andrews, Stephen 183, 185
Andrews, Steve 172, 173, 174, 175, 179–180, 181, 183, 185, 186, 189, 193, 195–196, 202
Angmering Park 219
Apperley, Charles 26–27, *see also* Nimrod,
Archer Shee, Colonel Jack 157, 159, 160, 162, 164
Ardingly 166, 175, 196, 230
Armsworth Park 146, 185, 203
Ashburton, Lord 15, 38, 43, 48
Ashe Park 18
Ashen Wood 146
Assembly Rooms 93, 149
Aston Wood 123
Atherton, Miss 159, 166
Atkinson, Mr 64
Aubertin, Major 59
Avington Park 227
Axel-Berg, Fiona (Sio) 208, 217, 221, 222, 229, 230, 232
Axel-Berg, Luke 217, 219
Aylward, Leslie 129, 134–135, 137, 138, 145, 149, 155, 161, 164, 167, 189

B
Badminton Park 209
Banks MP, Tony 217
Barclay, Mr 60, 77
Baring, Lady 64
Baring, Viscount 48
Barlow, Richard 196
Barnes, Gerald 131, 138–140, 169, 179
Barnes, Mary 140
Barnes, Sheila 140
Barnes, Sylvia 140
Barnes, Tom 140, 179, 203, 235
Barrett, Major 33, 34
Barry CB CBE, Major General R. H. (Dick) 157, 159–160, 162, 175
Basing, Lord 58, 80
Basingstoke 54, 59, 60, 77, 109, 179, 185
Basingstoke Canal 77
Bathurst, Earl of 60, 95, 142, 164, 195, 209, 219
Beaufort, Duke of 20, 120, 164, 195, 209, 219
Beaurepaire 27
Beauworth 30, 36, 47, 189
Beauworth coverts 47
Beauworth Woods 25
Becksteddle 188
Bedford, Duke of 20
Beeney, Darren and Alison 197
Begg, Mrs Pam 146, 203
Begg, Wing Commander 146
Bell, Isaac 78
Bennett, George 148, 216
Bentley 55, 58, 165, 210, 223
Bentley Green 46
Bentley Station 43
Bentworth 109, 138, 146, 169, 177, 181, 190
Bentworth Hall 146
Bentworth Lodge 167, 176–177, 219
Berens, Major 146
Berry Hill, Farringdon 61
Berry, Lord Julian 146
Berry, Simon 234
Bigge, Sir Arthur 78
Biggs, Will 26
Bighton Manor 185
Binsted 105, 216
Binsted Wyck 71
Bishops Sutton 21, 34, 77
Blackberry Lane 202
Blackmoor 57
Blackmoor estate 174, 230
Blackmoor Wood 109
Blair MP, Tony, 207, 232
Blakiston Bt., MC, Sir Arthur 131, 142
Bogrish, Peter 238
Bolton, Duchess of 19, 227
Bolton, Lord 16, 27
Bonham Carter, Lady Charlotte 171
Bonner, Major 152
Boodles Club 41, 46, 60, 219
Bordon Camp 60, 100, 133
Bordon Station 166
Bovill DSO, MC, Major Anthony C. 93, 100, 102
Bow, Gareth 219
Bower's Grove 154, 237
Bowman-Manifold, Michael 159, 169
Bowtell, Mr 161
Boyles, Dennis 145, 155, 161
Bradley Firs 221
Bramdean 146, 186, 197
Bramdean Common 42, 57, 67, 146, 166, 186, 195, 197
Brassey, Mr 60
Brick Kiln Farm 135
Brighton 217
Broadley, Richard 185
Brockenhurst 189
Brockwood 36, 146
Brockwood Copse 77
Brockwood coverts 146
Brockwood Dean 77
Brockwood Park 57
Brown, Chris 241
Brownfields 58
Buccleuch, Duke of 60
Bull's Bushes 77
Bullen, Charlie and Sarah 227
Burkham 109
Burkham House 130, 141
Bush Down 161
Bushy Warren 77
Butler Boys 185, 186
Butler, Brian 140
Butler, Chris 202
Butler, Fred 186
Butler, Jim 186
Butler, Michael 186
Butler, Pete 186
Butler, Rose 186
Butler's covert 154
Byas, David 208

C
Caldbeck 208
Calmady, Admiral 21, 25
Calthorpe, Lord 48
Camrose, Lord 146
Candover 25

– 249 –

Candover Valley 228
Cantelupe, Viscountess 130
Carlisle, Rosalind, Countess of 81–82
Carson, Willie 208
Castle Howard 82
Cavendish, Lucinda (Hopper) (née Corbett) 175, 177, 181, 183, 185, 189, 190, 195–196, 197, 201, 208, 210, 213, 214, 219–220, 230, 235
Cavendish, the Hon. John 189
Cazenove, Mr 77
Chalcraft, Austen 97, 112
Chalmers, Mr 119–120
Chawton House 37, 43, 77
Chawton Park 29, 34, 59, 67, 100, 112, 146
Chawton Park Wood 146
Cheriton Church 223
Cheriton Wood 34, 146, 166
Cheriton xiii, 33, 36, 160, 189, 241
Cherriman, Daniel 219
Chiffland 30
Chifney, Samuel 18
Chilcomb 64
Chilton Candover 241
Chilton Wood 34
Civil, Julie 186
Clare Farm 157
Cleveland, Duke of 35
Close, Carol 216
Close, Mick and Peggy 216
Coldstream 208
Colemore 177, 203
College Farm, Ellisfield 230
College Woods, Bighton 30
Collins, Bob 195, 196–197, 203, 206, 207, 208, 210, 214, 219, 221–222, 224, 234
Collins, Carol 196–197, 213
Collyer, Mr 30
Comb, Mr 46
Complin, John 83, 85, 86, 87, 97, 99, 100–102
Compton 25
Cooper, Angela 177–179, 188
Cooper, Harry 177, 188
Cooper, Jack 53, 67–68, 71
Corbett, Charlie 148, 189, 190, 214, 216, 223, 224
Corbett, Lucinda (Hopper) 160–161, 189

Corbett, Reverend Lionel 85, 97, 189
Coryton, Captain A. 39, 99, 145
Coryton, Frederick 53, 54–55, 56, 57–58, 63, 64, 67, 68, 81, 83, 85, 87, 93, 95, 97, 99, 112, 116, 145, 159, 189, 229
Courage DSO, Lieutenant Colonel Miles R. F. 127, 129, 131, 133–135, 136, 138
Coventry, Earl of 58–59
Cowen, Major Robin 189
Cowen, the Hon Mrs Shelagh (Toddy) 159, 167, 171, 176
Cox, Will 35
Crabwood 34
Cranbury Park 35
Craven country 32
Craven, Lord of 20
Crawley 219
Cricketers Arms, The 60
Crondall 58
Cumberland, Duke of 37
Cunynghame, Lady 19
Curre, Sir Edward 123, 195, 196
Curzon, Lord 70

D
Daly, General C.A. 100, 102
Daly, Louise 210
Daniels, Sarah 242
Darbishire, Mr 153
Davies, Dominique 199
Dawes, Mr 76
de Ferranti, Adrian 217, 221, 230
de Ferranti, Ludo 230
Deacon, Caroline 42
Deacon, Henry xii, 41, 42, 43, 44, 46, 47, 48, 49, 51, 53, 78, 135, 160, 237
Dicker, Gilbert 140
Dix, Rob 231, 235
Dogford Wood 107, 108, 123
Dogmersfield Park 226
Dora's Green 154
Downlands 174
Drury Farm, Bentworth 179
Dummer Grange 105
Dunn, Ellie 238
Dunn, Ralph 238
Dunn, Simon 231, 234, 235, 238
Durdens 77
Dutton, Ralph 202
Dyer, Ben 231

E
East Tisted 120, 146, 153
East Worldham 140
Easters 35
Edgar, Anthony 159, 167
Edgar, Roberta 162
Edgar, Robin and Esme 162
Edwards, Lionel 141
Eggar, Alfred 87, 95, 97, 232
Egremont, Lord 20
Ellen Wood 116
Ellisfield 77, 230
Eton College 173, 214
Evans, George Patrick Elystan – see Evans, George
Evans, George xiii, 69, 70, 71, 73, 74, 76, 77, 78, 81, 83, 84, 85, 86, 87, 93, 97, 106, 107, 108, 109, 110, 112, 116, 119, 120, 123, 127, 129, 130, 136, 137, 141, 154–155, 157–158, 171, 175, 176, 199, 227, 238
Evans, Jane 234
Evans, Major – see Evans, George
Evans, Miss Sally 231, 235–237, 238
Evans, Mrs Diana (née Stuart Smith) 107, 116
Evelyn, Squire xi, 15, 16, 27, 203, 243

F
Fanshawe, Captain Brian 174
Farleigh 18, 36, 230, 241
Farleigh estate 232
Farleigh House 232
Farleigh Paddocks 18
Farleigh Wallop 232
Farnham 20, 29, 46, 59, 138, 238
Farquhar, Captain Ian 195
Farringdon 61, 67, 129, 131, 161, 181, 189
Farringdon Vale 201
Faulkner, Frederick Ralph (Derick) 148, 175, 195, 201–203, 207, 210
Faulkner, Wendy 202
Ferdinand, Archduke Franz 80
Ferry, Otis 217
Filmore Hill 146
Fisher, Annie 227
Fisher, William 40, 42
Fitzhardinge, Lord 37
Fitzpatrick, Mr 48

Fitzwilliam Hunt Kennels 199
Fitzwilliam, Lord 20
Fletcher, Hamilton 57
Fletcher, Major 40
Floyd, Lieutenant Colonel John D. 159, 162, 164, 214
Floyd, Sarah 219
Floyd, Tom 207, 214, 219, 221, 222, 230
Foster MP, Michael 208
Foster, Richard (Dick) 21, 26, 29, 32, 33, 34, 36, 37
Four Lanes 47
Four Marks 213
Freeman, Kenny (Acker) 216
Frenchmere Copse 202
Frere, Mr 83, 84–86
Froyle 145, 157, 164, 203
Fryingdown Copse 109
Fulley 34

G
Gage, Lord 26
Gaick 86
Gamblin, Edward 120
Garth, Mr 46, 60
Gaston 181
Gaston Wood 109
Gearing, Mr 34
Gibbs, Annie-Lou 216
Gifford, Lord 33, 36–37
Glidden, Joseph 55
Globe Inn, Alresford 64
Godalming 224, 235
Golden Pot 36, 83
Goschen, H. Ken 145, 146, 149, 150–152, 153, 154, 155, 157–158, 159, 164–165, 166, 171–171, 175, 185, 188, 195, 201, 237
Goschen, Mrs Oney 127, 145, 149, 171
Gosling, Phil 16
Graeme, Charles 23, 25, 26, 46, 224
Gray, George 176
Gray, Gillian 189, 190–193
Gray, Joanna 189
Gray, John 157, 159, 160–161, 164, 167, 173, 174, 176, 184, 185, 188–189, 190, 195, 199, 203, 206, 207, 210, 216, 221
Gray, Pat 160, 166
Great Wood 181
Gregory, Alex 238
Gregson, Geoffrey 157, 159, 160, 162, 164, 166, 167, 169–171, 174, 175

INDEX

Gregson, Molly 160
Greywell 46, 140
Guildford 223
Guildford Station 133
Guildford, Bishop of 32
Guinness, Tim and Beverley 227
Gurkha Museum, Winchester 227
Guy, Albert 53, 64

H

Hackwood Park and estate 18, 19, 27, 70, 138, 145, 146–147, 179, 183, 202, 207, 210, 214, 216, 227–228, 231, 234, 235, 238
Hackwood Park Farm 235
Hagen, Miss
Hall Farm, Farringdon 138, 169, 189, 214
Hall Place 110, 112
Hall, Joe 16
Hambledon 25, 33, 35–36, 44, 47, 59, 60, 116, 146, 161, 188
Hamer, William 216
Hamilton, B 107, 119, 120
Harding, Oliver 235
Harkers Crossroads 116, 153, 167
Harmsworth xiii, 15, 16, 27, 32, 33
Harrap, Aileen and Jean 210
Harrap, Diana 210
Harrap, Giles 221
Harrap, Simon 177, 183, 207, 210, 217, 218–219, 221, 222, 226–227, 234
Harringay 140
Harting Hill 120
Hartley 105, 108, 109
Hartley estate 201, 202
Hartley Mauditt xiii, 57
Hartley Vale 161
Harvey, John 58
Harvey, Luke 209
Harvie, Jeremy and Oscar 226
Harvie, Rupert 217, 221, 224, 235
Hastings, John M. 107, 119, 120
Hatch Warren 18
Hatchmoor Farm, Greatham 183
Hatley Park 69
Hawkley 60, 108, 120, 162
Haworth, Captain Martin 33, 35–36, 42
Hayne, Mr 23
Hazely Row 34
Hazletine, Frank 159, 161, 166

Headbourne Worthy 58
Headley 223
Headley Wood Farm 174, 188
Healey, Denis 175
Healey, Mr 112
Heathcote, Sir William 46
Hedge Corner 60, 120
Heeney, Fiona (Floss) 140, 238
Hellfire Jack 16
Hen Wood 43, 109
Hennessy, Pop 26
Her Majesty The Queen, Elizabeth II 227
Herbert, the Hon. Geordie 190
Herriard 33, 36, 37, 234, 241
Herriard Church 116
Herriard Common 18, 109, 214
Herriard Grange 68
Herriard Park 43, 48, 54, 154–155, 162, 189, 199, 241
Herring, David 185, 186
Hewett, Fay 216
Hewett, John 148, 216
HH Inn xiii
Hickstead 140
High Wood 116
Highmoor, John 138, 145
Hinton Ampner 146, 202
Hinton Ampner House 201, 202
Hinton House 25
Hobart, Major 102
Hobart, Mrs Kathleen Stanley 93, 100–102
Hobbs Farm 135
Hockley House, Cheriton 189
Holden Farm 214
Holman, Mr 152
Holmes, Captain 141
Holroyd, Mr E. C. 138
Home Farmhouse 232
Hope, Brigadier General 141
Hope, Lieutenant Colonel 115
Horsedown Common 35, 171, 214
Horsham 219
Hothfield, Lord 63
House of Commons 49, 142, 173, 217
Houses of Parliament 208, 213
HRH Charles, The Prince of Wales 15, 18, 20, 36, 69, 78, 80, 112, 171, 173, 181, 228
Hudson, Miles 199
Hudson, Nicki (née Dimond) 221, 224, 227, 231, 235

Hudson, Will 214, 219, 221, 222, 226–227, 231, 235
Humbly Grove 35
Hungry Copse 181
Hunt Lodge 166, 176
Hunter, Lucy 241
Hursley 27, 46, 222
Hursley Hambledon 186, 190, 222
Hyde Park 207, 208, 213

I

Ikey Bell 107
Inadown, Newton Valence 160
Ings, Will 131, 135
Inskip, Mrs Anne 165
Irons, Jeremy 208
Isington 219
Isnage Farm, Bentley 165
Itchel Park 58
Itchen Abbas 16, 54, 160
Itchen Wood 146
Itton Court 123, 195–196, 199, 219

J

Jackson, Captain 60
James, Charles 133, 136–137
Jeffreys, Captain George – see Jeffreys, General Sir George
Jeffreys, General Sir George 71, 93, 98, 100, 110, 112, 130, 138, 141, 155
Jennings, John 26
Jersey, Lady 19
Jervoise family 234, 241
Jervoise, Arthur Tristram Ellis 53, 54, 55, 57–58, 64, 68, 71, 77, 78
Jervoise, Captain Edmund Purefoy Ellis 71, 76, 78, 80, 83
Jervoise, Francis Michael Ellis 33, 37, 38, 54
Jervoise, Jack 199
Jervoise, Major F.H.T. 154
Jervoise, Sir Thomas 54
Jones, Bob 145, 146, 150, 154, 155–156
Jones, Hume 190

K

Kanter, Ralph and Patricia 227
Kealy, Jack 138, 140, 142
Kemp, Miss Joyce 127, 133
Kempshott 18, 19, 20
Kempshott House 18, Kench, Zac 214
Kennet, George 39
Kilmeston 123, 213
Kilmeston Manor xi, 15, 16, 18, 20, 242

Kilmeston Westwood 59
King Edward VII 78
King George IV 18, 20, 78
King George V 68, 69, 78
King George VI 136
King Henry V 208
King, John 171
King's Worthy 34–35, 54
Kingscote, Thomas 21, 25, 26
Kingsley 166
Kitcombe Wood 112
Knight, Ben 181
Knight, Edward 29, 33, 37–38, 40
Knight, John 26
Knight, Montague 51, 53, 54, 55, 70, 83
Knightsbridge Green 74
Knox, Lieutenant Colonel 53, 54, 56, 103
Knutsford, Viscount 120

L

Lamerton 41
Langrish Farm 34
Langrish House Hotel 209
Lasham 18, 63, 105, 185
Lasham Station 109
Lasham, Church Farm 63
Latham, Mr Justice 199
Leconfield, Lord 90, 173
Lee Wood 157
Leigh Newton DSO, Major H. 145, 149
Lewis, Peter 216
Liphook 59
Liss 59, 102
Liss Place 54, 57
Little Somborne 23
Littleworth, Sidney 174
Llewellyn, Owen 89
Locks Grove 157
London Road 148
Longmoor Ranges 174
Lonsdale, Lord 86
Loriston-Clarke, Jennie 189
Lovington 162
Lower Froyle 83
Lower Green, Hawkley 162
Lower Lanham covert 135, 146
Lowther 196
Lowther, George 176
Ludshott Common 174
Lyndon-Skeggs, Andrew 222

M

Madron 208
Magdalen College 116, 197
Major, John 26
Mallalieu, Baroness Ann 208

– 251 –

Mangles MC, Lieutenant Colonel Frank 93, 102–103, 105–106
Manor Farm, Farringdon 58, 181
Mareland's Bridge 36
Markham, Richard 197, 206
Marsh House 58, 210, 222, 228
Marsh, Dave and Lou 179
Martin, Chris 199
Martin, Diana 186
Martyr Worthy 160
Marwell Hall 77
Matterley Gate 77
Maun, Fred 142
Maxse, Anthony 173, 181, 183, 186, 189
Maxse, John 169
Maxse, Sarah 190
Maxse, Sue 171, 181, 185, 193
Maynard, Dougie 214
McCowen, Simon 176
Medstead 54, 67, 181
Medstead Green 59
Meon Valley road 146
Milday, Sir Henry St John 18
Mill, Rev, Sir John Barker 33
Miller, Joan 105
Miller, Sir John 181
Mills, Peter 183
Milton 199
Milton Abbey 223
Milton Park 199
Milward, Clement 46
Mitchell, Colonel Frank 39, 120
Mitchell, Mrs 183
Mitchell, Tom 73, 95, 98, 105, 108
Momber, Frank 173, 183–184, 189, 193
Momber, Phil 183
Moore, Anne 216
Moore, Daphne 130
Morestead 34
Morpeth 208
Morris, Henry 120
Moseley, Jonathan 238
Mostyn, Sir Thomas xiii
Moundsmere 77, 135, 138, 176, 181, 189, 195, 203, 214, 221–222, 223, 224, 230, 238, 243
Moundsmere Manor xi, 136
Mounters Farm 127
Mozambique 64
Munro-Kerr, Duncan 177
Murphy, Michael 210
Mustill, Henry 179, 216

N
Napper, Mr 33, 37
Nason, Henry 39

Naylor, Mr 85, 97
New Cheriton 146
Newberry, Geoffrey 162
Newcomb, Jackie 210
Newcomb, John 210–211
Newcomb, Margaret 210
Newton Common 34
Newton Valence 107, 119, 120, 160, 161, 162, 163, 169, 175, 210
Newton Valence Place 171
Newton, Ursula (Urkie) 167
Nicholson MP, Mr W.Godfrey 64, 138
Nimrod 21, 26, 27, 29–30, *see also* Apperley, Charles
Noar Hill 153
Nore Hall 119, 120
Norsebury House 241
North End Farm, Cheriton 160, 166, 206, 210
North Waltham 105
North, Kruger 159, 164, 185, 186
Northbrook, Earl of 48–49, 93, 98
Northington 15, 58, 209, 228
Northington Church 227
Northumberland, Duke of 171
Norton Farm 175, 201, 202
Nunez, Mr 24
Nutley 36

O
Odiham 37, 49, 164
Old Alresford 32
Old Alresford House 123, 146
Old Down 103, 112, 146, 154, 213, 237
Old Down Wood 213
Old Rectory, Tunworth 222
Onslow, Augustus 33, 34, 35
Opik MP, Lembit 208
Opperman, Michael 183
Orbell, Joseph 37
Orred, Captain 93, 103, 105–106
Orvis, Will 77, 84, 85, 86, 95, 106
Osbalderton, Squire xiii, 38
Ovington 29

P
Park Copse 179
Parliament 207, 208, 231
Parliament Square 207, 217
Parry, Captain Brian 174
Payne, Harry 53, 68, 69, 70
Payne, Tom 77

Peacock, Sir Walter 80
Pearse, Robert 33, 37
Pelham Place 173, 181
Perryland 157, 213
Peterborough 107, 120, 123, 167, 175, 196, 199
Petersfield 46, 49, 102
Petre, Charlie 177
Phillis, Andrew 185
Pigott, Captain 45, 59
Pike, Charles 42
Pipers Hill 167
Plantation Bungalow 197
Plas Machynlleth 208
Plash Wood 201, 203
Pole, Major 60, 70–71
Poole, Willie 219
Popham Lane 16, 18, 58
Porter, Michael R. 173, 174, 175, 176, 183, 188, 195, 200, 201, 214
Portsmouth DL, Lord Quentin 217, 231, 232–234, 235
Portsmouth, Annabel 232
Pountney's covert 58
Powlett Powlett, William 21, 23–25
Powlett, Rev. C. 16, 190
Powlett, Sir Richard 54
Poyntz, William 18, 19
Preston Candover 25, 59, 77, 136
Preston House 127
Preston Oakhills 18
Preston Wood 25
Pullinger, Mrs 61

Q
Quarmby, Ron 167, 169, 171
Queen Elizabeth 136
Queen Victoria 67

R
Raby Castle 35
RAF Odiham 148, 179, 238
Randall, David 167
Rank, Lord 167
Rayson, Tommy 177
Reynard, Frank 120
Richardson, Mrs 100–102
Ridge, Thomas xi, xii, 15, 16, 18, 19, 20, 21, 23, 24, 25, 242, 243
River Itchen 23, 25, 33, 227, 242
River Lodden 18, 43
River Wey 58
Rivers, Michael 34
Roberts, Charles 37
Robinson, A. P. 89, 93, 95, 98, 99–100, 135
Robinson, Ben 149, 238
Romsey 20, 24
Rookery Copse 206
Ropley Church 110, 112

Ropley Cottage 42
Ropley Kennels 176
Ropley school 53, 64, 229
Ropley Station 67
Ropley Tennis Club 112
Ropley Wood 146
Ropley xii, xiii, 33, 34, 36, 41, 49, 53, 54, 55, 61, 63, 71, 73, 74, 86, 103, 110, 116, 123, 127, 131, 136, 140, 146, 150, 157, 166, 167, 172, 174, 175, 176, 186, 195, 203, 210, 219, 222, 224, 235, 238
Rotherfield coverts 36
Rotherfield estate 37, 47, 112, 119, 153, 159, 173, 177, 179, 181, 190, 203, 216
Rotherfield Park 67, 74, 105, 112, 116, 119, 145, 146, 154, 155, 166, 167, 201, 222, 237
Rowe Wood 36
Rowlands, Chantelle 199
Rowse, Peregrine 221, 223–224, 230, 235–236
Rowsell, Giles 179, 227
Rowsell, Hamish 201
Rowsell, Mrs Nicola 221, 230, 232, 241
Royal Naval College, Greenwich 83
Rupells, Mr 48
Russell, Lord John 18
Rutland, Duke of 60
Rycroft, Sir Newton 110
Rycroft, Sir Richard 83
Rye Common 189

S
Sabretache 69
Sandhurst 173
Sarajevo 80
Savile Row 115
Sawyer 29
Scholte, Frederick 115
Scotland, Mr 30
Scott Bt., DL, JP, Colonel Sir Jervoise 155–156, 162, *see also* Scott, Captain Jervoise Bolitho
Scott, Alex 183
Scott, Captain Jervoise Bolitho 93, 105–106, 107, 110, 119, 120, 129, 136, 155
Scott, James 33, 37
Scott, Sam 155
Scott, Sir James 135, 177, 189, 195, 201, 203, 216
Scott, Will 107, 109, 110, 123, 127, 129, 131, 133, 135, 136, 137
Searles, Mr 153

INDEX

Selborne 116, 120, 201, 230
Selborne Common 107, 116, 153, 183, 207
Selborne, Lord 89, 93
Selby Lowndes DSO, Brigadier M.W. (Boy) 131, 140, 141, 142, 146, 155
Seth Smith, Mr 85, 97
Shalden 25, 214, 219, 238
Shalden Farm 177, 193, 203, 224
Shalden Plantation 219
Sharp, George 18, 20
Sheetlands 43
Shell Lane 146
Sherfield 43
Shirley, Jack 33, 34–35
Shirvell, Andrew 203
Silvesters Farm 157
Sinclair, David and Gail 219
Slade Heath 157
Slade, Josh 235
Slys Farm, Bramdean 186
Smith, Dick 161
Soberton 24
Sole, Chris 241
Sonny's Bank 177
South Warnborough Manor 167
Southampton 185
Southampton, Lord 87
Spalding, Mr G.B. 15, 16, 34
Sparsholt Agricultural College 222
Speid-Soote, Captain 145
Spencer, Earl 23
Squires, John 36
St Leonard's Church 57
St Maurice's Covert 229
St. Clere estate 16
St. John's House 23
Stanford, Lieutenant Colonel Bill 230
Stanford, Margaret 230
Stansby, Will 40
Stanwick, Captain 86
Stawell, Lord 20
Steep 60
Stephens, Fred 46
Steventon 77
Stoke Charity 179, 228
Stoner Hill 109
Stoner Wood 123
Stoney Brow 201
Straker, Mr 60
Stratton, Jas 64
Stuart Smith, Diana 107, 110, *see also* Evans, Mrs Diana
Stuart Smith, Mr 84, 85, 97, 134
Summers, Alfred 53, 54, 57–58, 64
Summers, William 33, 37
Surtees, Robert Smith 169

Sutton Scotney 167, 230
Sutton Wood 43, 67, 103, 154, 213, 237
Swaines Hill Manor 228
Swan Inn, Alresford xii, 16, 23, 24, 25, 26, 40, 43, 54, 59, 242
Swarraton Farm 228
Swinburn, General Sir Richard 177, 193
Swinburn, Janie 177

T

Tattersall Tavern 74
The Butts, Alton 146, 195, 199, 221, 226
The Grange 15, 16, 34, 58, 209, 228
The Gullet 67, 176, 181, 213, 237
The Lunways Inn 77
The Purefoy Arms 59
The Star Inn, Bentworth 169
The Straights 166
The Swamp Donkeys 228
The Swan Hotel, Alton 87, 105, 112
The Wakes 116
Thedden estate 177
Theyer, Ormond 186, 195, 197
Theyer, Rose 197
Thomas, Edward A. 159, 167, 171
Thomas, Hugh 167
Thomas, Ruth 167
Thorny Down 34, 77
Thurgood, Lee 234
Tichborne 19, 24, 33, 35
Tichborne Down 34
Tichborne estate 160
Tichborne, Sir Henry 55
Tisted 129, 241
Tisted Station 112
Titheridge 74
Tormarton 219
Totnes 42
Tredcroft, Edward 33, 39–40, 42, 135
Treloar Hospital 146, 189, 199
Trimmer, John 154
Trinity Firs 181
Trinity Hill 123
Tristram, Molly 181
Tristram, Ruth 181, 190
Trodd, Mr 24
Tufnell, Wynne 216
Tunworth 193, 222
Turnbull, George 120
Twyford 25, 34

U

Uloth, Margaret 153
Upper Kempshott Wood 18
Upton House, Alresford 64

V

Vale, Ramle 154, 161, 167, 169–171, 175
Venning, Mr 145
Vernon, Mr 16
Villebois, Frederick 33
Villebois, John Truman 21, 25–27, 29–30, 32, 33–34, 46, *see also* Squire Villeboy
Villeboy, Squire 26, 27, 29, 32, *see also* Villebois, John,

W

Wall, George 37
Wallace, Captain Ronnie 189
Waller's Ash Tunnel 34
Walters, Brian 159, 166, 169
Ward-Thomas, Anthony 228
Ward, Rowland 110
Warner, Henry 120, 137, 138
Warnham Court 39
Warren, Peter 154, *see also* Vale, Ramle
Watt, Emmy and Roddy 227
Weatherill, Bernard
Webb, Nigel 213, 214, 227, 229
Webb, Tessa 213, 227
Welling, Bill 148, 216
West End Farm 202
West Stoke Farm 230
West Tisted Church 123
Westminster 41, 131, 207
Westminster Abbey 136
Weston Down 18
Weston Park 29, 230
Wheatsheaf Inn 16, 18, 19
Whitcomb, Susie 206
White City 140
White Hart, Winchester 16
White Horse Gorse 161
White-Spunner, General Barney 227
White, Rev. Gilbert 116
Whitehall 214
Whyte-Melville, George 232
Wield Wood 77, 110
Wilkins, Williams 15
Will Hall coverts 181
Will Hall Farm 199
William-Powlett, Barton 23–24
Willoughby de Broke, Lord 78
Wilson, Harold 175
Wimble Hill 157
Winchester College xi, 141, 154, 199, 237
Winchester Guildhall 188

Winchester Nursing Home 116
Winchester xii, 16, 18, 19, 21, 23, 24, 35, 42, 54, 55, 58, 59, 138, 169, 179, 188, 222, 227, 229, 241
Windmill Hill 80, 83
Wingate Gray, Colonel 154
Withey, Eric 152, 159, 162–164
Wonston 179
Wood, Arthur H. 53–54
Woodcote 25
Woodmancote Holt 29
Woodridden 109
Woods, Ginger
Woolmer Forest 102
Worthy Down 23–24, 177
Wyards Farm 181
Wyndham Bt., GVCO, Sir Charles Henry 173

Y

Yew Tree Pub 203
York, Duke of 20
Young, Jo 234

About the Author

Adrian Dangar hunted the Stowe Beagles before becoming Master and huntsman to the Spooners and West Dartmoor when 24 years old. He moved from the West Country to take up the same appointment with the Sinnington in North Yorkshire and from there to High Leicestershire where he became the second amateur huntsman in 300 years to be appointed MFH to the Quorn. He hunted hounds for 17 years in all and is currently serving a second term on the MFHA Committee in addition to joining the board of the new British Hound Sports Association.

Adrian founded Wild & Exotic Ltd, a niche travel company specialising in riding safaris and holidays around the world in 2000 and continues to work as an independent travel consultant.

He has written for a wide range of publications including *Country Life*, the *Daily Telegraph*, *Daily Mail*, *The Field*, *Horse & Hound* and *Trout & Salmon*.

The Hampshire Hunt 1749–2022 is his fourth book.

In addition to hunting, his favourite pastimes are gardening, the pursuit of woodcock in wild places, and trying to catch the occasional salmon from remote streams on the west coast of Scotland.

Other books by Adrian Dangar:

True to the Line
Life on the Edge
The Work of the Sinnington Hounds 1994–1998

Acknowledgements

This book would never have been possible without the help and support of so many individuals. Top of the list are Charlie Corbett, Nigel Webb and Hopper Cavendish, whose combined enthusiasm and knowledge have helped drive the project forward from the outset. I have often wondered what it must be like for a writer to have the benefit of a full-time researcher for a book of this nature, and now I know. Hopper's tireless energy and deep understanding of hunting and the countryside are combined with an unfailing ability to identify those important people – such as Ormond Theyer and the Butler Boys – who are integral to the success of every Hunt, but sometimes overlooked when its history comes to be written.

We have the Hampshire Record Office in Winchester to thank for so many intriguing anecdotes, especially those from beyond living memory. I am particularly indebted to Nigel Webb and Hampshire County Councillor, Mark Kemp-Gee, whose diplomatic liaisons resulted in seven large boxes of fascinating archive material arriving at my North Yorkshire home in July last year. That such illuminating records existed at all is entirely thanks to the likes of Frederick Coryton, Evelyn Baring, George Evans, Joyce Kemp and Michael Bowman-Manifold, whose carefully maintained diaries, letters and scrapbooks have provided so much hitherto unpublicised information. Thanks to the diligence of successive Hon. Secretaries from the late eighteenth century onwards, I have been able to draw on meticulously recorded minutes of the Hampshire Hunt Club. The earliest were written down in immaculate copperplate handwriting, which later gave way to writing that was much harder to decipher; it was a huge relief when my research reached August 1935 and the first typewritten minutes appeared.

Many thanks to those who have contributed to the recent history of the Hunt by sharing their own thoughts and memories. The list is too long to name everyone who has helped, but I should like to record my gratitude to Peter and Rosemary Andreae, John Jervoise, Gillian Gray Knight, Giles Rowsell, Sue Maxse, Derick and Wendy Faulkner, Simon Harrap, Luke and Sio Axel-Berg, Tom Floyd, Peregrine

Rowse, Rupert Harvie MFH, Nicola Rowsell, Quentin Portsmouth, Will Hudson, Lee Thurgood and Sally Evans MFH.

Others, such as Robin Greenwood, who made his research on racing in Hampshire available, have generously granted access to their own records. Simon Harrap provided the point-to-point scrapbook, Charlie Corbett sent information on the Hunt Scurry, Nicola Rowsell on the Pony Club, and Charles Gregson offered his father's hunting diaries from the sixties and seventies. Major Mangles's grandson, Edward Mangles from Yorkshire, kindly came up with the frieze and other images that embellish chapters seven and eight. Many of the images reproduced in the early chapters of the book have been taken from archive material held at the Hampshire Record Office, but some of the nineteenth century paintings have been reproduced by kind permission of their current owners. Thanks to all those who have generously provided their own photographs for the inclusion in the book, including Carol Collins, Anna Rainbow and Sio Axel-Berg. These and other images were most professionally scanned by the staff at Richard Greenly Photography.

I am grateful to Lord Ashburton for welcoming hounds to The Grange on the occasion of my visit in November 2021, and for allowing his magnificent example of Greek Revival architecture to be the setting for a photograph of current Members of the HH Club, 176 years after their predecessors were painted at the same location by Mr Spalding in 1845. Phil Momber has drawn her own delightful version of The Grange and other historically important houses within the HH country for the charming endpapers. Susie Whitcombe (artist) and Gillian Gray Knight (owner) have kindly allowed us to reproduce Susie's beautiful painting on the front cover. As Chairman of the Hampshire Hunt Club Trustees, Sir James Scott has not only offered his unstinting support throughout the project but also penned a delightful foreword.

I am indebted to Becky Bowyer for her constant advice as the book has unfolded and for her skills in designing the finished work that you see before you today. This would have been riddled with grammatical errors were it not for Becky, and the eagle-eyed scrutiny of proofreaders, John Cavendish and Nicola Rowsell, who kindly gave up their time to trawl through the manuscript with a fine toothcomb.

Copyright © 2022 Trustees of The Hampshire Hunt

First published in the UK in 2022
by Muscoates Publishing

ISBN 9978-1-9163100-2-5

All rights reserved. No part of this book may be reproduced or transmitted in any form or by any means, electronic or mechanical including photocopying, recording or by any information storage and retrieval system, without permission from the publisher in writing.

Photographs and other archive materials are the copyright/property of the publisher unless otherwise stated and credited. Whilst every effort has been made to obtain permission from copyright holders for all material used in this book, the publisher will be pleased to hear from anyone who has not been appropriately acknowledged.

Design by Becky Bowyer

Front cover: John Gray MFH and Bob Collins with hounds at Rookery Copse, 1996. From the original painting by Susie Whitcombe.

Printed in the UK by Gomer Press

Muscoates Publishing
Muscoates Grange, Nunnington, York YO62 5XF
E-mail: info@muscoatespublishing.com
Instagram: @adriandangar
Website: www.muscoatespublishing.com

2. Moundsmere Manor

3. Farleigh House

1. The Grange